The Story
of the
Country House

The Story
of the
Country House

·CLIVE ASLET·

YALE UNIVERSITY PRESS

New Haven and London

First published by Yale University Press 2021
302 Temple Street, P. O. Box 209040,
New Haven, CT 06520-9040
47 Bedford Square, London WC1B 3DP
yalebooks.com | yalebooks.co.uk

ISBN 978-0-300-255058 HB
Library of Congress Control Number: 2020952054
10 9 8 7 6 5 4 3 2
2025 2024 2023 2022 2021

Edited by Henry Howard
Text designed and typeset by Tetragon, London

Illustrations by Bethan Scorey

Printed in Great Britain by TJ Books Ltd, Padstow, Cornwall

To Marcus, Michael, Jeremy, John and Mary;
and in memory of John and Giles

CONTENTS

ACKNOWLEDGEMENTS

There are many people whom I must thank for their contribution to this book, foremost among them being the owners of many country houses I have visited over the years during a long association with *Country Life*. My colleagues in the architectural department of that magazine have been an unending source of erudition and delight. Today the flag is kept flying by John Goodall, with whom I have travelled Britain, entranced by his incomparable expertise in old buildings. John has been generous enough to read the manuscript, as did Tim Brittain-Catlin and Simon Thurley: their comments have been pure gold. Others who have shared abundantly of their knowledge are Mary Miers, James Stourton and James Knox. Any error is mine.

My first book, *The Last Country Houses*, was published by Yale in 1982; in 1990, the same press brought out *The American Country House*. After something of a break, I am delighted to find myself again racing under Yale colours. I would like to thank Heather McCallum and Sophie Neve for making this possible. Henry Howard has been the copy editor of my dreams.

My wife Naomi and sons William, Johnny and Charlie have tolerated my architectural obsessions over the years – and William has come to share some of them, while outshining his father, by studying for a PhD on James Gibbs. Deepest love and thanks to them all.

INTRODUCTION

Eric Ponsonby, 10th Earl of Bessborough loved Stansted Park. This was something of a surprise to his friends, since the house, near Chichester, was rebuilt after a fire in the Edwardian period and, in the early 1980s, Edwardian architecture was regarded with scorn. I disagreed; Yale University Press had just published my book *The Last Country Houses*, a study of country houses from 1890 to 1939. Which was why he asked me, as an eager young architectural historian, to help him revise his book about it, *A Place in the Forest*. Eric's partiality sometimes got the better of him, yet how nice it would be to believe, as he did, that Roman legionaries really had once tramped down the long avenue.

Outwardly Stansted may have been Edwardian but, like many country houses, it was more than that. For at least eight-hundred years, the people who owned it – a colourful crowd, rarely related to each other, since they were singularly bad at producing heirs – had been nurturing, reimagining and loving it perhaps as much as Eric did. Standing in immemorial forest, the first Stansted was used by Henry II as a hunting lodge in the late twelfth century. In 1480, the 12th Earl of Arundel replaced the lodge with a sprawling mansion in the ultra-fashionable material of brick. This building suffered a small bombardment during the Civil War and subsequently decayed so that all that now survives from Lord Arundel's time is a fragment of rose-coloured brick on the outside of the chapel. In the 1680s, a new Stansted arose on a different site nearby, with a hipped roof, dormers and pediment, for the 1st Earl of Scarbrough, a favourite of Charles II and one of the statesmen who invited William III to the throne (fig. 1).

The following century saw the levelling of the formal gardens to make a landscape park, the construction of a triangular tower by the 2nd Earl of Halifax in 1772 and the arrival of yet another owner, the

East India Company merchant and MP Richard Barwell, who 'made it his study to render himself obnoxious to persons of all ranks', according to a diarist, by shutting up the park; Barwell also remodelled the house. On Barwell's death in 1804, Stansted was bought by Lewis Way, who would have become a clergyman if his father had not made him study law. After working for a wealthy but unrelated client who shared his surname, Lewis Way found he had been left £30,000. A member of the London Society for Promoting Christianity Among the Jews, Way transformed Stansted into a college where young, impecunious Jews could stay, be shaved and baptised, and train as missionaries to be sent to their own people. A donkey-riding school prepared them for travel in distant lands. It was Way who made the chapel out of surviving fragment of the Tudor house. During the three-hour service of consecration, the poet John Keats had ample time to study the stained glass in the north windows, where the arms of the Earls of Arundel inspired a stanza of *The Eve of St Agnes*.

In 1840, the exuberant Thomas Hopper built a stone conservatory for the new owner, a port wine merchant called Charles Dixon who

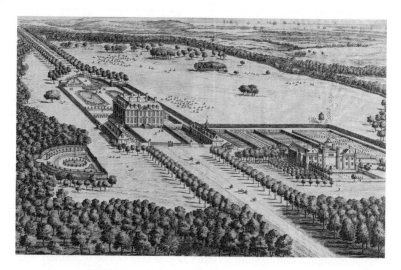

FIG. I *Stansted Park, near Chichester: a country house that, like others, has undergone many transformations since it was first built in the Middle Ages. In the right foreground is a fragment of a Tudor house, later turned into a chapel. This aerial view of 1708 drawn by Jan Kip shows the house built by the 1st Earl of Scarbrough in the 1680s; much altered, it burnt down in 1900 and was replaced.*

founded an almshouse for 'six of his less successful brethren'. Then, on the last day of the 1900 Goodwood Races, Stansted caught fire, in a blaze that lit up the country for miles around. Carvings by Grinling Gibbons, Italian ceiling paintings, pictures of the queens who were supposed to have slept there: all were destroyed. Stansted was rebuilt in an unexciting neo-Georgian style. This was the house bought by the 9th Earl of Bessborough in 1924, after Bessborough House in Ireland was burnt during the Troubles (fortunately, its contents had already been removed and some of its beautiful eighteenth-century pictures still hang at Stansted today). Bessborough asked his old Cambridge friend, the architect Harry Goodhart-Rendel, to come down in his Rolls-Royce and bring his new home up to date. The Sainte-Chapelle in Paris inspired a blue chapel ceiling, spangled with stars, and Rinaldo, as the architect was known, built a theatre modelled on the Duchess Theatre in London, which fired the young Eric with a passion for acting. In 1942 while watching a training film, a member of the Home Guard dropped a cigarette and the theatre went up in flames.

This book is an introduction to the history of places like Stansted. Stansted itself illustrates one of the difficulties of the subject: it went through so many iterations. Even country houses that strongly evoke a single period are often palimpsests where one era overwrites another, a process that may happen again and again until the deep past is no more than a ghostly, indecipherable smudge. The same place wears different guises. There is continuity in the place and idea of the country house, but the Stansted of today is nothing like the original hunting lodge. However, the long history of country houses like Stansted is a considerable part of their fascination. They are a document on which is written their owners' changing lives, tastes and sources of income. Generally I shall touch on only one aspect of the houses I discuss but many, like Stansted, were altered in almost every generation.

All of which prompts the question: what is a country house? That is not so easy to answer. The meaning changes depending on the historical period being discussed. Like 'castle', the single word we have in English to represent numerous, more specialised terms in medieval Latin texts, 'country house' is a catch-all. Chatsworth, in all its princely splendour, is a country house, but so is handcrafted Munstead Wood. Mighty Alnwick Castle, in the wilds of Northumberland – yes, that's undoubtedly a country house. Politely Georgian Kenwood House, on the edge of Hampstead Heath – most people would call that one too.

Historians used to think of a country house as being a gentleman's residence in the centre of a landed estate; rents from the tenanted farms that made up the estate paid for the house. It was a sealed and largely self-sufficient system, or that was the idea. That was the definition I was told to use when I began to write architectural articles in *Country Life* in the 1970s. These were the *seats* of gentlemen or peers, a word that conveyed settled occupation and the probability of a family vault in the parish church. However, this definition does not completely hold water.

In the Middle Ages, noblemen and women did possess seats – the place where the family had come from and members were buried – but there was nothing settled about their way of life. They were always on the move between castles, manor houses and hunting lodges; that is when they were not following the court, which was similarly peripatetic, or on campaign. Land was immensely important to them but the homes through which they passed were hardly what we would think of as country houses; indeed, the idea of a rural retreat would have seemed strange in a land whose towns and cities were tiny. Later, the great Tudor and Jacobean courtiers spent prodigiously on lavish building projects, sometimes ruining themselves in the process; they were loss leaders to impress the monarch, their cost unrelated to the income of the estate. Others built in places that were convenient for the court or the great money pot of the City of London; the suburbs of London have since swallowed them up. They were places of recreation, umbilically linked to the town.

With the Agricultural Depression that began in the 1870s and lasted until the Second World War, the link between country house and landed estate was pretty well severed. Land ceased to be the reliable and productive investment it had seemed since the Dissolution of the Monasteries in the sixteenth century. If Edwardian country-house builders wanted land, it was not because they thought it would finance their running costs. Rather, it conferred status and you could hunt and shoot on it.

But most people after 1900 did not want much land at all: Lutyens built his numerous country houses for clients who were looking for a different way of life from the stuffy, hidebound circles associated with Edward VII and George V. The *Country Life* definition did not apply (although paradoxically nearly all of Lutyens's houses were published by *Country Life*). After the Second World War, many new country houses did have land, because they were built by landowners who were downsizing from monster houses to more manageable ones built on the same site. Since the 1980s, however, when traditional landowners have been outnumbered in these stakes by hedge-fund managers and the owners of dot-com, life-science and new technology companies, land has been viewed differently. Field sports continue but rewilding has come up the agenda. Immense estates have been assembled in the Highlands for this purpose and nobody expects a Highland estate to make money.

This discussion has left out a species of country house that had a different name altogether: the villa. Villas were originally caprices – small, highly architectural buildings on the outskirts of towns, which could be visited for the day. In the eighteenth century they became more permanent dwellings. These days, many new country houses are of villa size and dependent on easy access to the city where the wealth that created them was made. Villas must have a place in this story, as do hunting lodges and the medieval hideaways known as pleasances. They have more in common with the twenty-first-century country house than the 1st Duke of Marlborough's Blenheim Palace or nineteenth-century Penrhyn Castle, built for a slate-quarry owner using money derived partly from his cousin's six slave-run sugar estates in Jamaica.

My definition of the country house is this: a work of domestic architecture in a rural location, surrounded by its own land (although not necessarily a landed estate) and intended to seem a self-contained unit: its own 'little kingdom', as nineteenth-century writers liked to call it. It is not a working entity like a farmhouse, although work may be done from it. The inhabitants value it for many things: love of the land, status, self-expression through architecture and, not least, the pleasure to be had there, with gardens, horses, dogs, art, collecting – delete as applicable. It has probably been made into a mini-Arcadia, where owner and loved ones can find refuge from a harsh or giddy world. Size is not the issue. The country house is an idea, and it changes with each generation.

This will be a narrative history, covering the whole of the British Isles. I confess that England plays a larger part than Scotland, Wales or Ireland, but this is unavoidable: from the Middle Ages onwards, it was economically dominant. Its peasants could produce a surplus, however modest, because of the kinder climate, while those of the other countries struggled to subsist. This meant that English landowners could collect more rent. They could also keep more sheep, at a time when wool was one of the few internationally traded commodities. English kings owned parts of France and, while they often had to fight expensive wars to keep or regain them, victory could yield a bonanza as towns were sacked and the booty distributed among the leaders of the winning side. There was simply more money to spend on domestic architecture in England, with a special incentive to build around London, where the results would be seen by people of influence.

Of course, the individual histories of the different countries of the British Isles make it impossible always to treat them as a single geographical unit. Ireland was a colony, Scotland a separate kingdom. Wales was conquered by Edward I at the end of the thirteenth century but its princes and warlords did not take occupation lying down; integration with England only came under the Tudors. These countries had their own architectural traditions which lasted into the eighteenth century, before, in the case of Scotland, being revived. The regional strands are spun together after the Scottish Act of Union of 1707, when Scotland was joined to England and Wales, and the Irish Act of Union of 1801, when the United Kingdom was formed. Southern Ireland won independence after the First World War. Inevitably, then, there are differences, but also shared features. Regional traditions merged with the architectural mainstream during the Georgian period and local singularities became a matter of nuance; by the late eighteenth century, the same architects were being used throughout Britain and their clients travelled, visiting other country houses as they did so; they may have owned several houses themselves. It is notable how many distinguished country-house architects were Scottish.

The story of the British country house reaches out further still beyond its immediate locality to embrace a wider world. Richard Barwell's fortune derived from India, Charles Dixon made his money in the wine trade, the Bessboroughs had estates in Ireland, and Lewis Way took a particular interest in the Holy Land. These places of retreat had global connections: trade, war and Empire provided the resources to build them.

Only the very rich could afford the luxury of a country house, but modern historians increasingly recognise that behind them and their architects stood dozens if not hundreds of others – labouring on the land, in counting houses, down mines, on men o' war, in cotton mills, sweating in the cantonments of India or enslaved on the sugar plantations of the West Indies. Without these usually anonymous toilers there would not have been the money to make the country house possible. The story is not for the faint-hearted. Owners amassed or inherited enormous wealth, often through what can now seem to be inordinate, grasping ambition, riding roughshod over both their political rivals and the poor on their estates, whose miserable existence stood in signal contrast to their own splendour. There were exceptions: some landlords could be kind. But even they could ignore what to us seem the glaring moral iniquities of the ultimate sources of their fortunes: slavery is an obvious example. The connections of this shocking evil with the Georgian economy are now receiving much scrutiny. Alas, it is not the only form of human exploitation whose fruits were the country house. Coal mining was an immense source of wealth but the consequences, we might think, were as bad for the environment as they were for the lungs of the miners engaged in it. Medieval serfdom was little better than slavery – and where, in the hierarchy of past sins, should we place the sacking of towns by soldiers eager for booty, the marriage of twelve-year-old heiresses to middle-aged men for the sake of their inheritance or the imperial adventurers known as Randlords, Cecil Rhodes's friends, rich from the gold fields and diamond mines of South Africa and chief flag wavers for the Boer War? Were those who did not directly commit abuses against fellow human beings complicit by failing to condemn them?

These are deep questions. I believe we should beware of attempting to retrofit modern morals onto previous eras of history which operated according to different codes. 'The past', as L.P. Hartley famously wrote, 'is a foreign country. They do things differently there.' Few areas of study better exemplify that observation than the country house. Historical research reveals how dissimilar – sometimes radically so – past lives, expectations, religious convictions and social mores could be from our own. Before passing judgement on men and women who lived prior to our own supposedly enlightened times, should we not pause to reflect on the globalised economy of today? Jane Austen's England did not morally confront the source of its sugar (West Indian plantations run by slaves) which seems unforgivable; but how many people in our own age can be sure of the conditions in which the rare minerals needed for electric car batteries are mined, cheap garments made or the parts of their mobile phones produced? Slavery 'exists in the supply chain of nearly every business', according to the investment managers CCLA. The past may not be such a foreign country after all.

The story of the country house is not only male. Even in the Middle Ages, some women – widows, abbesses – could be rich and independent; they might also have been educated to a high standard in convents, an opportunity generally denied to girls after the Dissolution of the Monasteries. Bess of Hardwick, Lady Anne Clifford and Sarah, Duchess of Marlborough were all builders. Wives like the Jacobean Lady Lisle at Penshurst supervised architectural works and estates while their husbands were away at court, in the army or making their fortunes overseas. During the English Civil War, this could extend to defending the country house against siege, which the Puritan Brilliana, Lady Harley did with great spirit, even though the privations killed her. Men may have generally taken the big decisions on architecture, landscape, collecting and furniture – subjects that they discussed in their clubs without female involvement – but some couples, like the 1st Marquess and Marchioness of Lansdowne at Bowood, did everything together. Women were likely to spend more time in the country than their menfolk, whether they liked it or not; one thinks of Lady Leicester, stuck in the building site of Holkham Hall, while her husband, the 1st Earl, pursued a quasi-bachelor life in London. Country houses have always been family places. Today, they are often acquired by couples when they start to have children; owners in the past were family-minded in a different way – they saw country houses as dynastic seats, and wives underwent a constant round of pregnancies to produce heirs. (One reason that babies were put out to be breast-fed by countrywomen was to allow the mother to conceive again as quickly as possible.)

There were no women architects to speak of before the twentieth century: society would have frowned on unaccompanied site visits and client meetings and it would have been difficult to go up scaffolding in long skirts. But feminine influence inside the country house cannot be overlooked. The wife ran the household, bottling fruit, dispensing home-made medicines, ensuring that epic deliveries of raw ingredients for the kitchen were properly stored, that carpets were beaten and copper pans scoured. Modern historians are apt to regard needlework, shell grottoes or creations such as the feather hangings that the bluestocking Elizabeth Montagu worked at her Berkshire country house, Sandleford Priory – the subject of a poem by William Cowper – as unacceptably 'gendered'. However, such 'ladies' work' (as a previous generation of historians called it) not only occupied hours of labour but softened the appearance of the home. At the end of the nineteenth century, Lutyens's career would be unimaginable without the help of the craftswoman and gardener Gertrude Jekyll.

As well as requiring a multitude of workers to create the wealth from which they were built, country houses themselves contained large numbers of people: that was the point of them. Before 1600, a noble retinue might run to hundreds of people. At one party in 1732, the future Marquess of Rockingham welcomed 'about one thousand' guests, serving them 'two hundred and twenty-five dishes'; it was part of a strategy to keep Yorkshire on the side of the Whigs – no wonder he rebuilt Wentworth Woodhouse with the longest façade of any country house in Britain. The connection between politics and country houses continued into the Jet Age, with Harold Macmillan still cultivating the impression of governing Britain from a grouse moor in the 1960s. Country-house weekends provided a forum for conversation. Deals could be done away from the general gaze and bonds cemented between the owner and guests, be they from the surrounding neighbourhood, the county town or London. Until the Second World War, *noblesse oblige* required traditional landowners to throw huge parties for their eldest son's coming of age and other dynastic events. They were at the centre of what the Middle Ages called an affinity and the Georgian period a connection. We might call it a social group or community.

In the medieval period, this was expressed in the great hall. Today the ubiquitous live-in kitchen is another multipurpose space, where what, until a quite recent date, would have been regarded as a highly private activity – the preparation of food – is thrown open to public view. By public, though, I mean that of a small group of family and friends. For people now buy or build country houses to be private. Indeed, the story of the country house could be told as a journey towards the modern ideal of privacy. We live in a society that is anxious to protect data, preserve personal space and escape (in the case of celebrities) paparazzi and mobile-phone cameras. Privacy has always been a luxury but now is more important to us than ever. If there is one place it can be found, it is in the country house. There are no passers-by and probably few guests, to judge from the small number of bedrooms in most new country houses.

We do not always remember how odd our privacy fetish would have seemed to other ages. For most of history country-house owners lived in close, sweaty proximity to other people on whom they relied for the necessities of existence. Before the eighteenth century, servants routinely slept outside bedroom doors (how else would they know to be available when called before the proliferation of the wired bell pull in the Regency?). It was only at their devotions that people were alone, and then they had God for company. Complete solitude might even have seemed frightening. But magnates still longed to escape the crowds of retainers who surrounded them. Medieval kings built fancifully named hideaways to which they could retreat with loved ones or a few chosen friends (and the servants who would look after them). Eighteenth-century gentlemen found seclusion in the follies of their landscape parks. On the edge of Ullswater in the Lake District, the 11th Duke of Norfolk built Lyulph's Tower, as an escape from Greystoke Castle – which was itself considerably smaller and more remote than his main seat of Arundel Castle, on which he spent heavily. Several country-house owners, particularly in Ireland, built tunnels so they could avoid contact with their servants. In the twentieth century, washing machines, vacuum cleaners and dishwashers made it possible for owners to live more independently of staff. Butlers are supposed to have become more plentiful in this age of billionaires, but few new country houses are equipped for many staff to live in; neither employers nor employees want a return to the below-stairs world of the Edwardian era. Privacy is closely guarded by both.

Country houses are inherently fragile, depending on the success of their owners in keeping them going. The *Destruction of the Country House* exhibition in 1974 revealed that well over a thousand had been demolished over the previous century. There have been other waves of destruction. During the English Civil War, which engulfed all parts of the British Isles, castles and country houses that were not wrecked in fighting were deliberately blown up or 'slighted' to prevent them from being strongholds in the future. Extravagance, racehorses, gambling and bad marriages have also brought ruin in their wake. The 1st Duke of Chandos's princely Canons Park, in Middlesex, lasted a mere twenty-three years after its completion before the 2nd Duke broke it up. Close to London, Canons was built to show off the 1st Duke's artistic taste and inordinate wealth; when duke and wealth were gone, it had no purpose. Hamilton Palace in Lanarkshire, begun in 1695, was not finished by the 10th Duke of Hamilton – Il Magnifico, or as one writer called him, the 'very duke of very dukes' – until 1842; but the contents were sold in 1884, the country house undermined to extract coal and demolished in 1921. The vagaries of inheritance meant that some owners possessed too many homes for their needs. When the 6th Duke of Devonshire succeeded his father in 1811, he had eight. They all survived his tenure but the 4th Earl of Dysart, that 'miserly old cormudgeon [*sic*]', as Horace Walpole called him, demolished two of the four properties that came to him, Harrington Hall in Northamptonshire and Woodhey Hall in Cheshire, both reputed gems. Terraces were levelled, gardens ploughed up, fruit-walls torn down. He kept Ham House outside London and Helmingham Hall in Suffolk.

Past losses can be lamented but in recent decades the country house has revived. Often owners have built on sites of demolished mansions, to take advantage of the opportunities for planning permission as well as the mature landscape. This is a story of resurrection as well as death.

There is also the subject – not to be forgotten if less fashionable than it once was – of taste. As Andrew Boorde, the first English writer to discuss the architecture of houses, wrote in 1554:

> For the commodious buyldyng of a place doth not onely satifye the mynde of the inhabitour, but also it doth comforte and reioyseth a mannes herte to se it, specially the pulcrose prospect.

Pulchritude is in the eye of the beholder and, in their hunt for beauty, owners did not always follow the pack. This point must be emphasised, lest the story told here creates an impression of inevitability in the onward march of style. Country-house aesthetics do not only move forward. Here of all places owners could suit themselves. It is impossible not to notice how many of them wanted to evoke the glories of an idealised past. The late country-house historian John Cornforth used to call this the 'backward look'. Owners might diverge from the mainstream of taste to create places of special meaning to themselves that expressed religious belief, a nostalgia for the age of chivalry, an assertion of ancient lineage that conveyed status, a vindication of their politics, or an idea about British history, claiming Roman origins that did not exist.

I opened this introduction by saying that Eric Bessborough loved Stansted Park. Readers are unlikely to remember that for a brief period in the 1970s he was Edward Heath's Minister for Technology – just the sort of person, one might have thought, to espouse the machine aesthetic of Modernism. There was, however, no sign of it at Stansted beyond an early adoption of cordless telephones. Stansted corresponded to everything he and his generation had been brought up to believe that a country house should be: a grand sort of place, well supplied with sofas, reading matter, jigsaw puzzles and guest bedrooms, where you would never be short of entertainment, be it shooting in the woods or admiring Liotard's portrait of the 2nd Earl in Turkish dress. Some of Eric's contemporaries broke the mould. When Sir Gawaine Baillie, 7th Baronet, needed a country house for himself after his mother had put Leeds Castle into a trust, he employed Tom Hancock, in association with Tony Swannell, to demolish a Victorian house to build Freechase, in the same county as Stansted, in 1975–7. There are other examples of country houses in the Modern style from the twentieth century but they are outnumbered by those that are Classical or 'contextualist' (taking their cue from their surroundings).

The appetite for experiment may be greater today but many owners remain unwilling to throw over the past. There is plenty of precedent for their conservatism. Despite upswings of innovation and the obsession of some periods with novelty, a counterweight existed in preconceived ideas of the nature of a country house, inherited from previous generations. To many owners, the fact that they could build a country house at all said much more about them than its style. They wanted to display their new-found status while pretending, in some cases, that it was not new-found at all; they identified with the ancient families of the realm and the way things had always been done. This was a greater issue for the country house than for London, where taste was more cosmopolitan and febrile. Outside the capital it was often deeply traditional and celebrated antiquity; and this reverence for the past led to some specially British features. Medieval great halls were open to the roof because that was how England did them: as a result, English carpenters developed that feat of engineering known as the hammerbeam roof, enabling them to span a hall that was wider than any individual timber without the need for supports on the ground – an achievement that was of less relevance to the Continent of Europe with its preference for coffered ceilings. Owners cleaved to central hearths in the hall long after the wall fireplace could have replaced them. In Scotland, the form of the great late seventeenth-century palaces of Thirlestane Castle and Drumlanrig Castle – I use the term palace to denote any exceptionally sumptuous country house – can only be explained by a native love of castles. If we look to such distinctively British contributions to European architecture as the Tudor manor house, romantically revived at the turn of the twentieth century, the landscape park of the Picturesque Movement, the antiquarianism of Horace Walpole and his friends in the mid-eighteenth century, and the Victorian phenomena of the Gothic Revival, Scots Baronial and the Arts and Crafts Movement, we see as often as not an association with the country house. There is frequently a desire to revive a Golden Age (not always the same Golden Age). It is integral to this building type.

Generally, the country houses we know today are only those which, by happy chance and good genes in the owning family, happen to have survived. They may no longer be lived in. The randomness of the sample that exists can skew the picture. This is compounded by the frozen-in-time quality of many country houses now open to the public, in which the evolution of family life has suddenly stopped, as when, in my youth, the needle was lifted from the gramophone record in a game of musical chairs. Even that great institution the National Trust has been the subject of criticism in recent years: the custodian of over two hundred historic properties, it faces the challenge of maintaining its reputation for scholarship and curatorial elan that it achieved in the late twentieth century, while also appealing to new and broader audiences. Let us remain positive. The country houses are in good repair; they are rich and astounding objects of study, whose almost numberless treasures deserve to be celebrated and interpreted. What some scholars and aesthetes regard as the new Dark Ages will not last forever; once over – and the financial toll taken by the 2020 pandemic also forgotten – the buildings and contents of the National Trust will surely still be there, ready to burst back into glory under the enthusiasm and scholarship of a new generation. I hope this book will encourage the process by showing that country houses can excite interest on several levels, from social and economic history to iconography and the owners' self-image. Meanwhile, among the families who live in old country houses or build new ones there is, despite Covid, greater optimism than at any point during my lifetime. The story has not ended and perhaps never will.

PROLOGUE

The story starts in a damp field in the Cotswolds. There is a river, a straggle of willows and a lot of molehills. Yet few molehills can be seen on the slightly elevated ground towards Halewell, a country house that may owe a major phase of its development to an Elizabethan Bishop of Worcester who needed somewhere to house the first wife he had scandalously divorced. Something attracts the moles to this patch, and the answer may lie in the specks of dull reddish brown amid the soft tilth of the molehills. Pick up one of the specks and clean it off; you see that it is a fragment of tile. A cursory examination shows that many of the molehills contain these little chips. There is no agricultural reason to have built a barn down here in the eighteenth century or Victorian age. Rubbed smooth by time, the morsel of burnt clay that you now have in your hand almost certainly dates from the early centuries AD. Archaeologists have identified this as the site of a Roman villa. An archaeological dig is being planned as I write.

This part of Gloucestershire was heavily populated with villas in the Roman period. Mosaics from another villa, which is close by, are in the British Museum. They were made at Cirencester where there was a famous school of mosaicists. Two miles away from Halewell is Chedworth where the National Trust owns a villa that was excavated in the nineteenth century. The Romanised owners of Chedworth led a life of some luxury. The area is still home to a population of large snails (*Helix pomatia*), introduced for their table. The family had their own courtyard, separate from the agricultural activities of the estate. They could relax in a heated bath house, with mosaic floors patterned with geometrical motifs that can be seen throughout the Empire; the walls of their apartments were decorated with painted plaster; they ate off fine pottery using silver utensils; they wore elegant rings, which sometimes slipped from their fingers while they were bathing and ended up in the drain beneath the bath house; the ladies wore their hair in fashionable styles, with numerous pins to keep it up. The owner's wing was elegant and exclusive: too small to have been shared by more than the family and their personal guests, tended by servants or slaves. The Romano-British valued their privacy.

Generally British villas were not as sumptuous as the best in Italy and high-status Romans no doubt regarded them as provincial. But they aspired to the same culture, as can be seen from elements of Classical architecture such as columns and pediments. Classicism is a means of articulating space using mathematical proportions and a system of repeating units based on the column, evolved ultimately from the architecture of Ancient Greece, and even Britannia, at the ends of the Empire, subscribed to it. Not that the Chedworth buildings looked much like those in Rome or Athens. They were rural, relatively humble and, because this really was not the Mediterranean, covered with heavy roofs to keep out the elements, rather than having shady colonnades and courtyards open to the sky. But they followed, as best they could, the same principles; they used, albeit in a thick local accent, the same language. For it was a universal language. In later centuries, the country house returns to it again and again.

What happened after the legions were withdrawn from the province of Britannia in 410 AD? The luxuries of life disappeared. Pottery and glass, as well as wine and olive oil, had come from other provinces in the Empire. When the imperial system of trade collapsed, so did the life of Britannia's villas. Scholars debate how long this took but ultimately even such basic skills as use of the potter's wheel were forgotten. Brick making stopped. No brick or tile would be made in Britain until Flemish craftsmen came to East Anglia in the early Middle Ages. And yet the same agricultural units went on being farmed, probably by the same peasants. There is evidence of such continuity around Halewell.

In time the villas themselves fell out of use. This is, on the face of it, puzzling. Here were substantial structures, often laboriously built of masonry or brick; why did the new rulers not take them over? They could have been adapted, surely. It would have been easier than building from new. The explanation does not only lie in the breakdown of the imperial economy. New people came from the north of Europe and they followed a different way of life that was Germanic or Nordic in character, and they built of wood, which was easier to work than stone. Wood leaves fewer traces than brick or stone but it has been possible to reconstruct, tentatively, some princely sites in Northumberland and Kent. They were made up of a cluster of buildings, focused not on the private space of the bath house but the communal one of the hall. Although the only evidence of these halls comes from the footings of the vertical timbers that survive as postholes left in the ground, we can imagine them and their importance from early literature such as the epic of Beowulf written around the year 1000 AD, in which the hall of Heorot 'towered up, high and wide-gabled'. This does not give us much to go on in forming a picture of the building. What is clear, however, is the social, even mystic importance of the hall as a place where a whole community ate together. This was where warriors formed their bonds of allegiance; a lord would fight surrounded by his loyal 'hearth guard', as an Old English poem about the Battle of Maldon described it. When some warriors shamefully run away from the fight, another rallies the rest of the troops by remembering the times that they had drunk mead together as 'heroes in the hall'.

The Saxon hall provides an entirely different model of social organisation from the Roman villa. Both are physically lost to us, except through excavation. But each represents an idea that recurs time and again in the subsequent story of the country house. Indeed that story could be described as constant dialogue between the two archetypes: the hall and the villa, the public and the private realm, the Northern vernacular, gathered cosily around a glowing hearth, and the architectural discipline of sunlit Mediterranean lands.

CHAPTER ONE

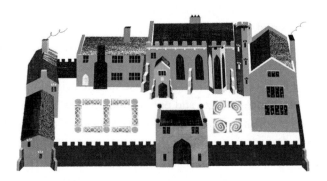

Medieval

K ING John rarely stayed more than a few days in the same place. While he was a restless and worried man, whose showdown with his barons led to the signing of a 'great charter', Magna Carta, in 1215 – which he subsequently revoked – his state of perpetual motion was not solely the result of neurosis. It was normal for monarchs, bishops and noblemen to travel constantly between their many properties. In fact the ruling class was forever on the move. The court and royal administration followed the king and knights might be away for months on campaign. A great territorial estate was not likely to form a single block; the result of inheritance, royal favour and marriage, it might be scattered throughout the kingdom. The lodgings that great people built for their own accommodation were precisely that: rooms where they lodged before going on to somewhere else. There were few pieces of furniture and nothing except the four walls was permanent. The colourful tapestries with which the walls were hung could be rolled up. Medieval lords took their domestic possessions with them, in a great series of carts – seventeen carts 'at every remevall' for one earl – and the travelling chests were unpacked on arrival and packed up again when the lord left. Meanwhile, a castle was left in the charge of its constable and manorial officials supervised the fields and woods of a manor in the lord's absence. But the great rooms were as bare as a theatre between performances. Home did not take on the modern association of comfort, emotional security and belonging until the Tudor period.

The landscape across which John rode would strike us as empty. England had a population of around three million people and nearly everybody lived in the countryside. Towns and even cities might be no bigger than modern villages and only London had as many as twenty thousand inhabitants. Peasants tilled strips of land, in big open fields; their animals roamed across great areas of common or rooted for acorns or beech mast in the woods. Whole swathes of England were preserved for the king's stag hunting, in rigorously controlled 'forests' composed of glades, woods and splendid free-standing trees. It was for most people a harsh life, in which the lowest tier of the strict hierarchy were practically slaves. The English climate was kinder than that of the other kingdoms of the British Isles; in the south, peasants could make a small surplus – some hens, a hide, a fleece – which they could sell or barter. This was more difficult elsewhere. It made England richer than its immediate neighbours. Natural obstacles, like the mountains of Scotland or Wales, were formidable, while the Fens of East Anglia and the bogs of Ireland had yet to be drained. King John's baggage train was famously drowned as it crossed the treacherous bite of tidal mudflats known as the Wash, with the loss of the crown jewels.

There were as yet few stone spires on the horizon, belonging to churches and monasteries – they were a product of the later Middle Ages. Most buildings, even in areas like the Cotswolds where stone was plentiful, were made of wood. It was a world shaped by human muscle, aided by horses and oxen. Prising stone from the face of a quarry was effortful and iron chisels might not last the day. Blocks had to be dragged to the building site, shaped and hauled into position, perhaps using a crane powered by a man walking inside what looked like a giant hamster wheel. Wood was easier to work and not only provided the timber for walls but nearly all articles in everyday use – carts, stools, spinning wheels, spoons. Every so often a stone building of immense size rose above the surrounding land: an abbey, a cathedral or a castle. For different reasons, both the religious buildings and castles inspired awe.

Castles were a Norman idea. Several date from the years after William the Conqueror's invasion of England in 1066. They grew up over generations, beginning, perhaps, with a tower keep and expanding to embrace an ever-greater area of land, with curtain walls and gatehouses. Often built on hills, they could be seen from miles around. These buildings were, to the medieval mind, so massive, so immemorial that they could only have been begun by legendary figures such as King Arthur, Julius Caesar or giants. They might be visited for long periods by the lord who owned them, in which case they would be fitted with comfortable apartments and become palaces. Or they might fall into a state of neglect, which could last many years until, perhaps, a new use was found and a flurry of building activity put them straight, fitting them for the accommodation of another lord. They reminded England that it was a conquered territory whose monarchs were often more interested in their dynastic possessions in parts of France and whose ruling elite spoke French. John's son Henry III learnt some English from the wet nurse with whom he spent his early years but other lords must have relied on Anglo-French glossaries such as that compiled in the 1250s by Walter of Bibbesworth for the management of estates.

A powerful lord was likely to hold many castles and estates, as well as offices such as sheriff (the representative of royal authority in a shire, whose role could be abused to extort money through the court) and wardships (by which the holder ran the estates of orphans until they reached maturity, with profits going to himself), although a reverse of fortune could mean that they were taken away as swiftly as they had been given. Little was secure in the Middle Ages. England was almost perpetually fighting Scotland, Ireland and, until the late thirteenth century, Wales. The Hundred Years War with France, as the kings of England struggled to obtain the French throne, was pursued in numerous expensive campaigns in which the occasional stellar victory – Crécy, Poitiers, Agincourt – stands out against a background of wearisome sieges. To the uncertainties of war were added the dangers of court politics and local strife. Noblemen had to battle for their possessions. From his power base of Pembroke Castle, William Marshal, Earl of Pembroke, regarded as the most chivalrous knight in Christendom, launched a freelance invasion of Ireland to secure his wife's enormous inheritance, which included Leinster. Since the twelfth century, a Norman enclave known as the Pale existed around Dublin but Marshal's offensive helped secure Ireland as an Anglo-Norman colony: the beginning of an unhappy history.

Monarchs stayed in royal castles and hunting lodges. Hunting was a major preoccupation of the medieval elite, for whom good horsemanship was an important military skill, and hundreds of deer parks were created, many with lodges to accommodate a hunting party. However, castles and hunting lodges were not the only large domestic buildings in the countryside: there was a much greater number of manor houses. The manor house was a product of the feudal system, imposed on England and Ireland by the Normans and copied in Scotland. Under feudalism, land was parcelled up among the king's most important supporters, who in turn subdivided it: possession depended on the owner providing services to his superior. Peasants worked on the lord's land in return for their own strips of ground and rights to graze their animals and gather wood. (Disputes were settled in the manor court, which was a significant source of profit to the lord. He could extract fines or fees for almost any economic activity.) Ultimately this pyramid supplied the king with knights to fight in his army. Everybody was somebody else's vassal, to whom he owed services in return for land, up to and even including the king; the king of Scotland was meant to pay homage to the king of England. Above even the king of England was the Pope, to whom King John, for example, paid homage; the Church formed a kind of alternative state, massively resourced, its priests subject to its own courts rather than the king's. Malefactors who were not priests could claim right of sanctuary on Church land which saved them from prosecution, and since the areas subject to sanctuary could be quite large, some debtors stayed there for years. The realm was often run by clerics who provided the administrative class.

Land meant power and riches in an economy fuelled by obligation and human hands rather than cash surpluses. With land went people who could work and fight for you. The unit of land on which this system was based was the manor, and manors were run from halls: the hall was the centre of administration, of communal life and the place where justice was given. To it could be attached chambers that the lord could stay in, making the complex into a manor house. Few early manor houses have come down to us because the wood from which they were built did not survive. We must imagine them as compounds of different structures within a ditch, rather than a single dwelling. The ditch kept livestock from straying; there were probably light defences against raids by thieves or unscrupulous neighbours. A rare stone building called Boothby Pagnell Manor House in Lincolnshire dates from about 1200: it now stands on its own on a lawn but would originally have been surrounded by other manorial buildings. There is a vaulted ground floor, like the crypt of a church. Historians used to call the room above it a first-floor hall but there was probably a large and separate hall built of wood somewhere nearby, perhaps connected by a covered way. What survives was really a great chamber to which the family would have retired to the comfort of the big fireplace that was set into the wall.

A woman who owned many manors was Margaret of Lincoln. Born Margaret Quincy, she had first married at the age of twelve. Her husband, who was twenty-seven years older than her, died in 1240, soon to be followed by Margaret's mother, the Countess of Lincoln. As a very wealthy widow in her early thirties, Margaret was considered a significant prize, still of childbearing age and ripe for another marriage. The man who won her was the fourth son of William Marshal: his three brothers had died before him and he was now 5th Earl of Pembroke. But Pembroke died in 1245, leaving Margaret, who was entitled as a widow to a third of his estates, a rich and independent woman in a man's world. Other women in her position found themselves bullied into a political marriage with one of the king's supporters, but she avoided this fate; when she did eventually remarry, it must have been to a man of her own choice since he was of inferior rank. Until then she had personal responsibility for her vast estates and many houses, which she ran herself. Fortunately, her plight was noticed by the greatest scholar of the age, Robert Grosseteste, Bishop of Lincoln. Then in his seventies, Grosseteste came from a humble background in Suffolk and rose through the Church; he could berate

Henry III in thunderous letters when he thought the king was trespassing on the Church's prerogatives, although he was also said to be a man of great charm. Lincoln was England's largest diocese, covering eight counties, so, like Margaret, he oversaw an immense estate, the officers and servants of which would have been nearly all men. He decided to give Margaret some advice in the form of forty-five rules, written in Norman French.

The first rule instructed Margaret to find out what she owned. This may seem strange to us, given the thoroughness with which property transactions are recorded; but ownership in the Middle Ages was vaguer. It depended as much on tradition, a knowledge of local landmarks and parish boundaries, and sometimes brute force, as it did on written evidence in the manorial court roll (most of the population could not read). Once Margaret had established the extent of her land holdings, she had to calculate what each manor was likely to produce. From this she deducted the seed corn to be kept for the next year and the food to be given as servants' wages, the result being what she could commit each year to the sustenance of her household. Each manor should be largely self-sufficient. Sales of wool and cheese yielded the cash with which she could purchase the few things that did not originate from the estate, such as wine, wax candles and clothes. Rule twenty gives the Bishop of Lincoln's household's recipe for bread.

To make sure that Margaret's property was run efficiently, her income maintained and the possibility of being cheated reduced, she had to visit in person. We can picture her on the road between her castles and manors with the help of the illuminated book of psalms made for the Luttrell family in Lincolnshire, known as Luttrell Psalter, now in the British Library; one of the decorations shows some ladies in a coach, which was no more than a long wagon covered by a gaily coloured awning, pulled by five horses in line (see fig. 2). Progress would have been slow and, without suspension, bone-jarringly uncomfortable for the occupants of the conveyance as it bumped over the deeply rutted roads.

Margaret did not travel alone but with her family, in Latin *familia*. Our meaning of the word, confined to parents, children and other blood relatives, did not emerge for another hundred years. In the Middle Ages it referred to everybody associated with a great lord – children, chaplains,

FIG. 2 *Households on the move must have been a common sight in the Middle Ages, as lords and prelates and their retinues moved between the many manors that a great family owned. This illustration from the Luttrell Psalter from around 1325–40 shows a party of ladies in a richly decorated, if uncomfortable wagon: the one on the left is being handed a pet dog, while the one on the right has a squirrel on her shoulder. © British Library Board. All Rights Reserved / Bridgeman Images*

poor relations, knights, squires, pages, ladies-in-waiting, steward, marshal, butler, pantler (the man in charge of the bread), veneur (huntsman), falconer, servants, clerk of works and the portable entertainment system known as a fool. A bishop or abbot, necessarily unmarried, had a *familia*, much like a noble's; it later came to be known as the household. There had been an inflation in the size of both royal and noble households during the Middle Ages. While Saxon kings kept no more than a couple of dozen men around them, the early fourteenth century household of Thomas, Earl of Lancaster comprised over seven hundred people, including guests and paupers; most of them were servants.

Households of this type had a long run, surviving in the retinues of clan chiefs in the remote Highlands of Scotland into the eighteenth century. At Castle Grant, Alexander Grant maintained a bard, armour bearer, piper and champion, the last two of whom were painted in full-length portraits in 1713, splendid in their tartan livery and trappings of office.

A household on the move must have been one of the sights of the countryside. The ladies were preceded by an advance guard of their household, to have ensured that their destination was ready to receive them. The lord and his friends went on horseback, hawks on wrists, footmen running by their sides to hold their stirrups when they wanted to get down. Their priests rode beside them on palfreys to provide conversation. Another party trundled after them with the furniture and fittings that would transform an empty building into a dwelling place, if not exactly a home. The journeys continued until agriculture changed in the late Middle Ages, partly because of the devastating plague of 1348–9 known as the Black Death. This reduced the population of England by a third, leaving fewer people to work the land: the attempts to control the inevitable rise in wages and increased bargaining power on the part of the peasants caused discontent, ending in a revolt. A boom in the price of wool meant that it was, in any case, more profitable to farm sheep, which needed only a few shepherds to look after them. So lords leased out their manors, taking a rental income but rarely visiting; when they did, the tenant might be required to move into the gatehouse to make way for them. The old peripatetic tradition was maintained only by a smaller number of energetic and easily bored figures like Henry VIII.

A great household could not stay anywhere for more than a few weeks. They ate their way through the food, and large numbers of people crammed into every corner, combined with poor sanitation meant that conditions soon became undesirable. So they furled up the tapestries, packed away the bedding and took apart the furniture, piling all of it, along with the pots and pans from the kitchen, onto the caravan of carts and set off, leaving behind them a bare shell that could be swept out and washed down. The huge size of noble households required equally large buildings to put them up. Major dwellings were arranged around two courtyards like an Oxford or Cambridge college: an outer court to which everyone had access and an inner one that was more private.

Most medieval architecture was built on a cellular principle, with different rooms being added as needed, rather like the carriages of a train; and the function of each element could generally be read from the outside. In any domestic building, college or inn of court, the most important room was the hall. It was both a practical space and an immemorial institution of great symbolic purpose – in a dwelling it was the place where the lord, his household and everyone associated with the manor ate together. This formed a bond of community which was regarded as of almost sacred importance, as it had been to the Vikings from whom the Normans were descended. Externally it could be identified by its tall roof and lantern. The space inside was warmed by a fire of logs, smouldering on a central hearth: smoke circled up towards the roof, blackening the rafters, until it drifted out through a turret with side openings at the top. The central hearth was a tradition that died hard; William I had a wall fireplace in the Tower of London and there is another at Boothby Pagnell, complete with a chimney, but it took until 1500 for wall fireplaces to be generally adopted. Owners cleaved to the central hearth, centuries after its apparent redundancy.

The best surviving example of an unaltered great hall is at Penshurst Place in Kent (fig. 3). Penshurst was built by Sir John Pulteney, a Leicestershire man who came to London to make his fortune as a draper (cloth merchant) and moneylender: he became Lord Mayor of London and died at the time of the Black Death owning land in eight counties as well as two big London houses. Like other Londoners over the years, he

FIG. 3 *Penshurst Place in Kent preserves the central hearth, which was for centuries a traditional feature of great halls. A hall was the centre of manorial life and seat of justice, around which chambers might be added for the accommodation of the lord and his family. Open timber roofs, such as this one, were a characteristic feature of English architecture.* © *Country Life Picture Library*

wanted a comfortable house not far from the City: Penshurst was chosen for its deer park, where he could hunt. Pulteney acquired it in the 1340s and built a manor house. The great hall has a lofty timber roof and tall windows that look as though they might belong to a church: there was no difference between the ornament used for religious and domestic buildings (though far more money was lavished on churches, abbeys and cathedrals than on domestic architecture). Later in the century, hall roofs developed into a phenomenon of carpentry, forming a daring geometrical structure in which the weight was distributed through projecting timbers and braces, the ultimate expression of which was the hammerbeam roof; spaces wider than a single timber could be spanned without the need for columnar support. Massive timbers were used, creating a spectacular and particularly English effect (other countries preferred flat ceilings).

A great hall was always busy. When the communal meal had finished, the trestle tables were taken down, straw mattresses spread out and many of the household dossed down where they had just eaten, clustering around the central hearth like campers around a campfire. Attendance was obligatory. As the Middle Ages went on, servants increasingly slept where they worked – in the kitchen, in the stables – but the lord's whole workforce coming together for a communal meal was an act of ritual. Even married men should not be allowed to go home to eat, according to Bishop Grosseteste; nor should anyone be permitted to take their food in a private room. Many years later, the Protestant scholar Desiderius Erasmus derided English floors, made of bare clay and covered in 'rushes from the marshes, so carelessly renewed that the foundation sometimes remains for twenty years, harbouring there below spittle and vomit and urine of dogs and men, beer that hath been cast forth and remnants of fishes and other filth unnameable'. As a Dutchman, Erasmus probably overstated the squalor. Certainly the etiquette books that were produced in growing numbers as the Middle Ages went on, and behaviour in the hall became codified, stress the importance of personal cleanliness in the form of handwashing. There must have been a hubbub of voices but marshals were on hand to prevent rowdiness and quarrelling.

The lord's table was raised on a dais and lit by a tall projecting window called an oriel. The high table was placed crossways and he sat on a chair with a hood over it or a carved beam behind; the tables for his household ran up and down the hall lengthways and men sat on benches (an arrangement still seen at Oxford and Cambridge colleges, the Inns of Court and City livery halls). Beside the lord on the high table would have been members of his family, important guests and the priests from his chapel – literate men who could also act as secretaries; all would have faced the body of the hall since tables were long and thin, only one side of them being used by diners, the other being left open for servants to access.

Opposite the lord, at the low end of the hall, was a wooden screen, generally with three openings. Behind it, a cross passage provided a means of going from one external court to another as well as ventilation to draw out some of the smoke from the hall. On the further side of the passage, aligned with the openings in the screen, were three doorways. One of the side doors gave into the pantry (a word derived from the French *pain*, meaning bread) where the dried goods and tableware were stored; a thick slice of bread called a trencher served instead of a plate. The other side door gave access to the buttery (from butt or barrel) where the drink and drinking vessels were kept. The division was not only physical but formal: each area was supervised by a different official, respectively the steward and the butler. Between these doors lay the third opening: this was for the passage that led to the kitchen, placed some way off in a separate structure because of the risk of fire.

Meals were served with pomp. First the bread and wine were brought in from the pantry and buttery, in a ceremony that may have reminded some diners of the Eucharist. Cooked dishes were then held high and led to the lord's table by the steward. At a great feast, they would have been accompanied by fanfares of trumpets. On extra special occasions, they may even have been preceded by an official on a horse. Further rites attended the cutting up and serving of the lord's food.

The layout of the hall remained constant for hundreds of years. Even when the central hearth was abandoned, the louvre in the roof above it, externally expressed as a lantern, was kept as part of the dignity of the architecture. A memory of it, in the second half of the seventeenth century, was the cupola (small dome) that decorated the roofline of many country houses.

Over time, the lord and his family stopped eating hugger-mugger in the hall, where the heavy smell of woodsmoke cannot always have been successful in masking other odours. They retreated upstairs to the great chamber: a habit bemoaned by the fourteenth-century poet William Langland in *Piers Plowman*. One of the best descriptions of the way a great chamber was used comes from an unlikely source: official accounts of the murder of Thomas Becket in 1170. Four knights arrived from Henry II's court in France, intent on a conversation. They went first into the hall of his palace at Canterbury. He was not there – only the servants who, having just served the archbishop, were now eating. Laws of hospitality dictated that the knights should be courteously greeted, as they were by the chief officer of the hall, Becket's steward, who escorted them upstairs. Becket had retired to the great chamber. He was found there, seated on his bed talking to a monk. His reception of the knights was deliberately rude and they pursued him into the cathedral, slicing off the top of his head. It will have been seen that the bed in Becket's great chamber was used for more things than sleeping: this expensive piece of furniture also served as somewhere to sit while talking to friends or senior officials of the household or estate. More formal meetings took place in the parlour – for talking, derived from the French *parler* (to talk) – beneath the great chamber, on the ground floor.

Far more splendid than anything to be found in a lord's house were the religious foundations that he supported, such as the church containing his family tomb. God was omnipresent in the Middle Ages and people constantly crossed themselves, sought the intercession of their chosen saints with the Almighty, and swore oaths by them and their relics. Some rich families had their own chapels, as well as portable altars that they could take on their travels, which were something of a status symbol since the convenience had to be paid for: services could only take place under licence. Really smart houses had, off the chapel, closets for reading holy books, such as richly decorated psalters and books of hours. The earliest of such closets were enclosed by fabric; later they developed into miniature rooms with their own fireplaces.

Manor houses formed their own self-contained world, complete with stables for horses, dairies to make cheese and slaughterhouses to kill beasts for the table – to be placed at a quarter of a mile's distance, according to the Tudor doctor Andrew Boorde in his *Dyetary of Health*. We have details of Sir William Hamilton's set-up at Newton Castle in Ayrshire from a court case brought against a neighbour for attacking it. This reveals that behind the high boundary walls were four courts, the outer three of which contained orchards, fishponds, two stables, brewery, granary, bakery, salt house, meat house, cheese house, coal house, fish houses and a larder.

Two of the most evocative medieval manor houses that survive today are Markenfield Hall in Yorkshire and Stokesay Castle in Shropshire (fig. 4). Stokesay was built by Lawrence of Ludlow, who became an extremely rich man running flocks of sheep and dealing in wool; he even lent money to the king. He acquired the manor in 1281, along with the right of free warren (meaning that he could hunt) and later a licence to crenellate. The latter allowed him to erect battlements; as the Middle Ages went on, battlements might be intended for show and status as much as defence, but

FIG. 4 *Stokesay Castle, Shropshire, on the Welsh border, was built by the very rich wool merchant Lawrence of Ludlow in the 1280s. While the tall windows of the great hall would have been vulnerable to attack, there were also two towers, one of them – seen on the right – quite possibly inspired by Edward I's contemporary Caernarfon Castle, on the coast of North Wales. Until the twentieth century, Stokesay was surrounded by a large village. Paul Hutchinson, Virtual Shropshire Drone Rangers, www.dronerangers.co.uk*

the border with Wales would still have been dangerous when Lawrence was building. While Stokesay must have helped Lawrence run his flocks and land, the scale and quality of the hall shows that he clearly intended to use it himself and wanted to make an impression. It has tall, pointed windows of plate tracery and a lofty roof made of crucks (large naturally curved timbers). The big expanse of window means that this was not a military building, although two stout towers indicate that Lawrence was taking no chances. One of the towers – an octagon – may have been inspired by the contemporary Caernarfon Castle, the most spectacular and sumptuous of the castles that Edward I built around the coast of North Wales. Stokesay was also protected by a moat, a wall enclosing a courtyard and a gatehouse – although the beautiful half-timbered gatehouse we see today is a Jacobean romance, built at the time that Stokesay became a gentleman's seat pure and simple, rather than the working centre of a manor which doubled as a grand residence. The 'jettied' or projecting wooden structure on top of North Tower is, however, largely medieval: a survival of the wooden structures that were often built on top of castle walls.

In Yorkshire, Markenfield Hall received a licence to crenellate in 1310. Like Stokesay it is moated, with a fine hall next to a battlemented tower. The family fled after the Rising of the North against Elizabeth I and, after falling into use as a farmhouse, it changed little. Today, one's heart stops when one sees it – ancient, idyllic and remote. In the fourteenth century, however, it was on a major road and the man who built it, John de Markenfield, was far from being a sensitive soul. Like other poor but clever children he took holy orders, not with the object of becoming a priest but gaining the education to become a royal administrator. His work for the ineffectual King Edward II was rewarded by the award of a number of Church livings in Edward's gift. For two years he served as Chancellor of the Exchequer. Royal favour protected de Markenfield from a charge of raping a widow. While Edward II's disaster at the Battle of Bannockburn increased the danger of Scottish raids and could have been one reason that Markenfield felt the need to fortify his manor house, they were also disordered times, and this violent and unscrupulous man also had his own enemies closer to home. Anywhere, disputes between arrogant and greedy neighbours could erupt into violence. One Norfolk manor house was stormed by 'riotous people to the number of a thousand persons', it was claimed.

As well as castles and manor houses, there was another precursor to the country house: the pleasance. The word means joy or delight, often in a sexual context – 'Wher he may finde Plesance of love, his herte boweth,' wrote the poet John Gower – and a playful name might be attached. Pleasances were built as an escape from the main residence of the estate: a place where the lord could get away from most of the household and enjoy a degree of privacy and frolic with his intimates – family, closest friends, sexual partners. John of Gaunt had the Bird's Nest in Leicester Forest and Henry V the Pleasance in the Marsh outside Kenilworth Castle. In the twelfth century Henry II would meet his mistress Rosamund Clifford at a house near Woodstock Palace, called either Everswell from the spring around which it was built or, for more obvious reasons, Rosamunds. Prelates did not commission sybaritic pleasances (at least not in name) but they also wanted time out; abbots and other senior officers of monasteries might be granted manors on which they developed bolt-holes: one example is Abbots Grange at Broadway, in the Cotswolds.

There was a pleasance at Sheen (later called Richmond) on the river Thames. This was where Richard II had his favourite palace, a few miles upstream from London. Sheen Palace had been erected by Edward III as a collection of wooden buildings within a moat. Here Richard would come with his court of over a thousand people. This was large, even by medieval standards, but is explained partly through its being, in effect, two courts. Richard adored his queen, Anne of Bohemia; teenagers when they married, they were inseparable and their courts merged. Richard added some luxurious new accommodation, complete with numerous lavatories and fireplaces, but for himself, Anne and presumably special friends, he went further. The court was, like all medieval courts, crowded, jostling but highly formal – and Richard, who had an extreme sense of his own majesty, was always the king. It was also the place where the business of government was transacted, something that bored this temperamentally theatrical young man. So he created a getaway called La Neyt on an island in the Thames, separated from the rest of the palace by water. Here he installed a large bathtub – *cuva ad Balneam* – with bronze taps for hot and cold water; two thousand painted tiles covered the walls of the bathroom. The court official who oversaw the maintenance of La Neyt, incidentally, was the first great poet to write in English, Geoffrey Chaucer: another sign of the sophistication that Richard enjoyed (not that Richard had a great liking for poetry and Anne never mastered the English language; fortunately Richard spoke excellent French).

We can form a picture of this pleasance. La Neyt provided the bolt-hole where a close group of sophisticated, loved-up young people went to have fun, out of the eye of the world. When Anne of Bohemia died in her late twenties in 1394, Richard expressed his feelings by having the whole of Sheen Palace destroyed. This was a response to overwhelming grief, typical perhaps of the histrionic side of Richard's nature, but a sign too that La Neyt, as a place, truly meant something to him. Sheen was more than a collection of rooms waiting to be filled with life when the owner arrived. It inspired an intensely emotional response. Many country houses would evoke a similar attachment from their owners down the ages. They would become, like La Neyt, personal Arcadias or refuges from the bitterness of the world outside.

Politically, escapism would prove a poor strategy for Richard. Scathingly described as a knight of Venus, the goddess of love, rather than Bellona, the goddess of war, he was deposed in 1399 and murdered the following year. These events would lead to the long and debilitating struggle between different branches of the ruling house known as the Wars of the Roses in the next century. But for the moment, Richard's pleasure in the domestic arts was reflected in a flurry of building, which included the first major dwellings to be constructed without fortifications. Dartington Hall in Devon, built for the king's half-brother John Holland, Duke of Exeter, was not a military building, nor was it merely a centre of manorial administration. The country house was in gestation if not actually born.

CHAPTER TWO

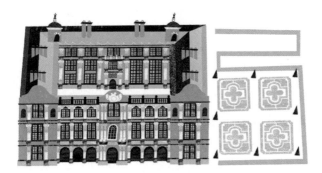

Tudor and Elizabethan

HALF a century after the death of Richard II in 1400, the different branches of the Plantagenet family quarrelled over the kingdom. The resulting Wars of the Roses were a sporadic series of skirmishes and some pitched battles between private armies, which may not have affected the country at large very much but took a dire toll of the ruling elite; around half of England's noble families were destroyed. With them, over time, went the great country houses that they built, which could only be supported by successful people who were able to shine at court and make rich marriage alliances. No trace now survives of the palace that William de la Pole, Duke of Suffolk built at Ewelme in Oxfordshire: Suffolk had virtually ruled England, such was his influence over the indecisive Henry VI. By 1450, a disastrous treaty, followed by war, had lost England most of its territories in France and the king was forced to commit Suffolk to exile. However, his ship was intercepted and his head summarily hacked off with a rusty sword. The house had been sumptuous – 'so rich that I did never see the like', according to a traveller in 1574. A unique feature appears to have been the use of iron bars to span the hall, rather than wooden beams. The only great Lancastrian country house to come down to us is Herstmonceux Castle in Sussex.

Massed artillery was first used in England at one of the battles in the Wars of the Roses in 1460. Gunpowder reduced the military importance of castles and made knights as vulnerable as common soldiers. So chivalry was dead – or so one might have thought. But almost as soon as the civil war had ended, with the Battle of Bosworth in 1485 and the Tudor dynasty on the throne, chivalry underwent the first of many revivals. When Henry VIII went on campaign, he travelled with a collapsible wooden castle, which for ease of assembly was erected with screws, iron plates and nuts and bolts rather than traditional pegged carpentry joints. Castles, even wooden ones, projected power; they displayed the venerability of their owner's lineage and his position at the top of the feudal hierarchy. They were also a key part of the imaginative landscape of chivalric romance, kept alive in the jousts and tournaments that Henry loved as a young man. Numerous country-house owners would fall in love with castles, however impractical, over the coming centuries, often displaying weapons and armour on their walls to enhance the warlike effect. Not that Henry's travelling castle was purely Gothic in style: it also incorporated Classical motifs such as 'great columns', in tribute to the king's self-image as a Renaissance prince.

In the 1530s the king broke with the Roman Catholic Church and dissolved its monasteries, destroying institutions which had previously owned vast swathes of England and Wales. It was a gigantic act of nationalisation. What had been Church assets, now owned by the king, were then sold or parcelled out among his supporters. The market in former monastic lands created a grand opportunity for Tudor merchants and courtiers, for whom landowning represented so much that they liked: status, a good return on their money, dynastic potential, political influence and hunting. It stimulated the building of country houses. Most obviously, there were more sites to raise them on.

Old abbey buildings were systematically pillaged for what could be sold – lead, which was difficult to mine, being stripped from the roofs and melted down; bells hauled away to be recast as cannon; stone carted off for use in the local town; precious vestments turned into bed hangings. And quite often the monastic buildings were converted into secular dwellings or served as a quarry from which materials were taken to construct a new country house. 'Abbey' was shamelessly preserved in the name of some houses, such as Lacock Abbey in Wiltshire (made out of the old cloisters; fig. 5) and Buckland Abbey, in Devon (converted from the very church). Remote abbeys and priories were left to moulder as ruins until rediscovered by the Picturesque Movement in the eighteenth century. Rich men got richer by farming sheep on land previously owned by monasteries.

And they no longer spent so lavishly on churches. During the Middle Ages, the richest, most beautifully made and adorned buildings had been cathedrals, abbeys and parish churches. In newly Protestant England and Wales, the doctrine changed. There was no longer the threat of purgatory, the time a soul spent being purged of its sins before judgment, which could be reduced by endowing chantries or donating stained-glass windows; so the money that would previously have been spent on masses

FIG. 5 *The name of Lacock Abbey in Wiltshire indicates that it was once a convent; the medieval cloisters were retained when the nunnery buildings were converted to a country house. The Dissolution of the Monasteries by Henry VIII provided a spur to country-house building, by opening up a market in land and giving ambitious men new estates.* © *National Trust*

for the dead could be redirected. Rich families still commissioned tomb sculptures but without the previous rites: they were an opportunity for Elizabethans to celebrate their lineage, real or made up, through heraldry. (Often the figures were shown as knights in armour, as they might have been in the Middle Ages: a deliberate anachronism that continued into the seventeenth century.) But otherwise the adornment of churches took second place to the country house.

Tudor monarchs, prelates, noblemen and magnates were not shy of displaying their wealth; on the contrary they flaunted it. This may have been just as true of medieval magnates but the sixteenth century justified display through a belief in magnificence. Sumptuous clothes made of expensive fabrics sewn with jewels, sideboards groaning with gold and silver vessels, splendid horses in rich caparisons, large numbers of retainers dressed in livery, stupendous feasts and extravagant building projects were expected of great people – it was almost, since their wealth was good for the country, their patriotic duty to provide them. Magnificence meant ostentation but was also associated in contemporary minds with benevolence and generosity. This was an age of spectacle and fantasy, luxury, novelty and show – and nowhere more so than in the country house.

In this Henry VIII set an example. He had a gargantuan appetite for buildings, owning sixty-three palaces and travelling between them in the medieval manner, with over fifty travelling trunks: each was packed with the contents of a room so the king would find the same configuration of furniture wherever he was. Henry improved existing palaces around London, Greenwich being the favourite of his early reign, and erected one of his own: Nonsuch in Surrey – whose name proclaims that there was nothing else like it in the world. From a distance, it looked like a fabulous, impossible, crazy castle, built largely of wood but decorated with rows of columns. Between the columns were panels of stucco ornament designed by the Italian artificer Nicholas Bellin who had already worked for Henry's rival, François I of France. The cloud-capp'd towers have now completely vanished although some of its panelling can be seen at Loseley Park in Surrey.

None of Henry's children – the boy king Edward VI, Mary Tudor who only reigned for five years, and Elizabeth I – followed his example in building. Elizabeth, who became queen in 1558 and lived until 1603, was more frugal than her father and did not want the cost of upkeep of so many buildings; instead she let her courtiers bear the cost of entertaining her when she made 'progresses' around the country, by staying with them. A royal visit was cripplingly expensive but worth it, in her hosts' eyes, if it enabled them to ingratiate themselves to the point of winning valuable monopolies and grants of land. They competed to outdo each other, so wherever Elizabeth went, she was treated to tournaments and theatrical pieces, often in elaborate if ephemeral architectural settings, that celebrated her and her reign in elaborate allegory. When she visited Robert Dudley, Earl of Leicester, at Kenilworth Castle in 1575, the dazzling entertainments lasted nineteen days (fig. 6). Fireworks could be heard twenty miles away. The prospect of a royal visit spurred country-house builders to such heights of spectacle and orgies of spending that their homes have come to be called prodigy houses.

FIG. 6 *Great castles were a phenomenon of the Middle Ages, built over many campaigns and some so big it was thought they could only have been constructed by legendary figures or giants. Kenilworth in Warwickshire was begun in the twelfth century and developed by Edward III's immensely rich son John of Gaunt. Elizabeth I granted it to her favourite Robert Dudley, Earl of Leicester, who entertained her there in spectacular style.* © *Alamy*

Where did the money come from? Until his disgrace and death in 1530, the richest man in the kingdom after the king was his Lord Chancellor, Cardinal Thomas Wolsey. Wolsey was probably the son of a butcher and innkeeper from East Anglia but, like other clever boys, entered the Church: clerics could be administrators (like John de Markenfield in an earlier time) as well as clergymen and it could be a route to influence and wealth. Not only was he Archbishop of York but Bishop of Winchester, Bishop of Tournai and Abbot of St Albans, as well as a cardinal and the papal legate, meaning that he was vested with the Pope's authority. For most of his career he was on good terms with Henry VIII; although his supervision of the courts of Chancery and Star Chamber kept him in London, while Henry was hurrying between palaces – particularly at times of the alarming new plague known as the sweating sickness – they met once a week. So like other courtiers he would have received fees in return for offices distributed and favours done, that income being augmented by large presents given by aspirants for ecclesiastical posts. He owned four palaces, of which the most splendid, Hampton Court, had been bought with his own money and expanded in a style that included Renaissance roundels supplied by foreign artists; Wolsey had travelled as a diplomat and took a detailed interest in his many building projects.

Was Henry VIII jealous of Wolsey's achievement, as popular mythology has it? No. It was expected that great churchmen would live in splendour, with an official need for a processional route from their private quarters to the chapel (also a feature of royal palaces, since it was on the way to the chapel that the monarch could be petitioned by courtiers seeking favours). Wolsey pressed Henry to regard Hampton Court as his own, and he did, eventually taking it for himself.

Like Margaret of Lincoln, the noblewoman known as Bess of Hardwick acquired immense wealth through marriage; all four of her husbands predeceased her, so that she accumulated a spectacular portfolio of estates. She built Hardwick Hall in Derbyshire on the proceeds, having previously erected the first version of Chatsworth House with her second husband Sir William Cavendish (fig. 7).

Sir Walter Raleigh was another who rose to affluence through sex appeal. Six foot tall, at a time when that was unusual, he is portrayed in a

FIG. 7 *Hardwick Hall in Derbyshire is the great masterpiece of the Elizabethan country house. While the elevated site and towers recall the castle tradition, as does the symmetrical composition, the immense windows glittering with glass were expensive and new. Glass allowed country-house owners to admire the countryside from inside the house; they also poured light into rooms that were often decorated in bright colours.* © *National Trust*

miniature by Nicholas Hilliard as an exquisite and proud figure with jewels in his hair; Queen Elizabeth was smitten. She showered him with crown leases that he could sell, a patent or monopoly on the sale of wine that allowed him to extract money from vintners, the estates of the executed traitor, Sir Anthony Babington, and 42,000 acres in the Irish province of Munster. A Devon man, he was made an admiral, a role that might have brought great riches from captured Spanish galleons – although in the end when the fleet captured *Madre de Deus*, a Portuguese carrack laden with treasure, he was out of favour at court and his share of the booty was a relatively modest £2,000. He was also given a palace in London where he entertained the first Native American Algonquin to reach England from the New World. His country house in Dorset – New Lodge, later called Sherborne Castle – had chivalric battlements and towers to accord with his romantic self-image. He popularised the smoking of tobacco – spool forward to the smoking rooms and billiard rooms of the Victorian period. But courtiers who lose their influence with the monarch also lose their income: in a last act to recover his position, he set off on an expedition, funded by James I, to discover the legendary golden land of Eldorado. He failed and was executed on his return.

Historians used to talk of an altogether different class as being on the rise in these years: the landed gentry. The gentry provided most of the Members of Parliament and magistrates in England, their status often funded by the legal profession, by industries such as iron founding in the Weald of Kent and Sussex, or by wool. It is now thought that the landed gentry had been there all along: we have seen the fortune that Lawrence of Ludlow made out of wool in the thirteenth century. Nevertheless, the gentry of Tudor and Elizabethan England remain conspicuous from the country houses they built (fig. 8). This is now popularly regarded as the golden age of the 'manor house', although not every prosperous gentry house – or, in the Weald of Kent and Sussex, yeoman's hall house – had a manor of its own. They might, however, be buildings of equal size and ambition – a phenomenon particularly of England, rather than most continental countries, because of the nature of the economy. Lawyers, merchants and wool men grew rich and wanted houses that displayed their status. They formed a proud local society, in some cases displaying the symbols with which they marked their woolsacks rather than coats of arms; Brympton d'Evercy, in Somerset, even has statues of sheep on the skyline.

We tend now to see these beautiful houses through Edwardian eyes, because many of those that have come down to us, having fallen into neglect during the Georgian period, were romantically restored as family homes around 1900. Originally they would have been full of life but not always occupied by the people who built them. Already, prosperous individuals were likely to spend at least part of their time in London, whether visiting the courts of law or transacting sales with the merchants of the staple who held the monopoly on the wool exports. This had even been the case in the Middle Ages.

By descent, the Tudors were Welsh and it was during Henry VIII's reign that Wales was absorbed by England and made subject to English

FIG. 8 *Lytes Cary Manor in Somerset demonstrates the cellular principle on which early country houses were built. Rooms accreted around the great hall, the function of the different parts being plainly visible from the outside. The owners were a landed gentry family called Lyte with connections to the law.* © Alamy

laws, with the result that Welshmen had to take surnames. Ireland, meanwhile, was a divided into areas that had been conquered by Anglo-Normans, originally a small fortified Pale around Dublin, to which had been added Leinster and other parts of the South. The rest of the island was Gaelic-speaking and ruled by numerous chieftains in a state of constant warfare. English influence had been weakened by the Wars of the Roses but Henry VIII tried to reassert it by cajoling the native 'wild Irish' into submission and granting English titles to Gaelic noblemen. Plantations or colonies of English and Welsh Protestants were settled on former monastic lands or those that had been confiscated from rebellious chiefs. Ireland remained Catholic outside the English plantations, and its chiefs lived in tall castles. Those who built country houses were torn between the late medieval life that continued in traditional halls, with ritual feasting amid their retainers, and the Renaissance ideas that were the last word in England. Supported by Spain, the wild Irish opposed the further spread of English settlement, with the result that the biggest army to leave England during the sixteenth century – seventeen thousand men – was sent to colonise by force. It was such a disaster that its leader, the ageing Elizabeth's favourite Robert Devereux, 2nd Earl of Essex, was himself driven to rebel and was executed in 1601.

On marrying Henry VII's daughter Margaret in 1501, James IV of Scotland signed a Treaty of Perpetual Peace with England and created the first Palace of Holyroodhouse, next to an abbey in Edinburgh, for his bride; swept away by later building, it drew inspiration from both England and France and was given a backhanded compliment by a French member of the queen's retinue, who called it 'undoubtedly a fine building, little in keeping with the country'. James did not remain friends with England but revived the Auld Alliance with France, making an ill-judged incursion into English territory in 1513: only a few miles from the border the army was destroyed, the king himself, nine earls, fourteen lords and ten thousand soldiers being killed. James IV's son, James V, only a baby when he came to the throne, married a daughter of the King of France, François I; impressed with the French court, he wanted to emulate what he saw there. When his queen died after only a year at the age of sixteen, he took a second French bride, Mary of Guise. Not surprisingly, the architecture of his reign leant towards France.

♣

Tudor people loved novelty and two technical innovations and the arrival of new ideas from Italy and France helped shape their country houses. The innovations were brick and glass; the new ideas were those of the Renaissance. Brick was not in itself a new material: it was mentioned in the Bible and the Romans had used it in Britannia for engineering purposes. But after the Roman Empire collapsed, the inhabitants of Britain forgot how to make it. A revival came with itinerant brickmakers from the Low Countries in the twelfth century but it was very sporadic and largely confined to East Anglia. Only when Henry VI chose it as the material from which to construct his new foundation of Eton College in 1440, planned on an enormous scale, did brick become fashionable; Henry's Treasurer Sir Roger Fiennes followed his master's lead and used it for Herstmonceux.

Tudor bricks are thinner than Victorian and Georgian ones: the wood-fired kilns could not reach the high temperatures achieved with coal. Inconsistent in colour, they were laid with wide mortar joints which give a lightness to the façade. Furthermore, bricklayers discovered that these rosy rectangular cuboids of baked clay could create exuberant effects. Different coloured bricks were laid to make patterns, particularly lines crossing diagonally to form diamonds (diaper pattern). Chimneystacks, which proclaimed wealth and superiority to village houses where they were rarely seen, and which were so desirable that dummy ones might be erected, lent themselves to a fantastic variety of shapes. These techniques and more were used *con amore* at East Barsham Manor in Norfolk, begun in the 1520s by Sir Henry Fermor (fig. 9). Fermor was the richest man in the county, defying government efforts to limit the numbers of sheep owned by any one person by keeping no fewer than 15,500 of them in twenty flocks. The silhouette of East Barsham is all tower and turrets, crenellations and chimneystacks, while the surface of the gatehouse ripples with decorative bands, ornamental panels and heraldry. Such virtuoso displays required specially shaped bricks, whether formed in moulds or carved using a chisel once they were in place. Portrait heads

FIG. 9 *Brick was a relatively new material in the Tudor period. East Barsham Manor, begun in the 1520s and now partially demolished, shows the joy that Sir Henry Fermor, who owned enormous flocks of sheep, took in its decorative possibilities. Throughout, fancy patterns are created by exuberant brick laying. Gatehouses, such as the one here, on the right, were no longer needed for defence but were objects of display.* © Alamy

and heraldic beasts were glazed, which both made them shine and gave protection against weather.

Like brick, glass had been made for thousands of years. Stained glass was one of the glories of the Middle Ages but the sort of glass then available, whether or not coloured, was difficult to see through. Most came from abroad until a native industry developed in the late sixteenth century, reducing the cost. Elizabethan glass was thick, full of imperfections and could not be produced in anything but small panes, which admitted draughts when they got loose in the cames, or lead rods, that held them in place; but it was transparent. What joy it gave to the home. How windows sparkled when the sun caught them, and what an impetus the flood of light must have been to decoration, which could now be properly seen in all its bright colours. And for the first time, the inhabitants of a country house could look out over the countryside around them without going outside. While previous country houses occupied sheltered locations, away from the weather, the Elizabethans chose hilltop sites, recalling those of castles. Views were important to them. The great banks of windows could be seen glittering from afar. 'Bright as Holdenby', was one saying. Hardwick Hall was supposed to be 'more glass than wall'.

One of the first Englishmen to view himself as a Renaissance prince had been Duke Humfrey of Gloucester, Henry V's brother, who collected the precious Humanist books, copied by hand in Italy, that became the basis of the Bodleian Library in Oxford and who kept a court of scholars and poets at his pleasance at Greenwich in the 1430s. As yet, the visual culture derived from the ruins of Ancient Rome had not arrived. Shortly before Henry VIII came to the throne in 1509, the sculptor Pietro Torrigiani appeared from Florence; a couple of years later, Henry commissioned him to create his father's tomb. Torrigiani brought with him a flavour of the new style in art, with its study and celebration of the human body. The architecture of Classicism, last consistently practised in England when Britannia was part of the Roman Empire, was about to make a return.

Classicism is a system of proportion whose basic unit is the column. There are three principal types or orders of column, with different shafts and tops (capitals). The most severe is Doric. Ionic, whose capital has curved rolls of stone, called volutes, to either side, was thought of as being feminine. The Corinthian capital is largely made of acanthus leaves: this order was regarded as both magnificent and festive. These are the three orders described by the Roman architect Vitruvius in the first century AD but two subsidiary ones were added later: a rustic form of Doric called Tuscan and a more evolved form of the Corinthian, with volutes, called Composite. An entablature, or horizontal crosspiece, runs above the columns. There is an almost infinite variety of permutations that can be made from these basic elements; some façades are based on the proportions of one of the orders but the columns themselves are invisible and only implied. In however rustic a form, the Roman villas described in the Prologue would have been built according to this system. From the sixteenth century onwards, Classicism would become the commonest idiom of the country house.

Until the appearance of the architect Inigo Jones in the seventeenth century, most country-house builders did not understand Renaissance Classicism as a system of organisation but borrowed a rag bag of decorative details which they stuck onto buildings of a traditional form. Drawn from the designs published by the Dutchman Hans Vredeman de Vries and the Frenchman Philibert de l'Orme, in which harmonious proportions took second place to a fever of ornament, they were, for the most part, used in the manner of fashion accessories, signalling an awareness of the latest foreign trends. However, the Scottish King James V had a more intimate knowledge of the subject. In 1536, he had set out to meet his future father-in-law Charles V of France, caught up with him near Lyon and together they had journeyed through the Loire valley, then the largest Renaissance building site in Europe. At home, James began a series of building projects, not only fortifying Stirling Castle with a mighty gatehouse thought to render it impregnable but creating a hunting lodge out of Falkland Palace, one of the first Scottish buildings that was not defensive in character (fig. 10). A French mason was probably responsible for the run of Corinthian columns on tall bases and columns, and circular medallions containing busts of mythological heroes are displayed on the south front of Falkland. Fortunately, Falkland was rescued

FIG. 10 *Having visited France in pursuit of a bride, James V of Scotland was attuned to the Renaissance ideas being exhibited in the great building works there. The influence can be seen in the attached columns and roundels with busts at Falkland Palace, dating from the late 1530s. They may well have been the work of French masons.*

from collapse at the end of the nineteenth century by the Marquess of Bute who employed the scholarly architect John Kinross to restore it. At Stirling, the two new sets of lodgings built for the king and queen are similarly French in character, externally marked by carved figures standing on barley-sugar columns.

Like Duke Humfrey, James attracted a glittering array of musicians, poets and inventors to his court, as well as many 'cunning craftsmen', according to a contemporary chronicler, from Spain, Holland and England. They brought the court up to date, introduced 'many new engines and devices' and caused changes in 'men's behaviour' which gave the court a cosmopolitan gloss. Alas, the Renaissance sun that had dawned for Scottish architecture at Stirling and Falkland would go behind clouds during the turbulent reign of James V's only surviving legitimate child, Mary, Queen of Scots, and the troubled minority of her son, James VI of Scotland (James I of England). But it would burst forth again in the seventeenth century.

The men who were responsible for the design and construction of buildings in the Middle Ages had been masons and carpenters (not surprisingly, because of the technical difficulty of constructing stone vaults and hammerbeam roofs). The first person in Britain to be identified as an architect, in 1563, was John Shute, who paradoxically is not known to have designed anything; he was principally a painter. Indeed architects in the modern sense, as professional people who have been systematically trained and examined, did not exist before the twentieth century. But the emergence of the term in the sixteenth century reflects a change from an exclusively craft-based approach. It is significant that Shute's claim to fame rests on a book: *The first and chief groundes of architecture used in all the auncient and famous monymentes*, dedicated to Queen Elizabeth. This was the result of a tour of Italy that he had made in 1550. It illustrates the orders of architecture, after the manner of Sebastiano Serlio but enriched with his own ideas and observations. Books suggested learning and they disseminated ideas.

The first and chief groundes, though not specially influential in itself, showed a direction of travel: towards the orderliness of the Renaissance, with its rectangular outlines, flat façades bearing rows of identical columns and symmetrical disposition. The medieval domestic tradition did not favour symmetry, which was often a feature of castle keeps or indeed whole castles, such as Beaumaris on Anglesey, built by Edward I, but not country houses. Externally, a country house expressed the elements of which it was composed, with different roof heights and cross wings; the hall that formed the centrepiece of any composition was itself entered from one end, rather than the middle. Nevertheless, aestheticians say that symmetry makes an innate appeal to human beings, who are hardwired to recognise it in faces (two eyes either side of the nose) and the human body (two legs, two arms), and the Tudor world must have been astounded when it made its first grand appearance in country houses such as Longleat in Wiltshire, owned by Sir John Thynne. Thynne's prosperity had come as the result of his association with Lord Protector Somerset, who had run the country during the minority of Henry VIII's sickly male heir, Edward VI. From 1547, the Protector had spent a fortune rebuilding Somerset House on the Strand in London in a princely manner, with a gatehouse based on a triumphal arch. As Somerset's steward, in charge of his building works, Thynne had probably helped design it. He also largely designed Longleat himself – another departure, since medieval gentlemen did not design their own houses, which required the structural knowledge of specialist craftsmen.

Originally, Longleat had been a monastery; what we see now dates from after 1572. The entrance façade is symmetrical, with four bays of coupled windows. The roof line has a parapet, decorated with cresting and statues, behind which are pavilions on the roof. The grid-like façades are articulated with pilasters and decorated with circular niches containing busts. It is a tour de force of discipline and organisation which would influence all the major country houses built during the rest of the century.

One of the masons at Longleat, in its later stages, was Robert Smythson. Smythson was England's first architect in something approaching the modern sense. We have almost no architectural drawings from the Middle Ages. Smythson, however, left a hundred and fifty, some of which are surveys but others beautifully drawn designs. This cache may have survived by chance and perhaps other surveyors or proto-architects also drew their designs on paper; its existence, however, reflects a new way of conceptualising buildings: what will be experienced in three dimensions is rendered in two. A building that was fixed to the spot could be visualised and discussed somewhere else, without the need for a model. As a means of communicating the new ideas coming from France and Italy, drawing was invaluable.

Smythson was a member of the Masons' Company in London; he no doubt served an apprenticeship as a mason. He does not seem to have left England but he clearly knew some of the architectural treatises from the Continent – notably by Serlio and Vredeman de Vries. These two offered contrasting interpretations of Classicism, Serlio's being sumptuous but calm, that of Vredeman de Vries extravagant in its fantastic ornament. Smythson absorbed both and married them to the native Gothic tradition. Scholars now regard Hardwick Hall as his masterpiece but Smythson himself may have preferred Wollaton Hall in Nottinghamshire. Wollaton is an extraordinary creation, dramatic but indigestible, built for an owner of coal mines, Sir Francis Willoughby, who probably played a significant role in its design. Although rich, Willoughby was difficult, impulsive and rather paranoid – qualities that may have been exacerbated by the death of his parents when he was a child and the execution of his guardian for treason. Wollaton reflects some of the madness. Like other Elizabethan houses wanting to be seen, it stands on the top of a hill, in the castle tradition. The eminence is enhanced by Wollaton's most remarkable feature: a central tower that takes the place of what would normally have been an internal courtyard; lit by a clerestory, it rises high above the roofs of the rest of the house. It gives the impression of being a throwback to the castle keep. When Smythson died in 1614, his tomb denoted him as 'Architecter and Surveyor unto the most worthy house of Wollaton', built a quarter of a century before.

It has been suggested that Wollaton was intended to evoke the Temple of Jerusalem, built by the Biblical King Solomon and described in the Book of Kings. The allusion is not obvious today but the age that gave rise to Shakespeare was obsessed by puzzles and Biblical stories, as well as wordplay, heraldry, Classical learning, literary conceits, ingenious geometry, astrological prediction, complex sundials, alchemy – all things that were better expressed in words than art. Visitors to buildings such as Wollaton were mentally challenged to decode what they saw. Architecture became an extension of literature: a private world of the mind. The seven Corinthian columns above the porch at Kirby Hall, Northamptonshire, refer to Wisdom's seven pillars in the Book of Proverbs, associated with the hospitable 'killing of beasts' and 'mingling of wine'. The man who built it, Sir Christopher Hatton, Lord Chancellor to Queen Elizabeth, was a lawyer, and lawyers particularly rejoiced in erudite riddles.

The esoteric symbolism of Elizabethan architecture suggests an intensely rarefied world which only the privileged could enter. When the queen visited Sir Henry Lee, her recently retired champion, at Ditchley in 1592, he presented an elaborate allegory, in which he was the Old Knight or the Hermit; Elizabeth, as the Fairy Queen, was led through a grove in which knights had been turned into trees and ladies into leaves because of their inconstancy. The Hermit's cell was hung with 'enchanted pictures', all of which have elaborate meanings; although it would have been clear that the principal meaning of the whole production was that

Lee, who had established a ménage with the former lady-in-waiting, the disreputable Anne Vavasour, wanted to regain the queen's favour. Solitude, as espoused by the Hermit, was highly valued in the world of allegory, as can be seen from the many portraits of lovers or other melancholy gentlemen mournfully ruminating on love.

In real life, these poetic individuals might have found it difficult to evade their large retinues of servants and retainers, but there was one place that peace and quiet could usually be found: on the roof. Behind the parapet, roofs had flat stretches of lead on which the owner and his favoured guests could walk, a silhouette of a foot being sometimes made by running a sharp blade around the outside and cutting into the lead. A high vantage point revealed the geometry of the gardens, laid out as a chequerboard of formal walks and clipped hedge, and the intricate patterns that were formed in the compartments: knots, arabesques and labyrinths. The roof might also have had banqueting houses where an after dinner 'banquet' of sweetmeats and nuts could be eaten. Extraordinary roofscapes of turrets, obelisks, balusters, clock towers and heraldic beasts developed. Some owners built tree houses.

Hunting lodges provided another place of escape. Families would go there while their big house was being cleaned or when economies had to be made; the 5th Earl of Northumberland kept 'secret house' at his hunting lodge with a mere 42 retainers rather than the usual 166.

Two distinctive features inside the Elizabethan country house were the long gallery and the plasterwork. Like a particularly spacious corridor, the long gallery was somewhere that people could walk up and down on rainy days: the English were famously keen on exercise. The one at Hardwick is 170 feet long. Some ran to over 200 feet. It has been suggested that long galleries originated in France, and the earliest to survive in England, at The Vyne in Hampshire, was built for Sir William Sandys, a courtier of Henry VIII with close contacts with France; it dates from around 1520. Partly to save space, long galleries were sometimes 'skied', meaning located at the top of the house, in what might otherwise have been the attic. They were often used for the display of dynastic portraits that proclaimed the family's pedigree and status, along with a portrait of the queen to prove loyalty. As late as the 1690s in his work *Of Building*, the gentleman architect Sir Roger North described them as 'that noble accomplishment to an house'.

Elizabethan plasterwork was formed using wooden moulds; the result has a softer, bolder look than the bravura allegories of Italian stuccadores or the Adam brothers' brittle decoration in the Georgian period. High-relief figures were made by carving lumps of plaster when dry. Ceilings swirl with vine leaves, blaze with heraldry or riot with allegorical figures, painted in the rich colours that the Tudors loved, which only acquired their bluish, silvery hues with age. Geometrical patterns were punctuated by elaborate pendants, projecting downwards like thick stalactites. One room that came to be ceiled in this way was the great hall. Medieval open-timber roofs made it impossible to create another, more private room above them. Their tall pitch also created difficulties for the façade, when symmetry came into fashion. By the end of the sixteenth century, most great halls had ceilings as well as walled fireplaces (there would have been nowhere for the smoke to escape from an open hearth). They were also becoming lower, in all senses, being the place where servants ate and waited to be given tasks: the lord, his dinner and the ceremony that attended it had gone upstairs. Great value was attached to the route by which the great chamber was reached, via the increasingly splendid staircases that were being made possible by improvements in building technology both in stone and wood.

Surveyors, masons and country gentlemen sometimes struggled to find elegant ways to express the new ideas: the gauche and the glorious can be seen in the same building.

Burton Agnes was one of Smythson's last houses but, for all his experience, the need to regularise a front that had, in the centre, an asymmetrical great hall cost him some thought. He solved the dilemma by placing the front door in a projecting bay, at right angles to the façade: the effect is a little cramped (fig. 11). But that is forgotten once you have entered the great hall. Opposite is a monumental doorway carved with vines and Renaissance motifs, including four naked if somewhat skinny figures from Mount Olympus – Saturn, Jupiter, Mars and Venus. These though are nothing compared to the tiers of plasterwork – hampers as they are technically called – decorating the screens passage; they are crowded with

FIG. 11 *Carved and moulded plasterwork was a particular feature of the English country house. In the great hall at Burton Agnes, in the East Riding of Yorkshire, built in the first decade of the seventeenth century, the plasterwork above the screens passage depicts the owner's journey towards the Heavenly City at the top of the composition.* © *Dylan Thomas*

allegorical figures, depicting the spiritual journey of a Christian knight (presumably the owner of the house, Sir Henry Griffith, fashionably dressed in doublet and hose) towards the Heavenly City, the last stage of his quest being accompanied by angels.

The great secular allegory of the age was Edmund Spenser's *The Faerie Queene*. It was written in the 1580s, when Spenser was part of the administration in Ireland. One of its dedicatory sonnets is addressed to 'Black Tom', 10th Earl of Ormond. Ormond maintained his ancestral Kilkenny Castle as (according to his bard) 'a tower of light', its fires roaring and tables heaped with fruit and wine. However, the manor house he built at Carrick-on-Suir in 1565 reflected the education he had received in England many years earlier, as one of the noble youths in the entourage of the future Edward VI, then Prince of Wales. Plaster medallions of Edward VI and Queen Elizabeth alternate around the long room. Spenser acknowledged him as a man of 'civilitie' (civilisation) and wrote of his 'brave mansion': brave perhaps in two senses because as well as being handsome, it expressed Ormond's confidence that his prestige meant he did not need to resort to conventional defences to ward off his enemies.

In 1603, the Fairy Queen herself, Gloriana, as Elizabeth I was called, had the coronation ring removed from her finger: she had never taken it off in the course of her forty-five-year reign. Nearly toothless and caked in white make-up, she died in Richmond Palace. Sir Robert Carey galloped north, with a relay of horses, to Holyrood Palace in Edinburgh and in less than three days would kneel before James VI and I to acclaim him as King of England and Ireland. James had previously travelled to Denmark to marry Anne of Denmark but he had not so much as set foot in his new territories. A new age had begun, not least for the country house.

CHAPTER THREE

Early Stuart

I N 1603, James VI of Scotland, now James I of England, Ireland and – it was optimistically hoped – France, travelled south for his coronation. Along the way his subjects greeted him 'with great solemnity and state'. He emptied the gaols of Newcastle upon Tyne of all their prisoners, except those held for really serious crimes such as Papistry, and spent great sums of money, which he did not really have, releasing debtors. At York a conduit ran all day with wine. On 3 May, he arrived at Theobalds, in Hertfordshire, the princely residence of the elf-like, wily Robert Cecil, who from having been Queen Elizabeth's chief minister, would now translate into his own. James liked Theobalds so much that he soon coaxed Cecil to exchange it for Hatfield Old Palace, with an endowment to help towards the building of a new mansion, the present Hatfield House. Countless numbers of people streamed from London to see their new king arrive at Theobalds – so many that a private road had to be quickly made to let him through. Even larger crowds assembled along the remainder of the route. About four miles from London James was welcomed by the Lord Mayor and 'such unspeakable number of citizens, as the like number was never seene to issue out upon any cause before'. Finally he reached London, but after little more than a week announced that anyone who hoped for a knighthood would have to wait until the coronation, and removed to Greenwich. It was the nearest place to the capital where he could hunt.

A poor physical specimen who could not walk very well, James became a different man on a horse, and spent so many hours in the saddle that little else could get done. His ministers, needing decisions on matters of state, were furious, but James did not care. He called London 'that filthie toune'. The city had grown to the point that it could no longer be contained within the city walls and had a suburb in Southwark. It had yet to overtake Paris and Constantinople in size but was bigger than any other town or city in Britain. Then as now, the growth of the capital was concerning. Not only were boisterous apprentices prone to riot but gentlemen spent too much time at court. The year of James's coronation saw a devastating outbreak of plague which killed a quarter of London's population.

As London grew, so did the desire to create country houses, either for courtiers or rich merchants from the City of London, in the area around. Charlton House, just east of Greenwich, built by the Dean of Durham who was then tutor to James I's eldest son Prince Henry, is a surviving example. But the pull of the capital remained so great that James I was driven to issue numerous proclamations urging the aristocracy and gentry to return home 'to repair their mansion houses in the country, to attend their services, and keep hospitality, according to the ancient and laudable custom of England'.

Hospitality was related to the idea of magnificence. The lord would feed all comers, rich or poor, with an open hand; everybody was welcome at his table which groaned with good things to eat. Such generosity and abundance was not confined to England or James's native Scotland. When the English-born judge Luke Gernon visited an Irish tower house 'built very strong' in 1620, he was almost overwhelmed:

> The hall is the uppermost room, let us go up, you shall not come downe
> agayne till tomorrow . . . Salutations paste, you shall be presented w^th
> all the drinkes in the house, first the ordinary beere, then aquavitae,

then sacke, then olde-ale, the lady tastes it, you must not refuse it. The
fyre is prepared in the middle of the hall, where you may solace yor self
till supper time, you shall not want sacke or tobacco.

Breakfast next day was a repetition of supper and the ceremony of departure was marked with drinks at the door. Note the fire in the middle of
the hall: this household that followed ancient traditions.

When Ben Jonson wrote his panegyric 'To Penshurst' – the first poem
in the language addressed not to a person but to a country house – it was
the antiquity of the Viscount Lisle's seat that he praised, along with the
overflowing largesse of its owner. This was one of the ironies of the poem,
since the family were not enormously old, having risen with the Tudors
(another irony will be discussed later). Ancient lineage was enormously
important to those who possessed it, or aspired to the status that it conferred. Bored by Lord Lumley of Lumley Castle's recitation of his pedigree,
James I exclaimed: 'Oh mon, gan nae further, I must digest the knowledge
I hae gained this day, for I didna ken Adam's ither name was Lumley.'

Old traditions implied an old family. Lords had a duty to the poor,
whose wants would once have been relieved by monasteries but now relied
on the charitable instincts of the rich, and some old families lived up to
their responsibilities. Every year the Tichbornes gave flour or bread to the
villagers of Tichborne in Hampshire: an immemorial custom recorded in
a painting commissioned by Sir Henry Tichborne in the 1670s, which
shows family, servants and villagers in front of Tichborne House. The
modern idea of the country house, standing by itself in a park, dates only
from the eighteenth century, when Capability Brown and his followers
demolished the villages that had once stood nearby and moved them
to new locations. In the seventeenth century, country houses were not
only heaving with the life of the estate but embedded in the village that
belonged to them, so the poor were constantly in view. Usually the family
of a country house worshipped with their tenants in the parish church,
although, as Catholics, the Tichbornes would have had their own chapel.

Alas, the first two Stuart kings, James I and his son Charles I, did not
practise what they preached, both of them, for different reasons, shrinking
from their poorer subjects. After a traumatic childhood, when James had

been kidnapped for a year and his mother, Mary, Queen of Scots, was exiled and later executed, he was nervous of crowds; too many Scottish kings had been assassinated. Charles, for his part, moved in an exquisite world of art and make-believe and rarely showed himself to his people. Both had a weakness for favourites and spent most of their time with small groups of courtiers, whom they showered with manors, forests, honours, lucrative offices and monopolies: favourites became rich from the bribes they took to advance a petitioner's business with the king, to whom they alone had access. These kings wanted privacy, and it was also becoming a concern of the country house. Before 1600, owners had lived surrounded by large numbers of people in rooms that, of necessity, were flexible in terms of use; they could accommodate whatever function was required at the time, depending on who was present. There was more furniture than had been the case in the Middle Ages and some pieces, carved from solid oak, were monumental; but the effect was still sparse. In the seventeenth century, country houses acquired a greater number of defined spaces, each dedicated to a specific use. Rooms of this type implied that only certain individuals would have access to them. There was also more furniture to put in them, to judge from the number of surviving examples; and in Charles I's reign, new types of upholstered furniture were copied from France. Lords also began to live at a greater distance from their servants. In the Middle Ages, they had been surrounded by young men of a similar status to themselves: the sons of other lords for whom it was considered an education, if only in how to behave; they might go hunting or on campaign together. But the education gained by hanging around a nobleman's household now seemed inferior to that provided by the universities and Inns of Court, so lords were instead attended by servants of inferior rank. To Sir Henry Wotton in 1624, 'Every Man's proper Mansion House and Home' was not only the 'Theater of his Hospitality' but 'a kind of private Princedome'. Hospitality is the opposite of privacy. Two worlds were colliding.

Privacy played a particular role in the great spiritual movement of the age: the rise of Puritanism. Puritans believed that God was revealed through the Bible and should be worshipped through prayer, rather than the 'beauty of holiness' of Charles I's Archbishop of Canterbury, William Laud – incense, candles, music, sumptuous vestments and backward-looking

Gothic architecture. The intensity of the one-to-one relationship that Puritans had with God can be seen from the 'Booke of Remembrance' kept by Elizabeth Isham of Lamport Hall in Northamptonshire, written before and during the English Civil War and recently discovered in papers at Princeton University. It reads like a whispered conversation, in which every act or memory is interpreted according to its fitness in the eyes of the Almighty, who seems almost to be sitting next to her. Puritans disapproved of feasting, maypole dancing, Christmas celebrations and the dissolute Jacobean court. However, their sober appearance did not exclude all luxury: the black silks in which rich Puritans dressed could be extremely expensive.

Prayer required privacy. Reading was another private activity and a room for it began to emerge in these years: the library. In the mid-fifteenth century, Duke Humfrey's library at Greenwich had been composed of costly manuscripts, written out by hand and difficult to obtain; there were nearly three hundred of them, regarded as a huge benefaction when they were given to the University of Oxford, although nearly all of them appear to have been burnt during the Reformation. Since then, printing had made books more accessible, but until 1600 only the richest of collectors needed more than a shelf to store them. On his death in 1632, the 'Wizard Earl' of Northumberland – his soubriquet came partly from his interest in alchemy, partly also from the number of books he owned – had a library of fifty-two 'chests' (bookcases) with enough volumes to fill a further dozen. This represented well over a thousand books, perhaps as many as two thousand. They were kept in the long gallery at Petworth House in Sussex. Most were in Latin on subjects that included religion, witchcraft, history, travel, mathematics and (a critically important subject in the seventeenth century, from its use in navigation) the making of sundials. The early seventeenth-century library at Ferniehirst Castle in Roxburghshire, polygonal and entirely panelled in wood, including the ceiling, still exists.

Courtiers could impoverish themselves through building to display their status and welcome the king. This is the second irony of 'To Penshurst'.

While Jonson praises Penshurst for its old-fashioned virtues, Lord Lisle would certainly have updated it if he could; but he was chronically strapped for cash. In 1607 he wrote a sorry letter to his wife Barbara regretting that he had no money to meet the interest on his debts, 'nor to buy necessary clothes for this winter. . . . Christmas is likewise coming on, which to one that lives in the place that I doe brings on a necessary extraordinary charge.' Barbara oversaw what building works her husband could undertake but they were limited in extent. In 1611, his agent Mr Golding wrote wondering how he could enlarge the deer park when 'already you live in so great and continual wants', having been reduced to a 'ruinous estate'. While Jonson scorns flashy Renaissance palaces built of costly materials, splendid staircases and show-off lanterns, Lisle

FIG. 12 *With its seven acres of roof and four hundred rooms, Knole, in Kent, reached its zenith under the ownership of the scholarly Thomas Sackville, 1st Earl of Dorset, who, like Lord Burghley, had been Elizabeth I's Lord High Treasurer. Dorset improved on the buildings left by several previous owners, including an Archbishop of Canterbury, to create a house that resembles an Oxford or Cambridge college, with a gatehouse, courtyards, great hall and chapel.* © Alamy

would have been delighted to live like his neighbour Robert Sackville, 1st Earl of Dorset, at Knole (fig. 12) A poet, scholar, traveller, courtier and patron of the arts, Dorset was an old man when he gained control of the house in 1603, but nevertheless built lavishly, as a Lord High Treasurer was expected to do. The hall is an enormous room with a chequerboard floor of black and white stones and a flat plaster ceiling – a departure from the hammerbeam roofs of the previous century. Festive grisaille panels by Paul Isaacson decorate the staircase: as you climb it, you ascend symbolically to a higher level of understanding, thanks to exposure to *The Five Senses*. The king never visited Knole but the upper chamber was made ready for him. A recent restoration by the National Trust has revealed that scorched into the floor joists near the fireplace are burn marks (such as a double V for Virgin of Virgins, meaning the Virgin Mary) which would have deterred witches from coming down the chimney. James had written a book on witchcraft.

Country houses had always been an extension of the power games and money grabbing of the court; display proved your creditworthiness and standing with the king. The stakes were high and those who could not keep up might be ruined. Edward Seymour, grandson of Lord Protector Somerset, had to abandon his grand schemes for Berry Pomeroy in Devon in 1611. He managed to purchase a baronetcy (the selling of honours plumped out James I's shaky finances) but the house remains unfinished.

Two country houses now owned by the National Trust preserve the spirit of the Jacobean age, largely because later owners could not afford to bring them up to date. Blickling Hall in Norfolk was built by the lawyer Sir Henry Hobart who controlled the Court of Wards, a profitable appointment since families who received favourable treatment were happy to show their gratitude in the form of large 'gifts'. Hobart had received the position, no doubt paying heavily for it himself, through James I's chief minister Robert Cecil (now the Earl of Salisbury), owner of Hatfield, who also suggested the architect Robert Lyminge. Built around two courts, Blickling seems immense but looks like merely one of the wings of the much larger Hatfield – although Hatfield was itself intentionally manageable (clever Cecil) compared to even bigger courtier houses such as Audley End. Blickling's façades are symmetrical but congested – curly

Dutch gables, towers to either side, a central tower boasting a clock (clocks of this kind were something of a novelty; Hatfield has one, as does Burghley House built for Salisbury's father, Lord Burghley (fig. 13)). In a lawyerly way, the plasterwork of the long gallery ceiling is copied from plates in a book of moral verses, whose point is deliberately obscure. This can be a difficult house to love. Chastleton House in Oxfordshire is less pretentious, although the builder, Walter Jones, had a pedigree that showed his descent from Brutus, the Trojan who supposedly became the first king of Britain. Jones was also a lawyer, but on a smaller scale than Hobart: although a member of Parliament, his greatest office was that of Worcester town clerk. The family had recently done well through the wool trade and made some good marriages. Externally the house is plain but sophisticated, the composition made up of squarish bays that advance and recede. Instead of Blickling's hectic skyline, Chastleton has a series of

FIG. 13 *The splendid skyline of Burghley House outside Stamford, in Lincolnshire. This enormous house was built over three decades after 1555 for Sir William Cecil, later 1st Baron Burghley, Elizabeth I's Lord High Treasurer. Lord Burghley and his guests would have enjoyed walking on the leads of the roof and eating intimate 'banquets' or desserts of sweetmeats, fruit and wine in the rooms there.* © *Country Life Picture Library*

gables in front of a pitched roof; there is a battlemented tower at either end. It may be that Jones ran out of money before he had even finished the project, and certainly subsequent generations (partly through support for the king during the Civil War) were unable to make alterations; as a result it has come down as the most complete of Jacobean country houses. Inside are some of the tapestries and woven cloth hangings that even now suggest how brightly coloured it must have been, despite the carved panelling.

♣

The Jacobean country house was essentially the Elizabethan country house with bow windows, more ornament and a ceiling to the great hall replacing the open roof. A rupture was made with that tradition in the court architecture of the next reign. While James I had been bookish, Charles I was a connoisseur of the visual arts and assembled one of the greatest art collections in Europe. He was a fastidious man, twenty-six when he ascended the throne in 1625, and came to be devoted – once she had sent most of her large retinue back to France – to his young queen Henrietta Maria. Where he was distant, she was lively: both abhorred the oafishness and lubricity of the Jacobean court. Their favourite entertainment was the masque, a kind of theatrical presentation using words, music, dance, elaborate costumes and spectacular stage effects that had evolved under Elizabeth I. Masques were acted by courtiers and Charles and Henrietta Maria themselves would descend (sometimes from the clouds) to lead the dance. The mood was pastoral, idealising, chivalric – although the allegories that eulogised the king's rule could not have been wider of the mark, as the country descended towards civil war. Sets and costumes were exquisite, delightful and designed by Inigo Jones.

Jones streaked like a meteor across the Stuart sky, a painter, masque designer, antiquarian, connoisseur and all-round man of taste. In the European context, England had previously been provincial: Jones brought home the sophistication of Italy, where he had travelled and studied the ruins at first hand. His dazzled contemporaries may have thought he was full of himself: *Huomo vanissimo e molto vantatore* – an extremely vain man and very boastful – concluded an Italian, having watched him pronounce on some of Charles I's newly arrived Italian paintings. But he beguiled the king and his influence on the Georgian country house would be immense. Here was somebody who could speak the language of Italian classicism fluently, having bought, studied and annotated the *Four Books of Architecture* by Andrea Palladio, published in 1570. Palladio was the architect who had done most to revive the purity of the Classical tradition by direct reference to its monuments, and Jones admired his 'sollid, proporsionable . . . and unaffected' style. In Italy, Jones had met the aged and now blind Vincenzo Scamozzi, who had completed some of Palladio's unfinished projects. To Jones, Classical architecture did not merely consist of a repertoire of ornament that could be applied as decoration, but constituted a system of organising buildings based on mathematical proportions. It spoke to the men and women of the intellectual elite who read Ben Jonson's poetry, were steeped in Classical literature and fascinated by number codes.

Jones's few buildings were original, in the sense that they were far from copies of contemporary practice on the Continent; in the context of England, they were revolutionary. In 1617 he began the Queen's House at Greenwich, intended for James I's queen, the party-loving Anne of Denmark. But Anne died and with the royal finances in disarray it had to wait until Charles I was on the throne for the building to be completed for the new queen, Henrietta Maria. A change of design produced a building that had no parallel in Europe at the time: a crisp white box of severely rectangular silhouette, which would be the origin of hundreds of crisp, rectangular boxes across Britain during the eighteenth century.

The Queen's House was a witty building. Just as Sir Walter Raleigh had supposedly thrown down his cloak so that Queen Elizabeth would not have to step in a puddle – the incident, if it happened at all, took place at Greenwich – Jones built the Queen's House astride the public road that separated Greenwich Palace from its park. The queen could cross the road by means of this architectural bridge, without having to muddy her shoes or meet her subjects. The flat roof and first-floor loggia that faced the park provided viewing platforms for ladies to look out over the men hunting or watch other entertainments, and it may have played a role in the reception of ambassadors arriving at London by the Thames. The house was on public view but was also a place of retreat, filled with art treasures, for a couple who disdained the populace.

The Stuart finances were too chaotic to allow Jones to build other houses for the king, although he would make a further contribution to domestic architecture after the Civil War. Before that, his example was little followed and less understood. We see his influence, however, in Lodge Park, a courtly building rich in architecture, that stands alone amid Gloucestershire fields like a magical apparition from a court masque (fig. 14). It was built for John Dutton, known as Crump, a puny hunchback who owned Sherborne in Gloucestershire. Crump was a cavalier. The word originally means horseman, and he is supposed to have died after falling from his horse during a night ride. In the 1630s, he conceived Lodge Park as somewhere that he and his friends could watch deer being coursed

FIG. 14 *Lodge Park at Sherborne in Gloucestershire is one of a select group of pre-Civil War buildings that show the influence of Inigo Jones. It served as a party building from which the cavalier 'Crump' Dutton and his guests could watch deer being coursed (chased by dogs). Contemporaries recognised the influence of Jones's Banqueting House in Whitehall but the façade is more crowded and less pure in its Classicism than Jones's work.* © *Country Life Picture Library*

(chased by hounds down a straight road), gamble and regale themselves afterwards. At the end of the day, Crump and his party would have rolled back to the house they had come from that morning, Sherborne Park. Contemporaries saw the comparison with Jones: one likened Lodge Park to that 'goodly and magnificent Building the Banquetting House at Whitehall'. Inside, the Great Room is a double cube, the form that Jones used at Wilton House. But even at first glance Lodge Park seems a little too frantic with architecture to be comfortable. Pediments jostle shoulder to shoulder along the cornice line. The balusters of the parapet taper towards their feet. The less-is-more message of Jones's Classicism has only partly got through.

While the architecture of Inigo Jones brought a new degree of formality to the country house, it was not the only wind stirring the Stuart court. There was also, as in the masque, a strong element of fantasy. The most conspicuous of the resulting dwellings was Bolsover Castle, whose owner Sir Charles Cavendish was the youngest son of that indefatigable builder Bess of Hardwick. Work began in 1612, to the design of either Robert Smythson or his son John. Since Bolsover had been the site of a medieval castle, a new 'Little Castle' was added, with turrets and battlements but of little practical use as fortification (fig. 15). It is a castle of romance, in the form of a keep. The architectural historian John Goodall has made the intriguing suggestion that it may have been intended not only to evoke the Age of Chivalry but in the same way that the keep of Dover Castle was at this time called Caesar's Tower – imperial Rome. Cavendish died in 1617 and the work was continued by his son William. William Cavendish was a famous exponent of *manège* or *haut école*, a discipline similar to that practised by the Spanish Riding School in Vienna today. Control of the horse was considered a princely skill, being useful in war, and Cavendish taught *manège* to the future Charles II. At Bolsover, he built a riding school along one side of the courtyard; as a lover of the arts, he also decorated the Little Castle in a rich, up-to-the-minute but abstruse scheme, which includes paintings of the *Labours of Hercules* in the hall, *The Five Senses* in the parlour and *The Virtues* in the closet.

Cavendish led the Royalist horse to defeat at the Battle of Marston Moor and spent exile during the Commonwealth living in the house

of the painter Peter Paul Rubens at Antwerp. When he returned at the
Restoration, he resumed the decoration of the Little Castle, remembering, no doubt, the time that Charles I visited in 1633, when a masque
called *Love's Welcome*, commissioned from Ben Jonson, was staged for
him. Extravagant and fantastic though it seems, Bolsover was intended
as a retreat from the main Cavendish seat of Welbeck Abbey a few miles
away. The visit of the king must have seemed particularly intimate in
such a setting.

Bolsover may have influenced the general form of the palace built
by Cavendish's friend, the haughty Earl of Strafford at Jigginstown in
Ireland. Like the terrace range of Bolsover, which may owe something to
Giulio Romano's Palazzo del Tè at Mantua, the profile is low: Jigginstown
Castle (as it is called, although nothing like a castle) consisted of a single
storey of state rooms and family apartment, with a low attic above them
and tall chimneystacks. 'Without offence to Mr. [Inigo] Jones, or Pride
in myself be it spoken, I take myself to be a very pretty architect too,'

FIG. 15 *No sooner had the invention of gunpowder made chivalry obsolete on the
battlefield than it was revived as part of the imaginative world of the court. Bolsover
Castle was enlarged after 1612 by Sir Charles Cavendish, in a project only completed
by his son William. The latter, who taught the future Charles II to ride, built a* manège
at Bolsover, as well as decorating the Little Castle with allegorical paintings. © Country
Life Picture Library

he wrote, having presumably made the design. Not for the last time, Strafford's arrogance outmatched his abilities. Jigginstown was never finished and is now a ruin.

The Earl of Strafford was beheaded in 1641; Archbishop Laud followed him to the block four years later. Charles I's turn would come in 1649, as the kingdom was replaced by a Commonwealth and the country house took a new course.

CHAPTER FOUR

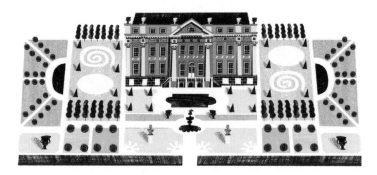

Commonwealth to Queen Anne

I N 1642, Charles I raised his standard at Nottingham and the English Civil War was unleashed. It split the nation between Cavaliers and Roundheads and brought terrible destruction upon the country house. Ladies like the Royalist Mary Bankes at Corfe Castle and the Parliamentarian Brilliana, Lady Harley at Brampton Bryan Castle defended their properties against besieging armies while their menfolk were away, but their homes were eventually subdued and reduced. After the siege of Basing House in Berkshire, the king's architect Inigo Jones, by then an old man, suffered the indignity of being carried out in a blanket; Basing House was later demolished on the orders of Parliament. Castles were blown up to prevent further military use.

Charles was beheaded in 1649 but a Scottish army held out until 1651 and in Ireland the war continued until 1653. Oliver Cromwell's campaign in Ireland was particularly brutal, as he suppressed the opposition and imposed Penal Laws against Catholics, who made up most of the native population. Estates confiscated from Catholics were distributed among his supporters, such as Sir John Ponsonby, colonel of a horse regiment, who was granted the estate of a rebel whose family had owned it since the thirteenth century. He named it Bessborough, after his wife, Elizabeth. The savage Cromwellian practice of hunting outlaws (known as tories or rapparees) to death, or pardoning their murder by other tories, was officially sanctioned until the 1770s.

The English Civil War scattered or crushed the old elite, who had taken their artistic lead from the court; some cavaliers fled overseas, where their exposure to the architecture of France and Holland would influence the country houses they built when they returned after Charles II's Restoration, while those who stayed in England were heavily fined and denied lucrative positions. But building did not come to an end. The new regime brought new people to the fore; and although some Royalists had been ruined, others managed to hang on and reach an accommodation with the new government. Politics remained fractious; London was febrile. There was plenty of reason to live in the country.

Royalists had particular grounds for keeping a low profile and staying on their estates. However, literary-minded Puritans also preferred the restorative quiet of country life to the hurly-burly and factionalism of the capital. Country-house poems praising 'retirement' had been something of a literary device before the Civil War but now had a practical application; they were written in increasing numbers. One of the best, 'Upon Appleton House' by Andrew Marvell, praises the seat of Lord Fairfax for its unpretentiousness; Fairfax, who had been the Parliamentary army's most successful commander, was now engaged in intellectual and religious pursuits at Nun Appleton, with Marvell as tutor to his daughter Mary. While Marvell was there, Fairfax enlarged the house with the help of John Webb, whose drawings for capitals to decorate it are now in the Royal Institute of British Architects collection. Webb's involvement may seem surprising, given that he had worked with Jones on the masques at Charles I's court. But architectural choices during the interregnum were not always dictated by politics.

What of Jones himself? According to Webb, he died 'through grief, as is well known, for the fatal calamity of his dread master'. Not quite.

Jones did not die until 1652, so the fatal effect of his broken heart was not instantaneous; it took three years. And Webb was writing after the Restoration of Charles I's son, Charles II: wanting to be Jones's successor in the Office of Works and being related to him by marriage, he seems to have overstated Jones's reaction to the king's beheading. In fact Jones had not done too badly: although fined, he was able to live at Somerset House, in the midst of some prominent figures in the Commonwealth, and died a rich man; respected for his abilities, temperamentally restrained – as it would seem from the occasional insight given by his notes – and dressing habitually in black, he may not have found it so difficult to blend in. Distaste for Oliver Cromwell did not prevent him from being closely involved with two country-house projects – Lees Court in Kent and Coleshill House in Berkshire – one for a Royalist, the other for a member of the new regime. Completely different from one another, each would be significant for the development of the country house.

Did Jones design these buildings? That question has been disputed by scholars and is, in any case, somewhat fruitless; until the mid-eighteenth century, country houses often had no one architect, but emerged from a collaborative process between the owner, his friends, an advisor with experience of architecture and the mason who would execute the idea. There were no working drawings which set out exactly what had to be done. At Lees Court and Coleshill, Jones was an important part of the mix. We see his stardust on the result.

The innovation of Lees Court is the façade of fourteen giant Ionic pilasters. Never before had a Classical order been used with such authority and discipline. Except for a broken pediment and coat of arms over the central doorway, there is nothing to distract the eye; the windows have no architraves or moulded surrounds but are simply punched into the smooth ashlar of the masonry. The whole composition is overhung by deep eaves reminiscent of Jones's church of St Paul's, Covent Garden. Here was architecture as a single bold and brilliant idea. The giant order would not be repeated on a country house until the 1680s, when the Duke of Devonshire began Chatsworth. Fortunately the entrance front of Lees Court survived a fire of 1911 after which the interior was rebuilt; lead from the melted roof is visible on the bases of the pilasters.

In 1952, Coleshill House in Berkshire was also devastated by fire in a blaze that was visible twenty miles away. Although now demolished, Coleshill is an important example of a new type of country house. By the standards of the prodigy houses of the Elizabethan and early Stuart era, it was modest in size. It was also symmetrical and compact: a (staircase) hall, in the middle of the entrance front, gave into a salon, in the centre of the garden front. To either side of this axis were two rooms – hence the term 'double pile' by which this sort of plan was known. There was no order visible externally, although the proportions imply one; it is, as it were, a Classical house from which the order has been removed (thus 'astylar'). On top, a tall roof with dormer windows is punctuated by soaring chimneys; in the centre of the composition is a cupola. We can see that this is surrounded by flat leads since a balustrade exists to stop anyone walking there from falling off.

The owner of Coleshill was Sir George Pratt, one of the Commissioners responsible for securing the peace of the new Commonwealth after 1649. He had inherited from his father, an Alderman in the City of London, in 1647; already elderly, though with a much younger wife, he spent his evenings in his study or gambling (his losses may explain why the house took many years to build). When the old house at Coleshill burnt down, he turned to his fashionable young cousin Roger Pratt for advice.

Roger Pratt had spent the Civil War on the Continent, rubbing up a knowledge of architecture. He came back as an educated gentleman who designed buildings, on a more than amateur basis – one of a group that would later include the mathematician and astronomer Sir Christopher Wren. His selling points were his knowledge of foreign examples, his study of 'the best authors of Architecture, viz, Palladio, Scamozzi, Serlio, etc.' and an ability to draw designs on paper. Skill in drawing was as yet relatively rare and put the architect in a superior position to the mason who would build the house; the latter's invention was kept in check. Even so, Pratt, about thirty, had no practical experience in architecture when Sir George approached him around 1650. Fortunately he had met the old and distinguished Jones. It is recorded that they were often at Coleshill together.

The absence of columns was not a Puritan trope. Some Parliamentarian country houses bristle with them, and in London, always strongly

Parliamentarian and now the centre of the new government, columns were much used, perhaps to evoke the example of the Roman Republic. But Coleshill's air of self-restraint did suit the mood of the times. The precedents – seen by Roger Pratt on his travels – were Dutch; and this may have struck a chord, given that the Dutch Republic was Protestant and a successful trading nation (too successful for comfort: England would soon be at war with it). Clearly this country house was planned for a different way of life. This can be seen most obviously in the complete elimination of the old-fashioned hall, with its hierarchy and hospitality; the big space that visitors first entered at Coleshill was a staircase hall. From now on, halls would not be entered by a screens passage. Nor was there provision for a household to eat together. Sir George, with his books and his gambling, preferred private amusements to communal life.

The prominence given to the staircase as the first thing a visitor saw on entering the house, was new. Elizabethan and Jacobean staircases could be spectacular, turning around elaborate newel posts sometimes surmounted by carved figures. They were often enclosed and, in latter years, part of a ceremonial route from the great hall to the great chamber. Coleshill eliminates the great hall and the ascent to the first floor is made through the space it might once have occupied. Hugging the walls for support, the staircase leads up to another novelty: a large dining room on the first floor. Rooms reserved solely for dining would become a standard feature of the country house. This one had a richly plastered ceiling made up of geometrical compartments, the dividers being decorated with garlands of fruit and swirls of leaves.

Pratt was knighted in 1668 for his contribution to replanning the City of London after the Great Fire but that year he married an heiress and stopped practising architecture, except to rebuild his own country house. The double-pile plan, however, was an immediate hit, as was the external composition of Coleshill. Houses with tall roofs, cupolas and dormers, with half-sunk basements, flights of steps leading up to the entrance and more often than not built of brick, remained popular until the end of the century. Ashdown House, on the Berkshire Downs, is a whimsical example, with very upright proportions: the dazzling white of its walls – made of clunch, a kind of hardened chalk – give it a fairy-tale quality. It was built by the Earl of Craven for Charles I's tragic sister, Elizabeth, the Winter Queen of Bohemia, whose husband, the Elector Palatine, was deposed from his throne after only one year; but she died before the house was finished. This style, like others in the seventeenth century, had no *parti pris*.

It was under the Commonwealth that the first portico appeared on an English country house. A portico is sometimes called a temple front: it consists of a row of columns with a pediment (like a triangular gable) on top of it. In 1653, John Webb attached one to The Vyne in Hampshire, a Tudor house that the Puritan Chaloner Chute had bought from its impoverished Royalist owner (fig. 16). Chute's tomb describes him as 'a lawyer of the first Practice of his day' and he was Speaker of the House of Commons under Oliver Cromwell's son, Richard. His effigy shows him as pensive but highly elegant, dressed no doubt in silk but accompanied by a Puritan's broad-brimmed hat. Having represented several prominent Royalists during their trials, he was not deterred by Webb's previous association with the court. The novelty of the portico can be seen from the

FIG. 16 *In 1653 John Webb added a note of Mediterranean Classicism to a Tudor country house, The Vyne in Hampshire, by applying a portico for the Puritan lawyer Chaloner Chute. Later, porticos would become a standard feature of the Georgian country house, although they had only been used for temples in the Ancient world.* © *National Trust*

nervousness Webb seems to have had about the engineering: the outer two columns are square piers, attached to a short brick wall. Overall the device was a cheap way to add a gloss of learned sophistication of what was probably a crumbling pile. It is easy to see why it would have appealed to the clever, immaculate Chute. Neither he nor Webb can have realised that The Vyne's portico would have been regarded as a solecism in Antiquity. In the Ancient world, porticos were not attached to domestic buildings, only temples. The mistake, however, had already been made by Palladio and Scamozzi in Italy. In England, three decades would elapse before architects took up the idea again but in the Georgian period porticos would be ubiquitous and a defining feature of the age.

In 1658, Oliver Cromwell died. He had ruled England and Ireland since 1649, having such difficulties with Parliament that in the end he dismissed it and made himself Lord Protector, in a ceremony that was almost a coronation. His son Richard inherited the title but was not equal to the task of government and resigned after nine months. In 1660, Charles II returned to claim his throne amid popular rejoicing. But when the king went to inspect Greenwich Palace, the gates had to be broken open to enter the park. The palace, unmaintained for twenty years, had been trashed; at one point the state rooms, perhaps as a calculated insult to the previous occupants, had been used a stable. Unlike the exquisite Charles I, Charles II was an easy-going voluptuary, whose sensual nature and love of luxury affected the mores of the court; but he never succeeded in his plans to turn Greenwich into the English Versailles or build a great palace at Winchester as he had hoped. The king could do little more than add a wing to Windsor Castle, leaving palace-building to his mightier subjects.

However, Charles does appear to have made one important contribution to architecture, since the earliest extant sash window is in the King's House that was built for him at Newmarket; it is thought to have been installed in 1671. Previously, country houses had casements that open outwards; wide windows were divided by thick bars of stone or wood called mullions, with casements in a pair to either side. The technology favoured squarish proportions. Sash windows are formed of two frames, divided by glazing bars (stout to begin with, but refined to the slimmest of profiles during the Regency period); to open them, one of the frames slides up or down. They are generally of tall proportions. It is thought that sash windows first arrived after the Great Fire of London in 1666 when the hectic pace of building work attracted craftsmen from the Continent: competition drove joinery and the making of window glass to new heights. After the King's House, sashes were adopted by country-house owners such as the Duke of Lauderdale, who remodelled Ham House outside London in 1672–4. The appearance of Tudor, Elizabethan and Stuart country houses was often significantly altered when their casements were replaced by sash windows in the Georgian period.

♣

To maintain themselves in exile many Royalists had sold everything they had, including their country houses. However, they were determined to make up for lost time, if they could. No longer were people fined for playing ninepins or going to the alehouse when they should have been at church. And if the 1660s were a time of readjustment, interrupted by the disasters of the Great Plague of 1665 and the Great Fire of London of 1666, the nation had recovered sufficiently for country-house building to resume on a grand scale around 1680.

On the Continent, this was the age of the Baroque. It was associated with the Roman Catholic Church and absolutist monarchs such as Louis XIV, whereas England, Scotland and Wales were strongly Protestant; there was no appetite to return to the religious conflicts of the Civil War and Charles II could only rule through Parliament, which held the purse strings. These differences were reflected in the development of the style: English churches replaced the gesturing saints and painted ceilings of France and Italy with virtuoso carving of garlands and other non-human ornament. But there was no such inhibition in the country house.

The Baroque was exciting, dazzling the eye not just through the splendour of the materials but the illusionism of the effects. Gods and goddesses seemed to burst out of walls and ceilings and into the rooms around which they had been painted. *Trompe-l'oeil* tricked the beholder into thinking that a flat surface had depth and painted violins (in the case of a door at Chatsworth; see fig. 17) existed in three dimensions. Architects became cinematographers, controlling the experience of people visiting their buildings by manipulating space. Jones's restraint and clear geometry were out. All was movement, spectacle, drama. Giant orders rose through the full height of the façade, with subsidiary orders scattered around them. Statues disported themselves on skylines. Gardens, laid out with gravel paths and clipped hedges, seemed to go on for miles. Staircases gave dizzying vistas to those who ascended them, looking through arches and across the immensities of stone-lined halls. Enfilades, meaning rooms lined up so you can see through all the doors, provided a receding perspective, ending in a window onto the further perspective of the garden. Mirror glass, now improved, provided glitter and delight. Showing off, with no regard to rules or restraint, was the order of the day. Whatever could be gilded was. Pediments were broken, columns blocked, liberties taken with Classical form. The muse of architecture had let down her hair and was on the ride of her life.

There was nothing private about the Baroque. A prince, whose power was embodied in his person, was perpetually on show. Louis XIV

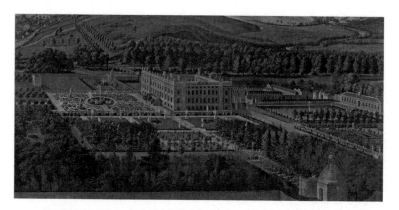

FIG. 17 *This detail of a 1699 painting by Jan Siberechts of Chatsworth House contrasts the formality of the 1st Duke of Devonshire's palatial country house and its double height Corinthian order, with the ruggedness of the Derbyshire landscape. The geometrically planned gardens are enlivened with numerous water features. Not visible here, a footman leaps onto the step behind a carriage pulled by six horses – evidence of the improvements in travel that were making country houses easier to reach.* © The Devonshire Collections, Chatsworth/Reproduced by permission of Chatsworth Settlement Trustees

would receive visitors while on the *chaise percée*. In the English court, the Groom of the Stool, who helped the king in such situations, did not occupy a menial office: proximity to the royal person gave influence. The rich aristocrats who built country houses, often from the profits from court appointments, emulated the ceremony of the court – indeed, lived in greater state than the king and queen. Modesty was not a Baroque characteristic; it was an architecture of display.

Where the double-pile house was compact, the Baroque palace spread its wings. It was not intended to serve the home life of a private gentleman, who enjoyed small private gatherings or solitary study, so much as the rituals of a princeling. Coleshill was planned so that the bedchambers could be reached without going through other rooms. Baroque palaces had enfilades. Disposed symmetrically on either side of a large central space – sometimes called, in deference to Italy, a saloon – would be two apartments, one for the owner, one for his wife (there might be another somewhere, the grandest of all, for the monarch). Each apartment would comprise an anteroom, a withdrawing room, a bedchamber and a closet. The rooms were experienced in sequence, and a visitor's importance could be judged by the degree to which he was allowed to approach the inner sanctum of the bedchamber. Decoration became richer by stages as they did so. As in the medieval great chamber, the bed was not necessarily used for sleeping in, so much as for show: a four-poster with elaborate canopy and hangings. It was an essential prop in the ceremonial process of getting up – the *levée* – during which a great person was open to callers, petitioners and secretaries. Close friends or valued associates were taken into a closet off the bedchamber, to admire small and costly curiosities and works of art.

Baroque country houses were built at a stunning cost (that was the point of them: to stun), using decorative effects that were beyond the range of most home-grown artists and craftsmen. Painted ceilings, let alone whole painted rooms, could only be afforded by grandees. In 1687, Antonio Verrio began work on the Heaven Room at Burghley, its walls and ceilings painted with a banquet of the gods on Mount Olympus, attended by the creatures of the Zodiac: all are making merry at the sight of Venus being caught by her angry husband Vulcan as she makes love to Mars (fig. 18).

FIG. 18 *The Baroque country house was intended to awe and amaze visitors. At Burghley, the Italian artist Antonio Verrio painted the Heaven Room as a complete scheme, in which the gods and goddess of Olympus seem to jump or fly forward, past the painted architecture and into the room itself. They are shown laughing at Mars and Venus who have been surprised by Venus's husband Vulcan. To the right we see Vulcan's forge and a bravura depiction of a rainbow. The Burghley House Collection*

The subject suited the Italian Verrio, who was a bon viveur and philanderer. Lord Exeter called him an 'impudent dogg' but for the most part they got on; the commission lasted a decade and during it Verrio's services were lent to Chatsworth for him to decorate the king's apartment with *The Return of the Golden Age* – a scarcely veiled piece of flattery.

England was fortunate during the Baroque years; it produced a carver of genius in Grinling Gibbons. Working in fruitwood, he specialised in the creation of illusionistic garlands of fruit and sometimes birds (in the next century, Horace Walpole would greet the French ambassador at Strawberry Hill wearing a limewood carving of a lace cravat). In other spheres, native talent was outclassed by the skilled Huguenots fleeing religious persecution in France. The silversmith Paul de Lamerie supplied wine coolers and sugar casters. The ironworker Jean Tijou wrought gates and railings. The carver and gilder Jean Pelletier made candle stands and fire screens. The joiner Peter Rieusset laid 271 yards of *parquet de Versailles* at Boughton House in Northamptonshire. The cartographer Jean Rocque drew decorative maps. The architect and engraver Daniel Marot brought the court style of Holland and France to England through his work as a decorative artist and designer, being responsible for some of the court furniture now at Knole. Covered in silver, how that must have wowed contemporaries when it was new.

Expanding trade around the world brought not only foreign artists and craftsmen but luxurious foreign goods. Inspired by the Hampton Court Beauties, eight full-length portraits of ladies of the court of William and Mary painted by Godfrey Kneller (from Lübeck), the 6th Duke and Duchess of Somerset created the Beauty Room at Petworth House in the second half of the 1690s. The Swedish painter Michael Dahl painted seven of the Somersets' young female relatives, in an enchanting series that was hung between tall mirror glasses which, used on such a scale, were themselves an expensive novelty. In front of the mirrors were tall blue-and-white porcelain jars from China, displayed on carved cedar pedestals. Chinese porcelain first arrived in England in the 1570s and 1580s and was so precious that, at Burghley House, gilded silver mounts were commissioned to display it. By the 1690s, it had become such a craze that the tiered shelves above corner fireplaces (an idea imported from Holland) were crowded with 'garnitures' of pots and jars. Another Dutch fashion was for tulips, whose precious, flamboyant blooms were displayed in specially designed Delftware vases with many separate mouths in which to insert the stems.

Royal service could be as much a route to wealth in Scotland as in England. Charles II's commander-in-chief in Scotland, General Thomas Dalyell, built towers at two corners of his House of the Binns in West Lothian and ornamented the interior with Classical chimneypieces. He gained the name of 'Bluidy Tam' from his brutal suppression of the Covenanters (from their signing of a National Covenant), extremists even by the standards of fervently Protestant Scotland; his Russian leather cavalry boots stand like sculpture on the walls of the dining room of his home, and water is said to boil if poured into them. The House of the Binns, however, is modest when compared to the Baroque palace of Drumlanrig Castle, overlooking the Nith Valley in Dumfriesshire. William Douglas,

1st Duke of Queensberry, rebuilt this ancient stronghold of his family from 1679. As High Treasurer for Scotland, Queensberry was charged with raising £40,000 each year for the king; but in the tradition of court appointments, he could keep anything extra for himself and he was merciless in his extraction of taxes and fines. Both Drumlanrig and Thirlestane Castle, which was built for the de facto ruler of Scotland, the 1st Duke of Lauderdale, have a skyline of towers and turrets recalling the vanished age of the castle. There is also an element of fantasy that evokes the chateaux of the Loire.

The architect of Thirlestane was the fascinating and glamorous Sir William Bruce. He had played a key role in the Restoration, persuading General Monck and his soldiers to support the return of the Stuarts and acting as an intermediary with the exiled court. After 1660 his star soared. He became a baronet, a Privy Councillor of Scotland, a collector of fines and taxes, and the Surveyor of the King's Works in Scotland, restoring Holyrood Palace in Edinburgh. Wearing a multicoloured robe, he looks haughtily out from his portrait in the Scottish National Portrait Gallery, a smile playing on his sensualist's rosebud lips. By 1665 Bruce could buy the Balcaskie estate, which he reimagined, aligning the house and its gardens on a volcanic outcrop on the other side of the Firth of Forth known as the Bass Rock. Ten years later he bought another site for himself outside the town of Kinross (fig. 19). To begin with, he only laid out the grounds of the future Kinross House, making an axis that runs from the entrance gates, through the centre of the house and out through the garden gate, this time aligned on the medieval Loch Leven Castle. This was where Charles II's great-grandmother Mary, Queen of Scots had been brutally imprisoned, until she charmed one of her gaolers into allowing her to escape – one of many romantic episodes in the Stuart myth. Bruce contrived that his mansion should lie at the exact midpoint between entrance gates and castle. Building began in 1686. Kinross was never fully completed by Bruce but must have astounded contemporaries all the same. Castles, it seems to declare, no longer impress; refinement lies in the accomplished use of Classical ornament, such as the Giant Corinthian order on the entrance front, and restraint. Nothing so self-assured had been built in Scotland, or indeed England, before.

FIG. 19 *The Royalist architect Sir William Bruce helped bring about the restoration of Charles II and made a fortune from official appointments in Scotland. He built Kinross House, between Dunfermline and Perth, for himself: a sophisticated essay in the Classicism he had seen during his years on the Continent, aligned on the island castle of Loch Leven where Mary, Queen of Scots had been imprisoned. Reproduced courtesy of Kinross House Estate*

Scottish country houses built of a grey stone, granite or covered with harling can seem austere; not so Kinross. Its grey sandstone strongly streaked with orange has a festive air. Screens ending in pavilions sweep forward to enfold the visitor. There are no dormers in the roof, as would be found in an English house of this date. Instead attic windows are inserted, quirkily, in a line between cornice and eaves: clearly Bruce had thought carefully about the way to simplify the design as far as possible. Over the entrance door, the garlands of flowers that take the edge off the severity of the façade do not project, having been carved out of the ashlar itself, as though they were bubbling up from inside the stone. It is a delicious house, to which our aesthetic response is controlled as though by a master dramatist.

Bruce may have begun Kinross in the expectation of receiving a peerage, but his star crashed to earth as quickly as it had risen. Owing everything to the Stuarts, he became *persona non grata* after the abdication of James II in 1688. Travelling through Britain in 1722, Daniel Defoe thought Kinross 'the most beautiful and regular piece of architecture, (for a private gentleman's seat) in all Scotland, perhaps, in all Britain'.

Bruce's story of prosperity under Charles II, followed by disaster when James II fell, finds echoes in that of many Irish families. For a time it was a golden period for the country house in Ireland. Land that had been confiscated from Catholics by Oliver Cromwell was returned to its previous owners. The king's viceroy, the 1st Duke of Ormond, set the pace. Ormond was English by birth, a convinced Anglican, but also the great-grandson of Black Tom, the Earl of Ormond who built the manor house at Carrick-on-Suir. Despite immense debts, the duke spent lavishly on Kilkenny Castle, which was said to surpass 'many palaces of Italy'. This was as much a part of what it meant to be a duke as his purchase of Moor Park, outside London, and the biggest house in St James's Square, which then had to be furnished in appropriate splendour (although Moor Park was soon sold as an economy). His redoubtable duchess, who had held Kilkenny Castle during the Civil War, lived in even greater state at nearby Dunmore. Food was provided according to rank, so that the duchess, her chaplain and ladies-in-waiting were served ten courses of four dishes each, her black page Scipio got two dishes and the scullions had to manage on leftovers. Many of the country houses built by Irish cavaliers in the late seventeenth century, like Lord Orrery's Cork seat of Charleville, named after Charles II, were destroyed in Ireland's disastrous three years of war against William III after 1688.

♣

The first Baroque palace in England was Chatsworth, beside the river Derwent in Derbyshire, begun in 1686; it was built for the 1st Duke of Devonshire (as he became): a fiery and dissolute man who fought several duels and gambled heavily on the races and cockfights at Newmarket. Devonshire's biggest gamble was to put himself forward as one of the handful of noblemen who invited William III to take the throne, compelling the last of the Stuarts, James II, a Catholic who had recently produced a male heir, to abdicate. The gamble paid off and a new Chatsworth was the result. Originally, the duke had intended to do no more than add a south wing to Bess of Hardwick's mansion but the project grew until, by 1706, the whole place had been rebuilt. Various architects were employed but the controlling genius and drive came from the duke himself. Nothing so splendid had been seen in the country house before.

The greatest architect of his age was Sir Christopher Wren and some gentlemen consulted him about their building projects; but his advice was not always followed and no country house can be securely attributed to him. He must have been too busy with St Paul's Cathedral, the City churches and his many projects as Surveyor of the King's Works to give much attention to domestic work. Nevertheless, the dome that he built over St Paul's introduced a new motif to the architectural lexicon, and his younger contemporary John Vanbrugh was quick to spot its potential for Castle Howard. Vanbrugh's client was the 3rd Earl of Carlisle, who had been First Lord of the Treasury under William and Mary. At court, he moved in a circle for whom architecture – and what it could say about their own position in the world – was a major preoccupation, shared by William III himself. In 1693, the year after Carlisle inherited from his father, the medieval castle of Henderskelfe burnt down. Five years later he decided to sweep away the remains of the castle and the twenty or so houses that comprised the village of Henderskelfe and replace them with one of the most ambitious houses in Europe, with a new name that trumpeted that of his family – Castle Howard. The somewhat bleak location would be transformed into a princely landscape of carriage drives, follies, gardens and woods. To build the palace, Carlisle turned first to William Talman, the Duke of Devonshire's architect at Chatsworth; but Talman and his client fell out. Vanbrugh saw his chance.

Before Castle Howard, Vanbrugh had designed precisely nothing. Now in his thirties, he had served as a soldier, and spent several years languishing in French gaols after having been arrested in Calais for lack of the correct papers, before bursting onto the London scene as a saucy playwright and a wit. With amazing confidence, Vanbrugh sketched out an enormous house, with two embracing wings and a centrepiece with a dome. Perhaps Vanbrugh's experience in the theatre had imbued him with an innate feeling for stage effects, for Castle Howard is nothing if not dramatic. Giant pilasters rise up the full height of the centre block, statues gesticulate along the skyline, wings sweep forward on either side. Vanbrugh's genius was made for the flamboyant Baroque style, of which Castle Howard is one of Britain's principal monuments. A painted and gilded hall rises up seventy feet into the dome. The design was intensely discussed by the aristocratic members of the Kit-Cat Club to which both Vanbrugh and Carlisle belonged, several of whom were building great country houses.

Vanbrugh took the first word in the name of Castle Howard seriously. Several of his houses have towers and his own home on Maze Hill in Greenwich took the form of a mock castle, which he called Bastille House – a memory of the time he had spent incarcerated in the Bastille in Paris as a young man. (Or is incarcerated too strong a term? Perhaps he spent some of his time on parole, walking the streets of Paris and studying the architecture.) Blenheim Palace, built by the nation to celebrate the Duke of Marlborough's victories against Louis XIV, erupts with flaming grenades (in stone) and martial trophies as well as columns and pediments (fig. 20). It was at Blenheim that Vanbrugh's quick wit led to the invention of a design aesthetic, by which a building was not valued for its intrinsic architecture but as an incident in a scene such as

FIG. 20 *Blenheim Palace in Oxfordshire was built by a grateful nation for the 1st Duke of Marlborough as a reward for defeating the French. All is movement in Vanbrugh's flamboyant and dramatic building, 1705–25, with its spectacular skyline adorned with what appear to be flaming cannonballs instead of urns. It stands amid the serenity of 'Capability' Brown's mid-eighteenth-century park, overlooking the artificial lake that submerged the lower floor of Vanbrugh's bridge. © Blenheim 2021*

'the best of Landskip painters can invent'. This was his justification to
the Duchess of Marlborough for restoring the old Manor of Woodstock,
in the grounds of Blenheim, for his own use, without permission: it
helped complete the scene and the associations that it aroused stirred
the imagination, as Sir William Bruce had found at Loch Leven. This
cut no ice with the duchess, but hundreds of country-house owners in
the later eighteenth-century turned the Picturesque improvement of
their estates into a cult.

And something else was new at Blenheim. 'The word Corridor,
Madam, is foreign, and signifies in plain English, no more than a
Passage,' Vanbrugh told the Duchess of Marlborough at Blenheim,
who evidently had not heard it before; 'it is now however generally
used as an English word.' He introduced corridors to Blenheim and
Castle Howard. Nobody would call these houses practical or cosy,
and we may suspect him of liking the receding vistas and other spatial
excitements that corridors made possible more than their usefulness.
But corridors also clearly had a practical value, by enabling people to
circulate around the house more freely rather than having to go from
one room to another in a line. In the first volume of Colen Campbell's
Vitruvius Britannicus, which appeared in 1715, it is only Vanbrugh's
country houses which have them.

This was an age of science and experiments often took place in
country houses, as well as apothecaries' shops and colleges. In turn, a
number of inventions had special relevance to the country house. We
know from Pepys that the design of coaches was of particular interest to
the scientists of the Royal Society; the natural philosopher and architect
Robert Hooke himself designed a Sailing Chariot, powered by the wind.
Country houses were often portrayed with a coach-and-four approaching
the gates, although the journeys undertaken by the diarist Celia Fiennes
in the 1690s were still made side-saddle.

Illusionism fascinated both scientists and artists. Walls were hung
with exuberant, hyper-realistic paintings by Dutch artists, and those
of tulips and other flowers, shown with droplets of water or butterflies
on their leaves, were highly prized. Engraved bird's-eye views by Jan
Kip and Leonard Knyff presented country houses, and their parks and

gardens, in dazzling perspective, from a viewpoint that could never have been attained by any human eye; the medium was ideally suited to the depiction of the complex geometry of the Baroque garden.

Gravel paths, topiary walks, avenues of clipped trees – all of them as straight as could be: failing the possession of wings, visitors could get the next best thing to an aerial view by climbing onto leads of the roof, and the ever-curious Celia Fiennes never visited a country house without doing so. On the ground, a walk along the interminable straight paths could have been rather dull: Baroque landscapes were neither intimate nor spontaneous. But another area of scientific advance came to the rescue: hydraulics. Dutch engineers were not only draining the Fens but applying their skills to enlivening gardens with numerous types of waterworks. These went beyond conventional fountains, ponds and rills. At Wilton House, the grotto included a range of practical jokes, including underground pipes that would suddenly spout water, artificial rain and statues that wept onto the people looking at them. Water also operated an instrument that, according to Fiennes, 'makes the melody of Nightingerlls and all sorts of other birds'. Once again, the Baroque country house was nothing if not theatre, calculated to amaze.

Queen Anne, the last of the Stuart dynasty, died in 1714. The country houses of the next reign would also amaze visitors, less through waterspouts or mechanical nightingales, more by epic scale, marble and landscape parks.

CHAPTER FIVE

Early Georgian

ON 18 September 1714, Georg Ludwig, Elector of Hanover, landed at Greenwich and took the throne as George I. At fifty-four he was the oldest monarch ever to have done so in England and the second oldest in Scotland. He never mastered English, cut an unimpressive figure and took little interest in building or the visual arts: he spent more on his racehorses than his palaces. Nevertheless, the richest of his subjects could build on a princely scale and new people were on the rise. The Duke of Marlborough's victories against Louis XIV in the War of the Spanish Succession, which ended in 1714, engendered a mood of self-confidence.

Banking, manufacturing, property development, marriage, inheritance – these were all routes to making fortunes, but often more profitable were government and Empire. They could intersect. Sir Robert Walpole built Houghton from the profits accrued from his role as prime minister. John Aislabie, who created one of the greatest gardens of age at Studley Royal in Yorkshire, was Treasurer to the Navy and Chancellor of the Exchequer, and managed the legislation by which the national debt was absorbed by the South Sea Company. When the South Sea Bubble burst, he had to repay £45,000 – although this still left him with £120,000, a figure that was almost certainly massaged downwards to prevent more from being taken. The Duke of Chandos had been paymaster of the army during Marlborough's Wars, from which by 1713 he had profited to the tune of £600,000. Many eighteenth-century country-house builders were MPs: country houses were part of the stock-in-trade of people needing to entertain their electorate and impress the neighbourhood. The Onslow dynasty which produced three Speakers for the House of Commons lived at Clandon Park, outside their power base of Guildford. It is possible to see London from the roof.

Adventurers risked their health and lives in India, where European trading companies battled to extract the fabled riches of the East, with the aid of private armies. In 1710, Thomas Pitt, governor of Madras, returned home with a colossal uncut diamond, weighing 410 carats: a portrait shows him wearing it in his hat although his correspondence suggests he was far too worried about it to do so very often. It represented the whole fortune he had made while serving – or competing against – the East India Company (the EIC discouraged its employees bringing back other forms of tradable cargo because it would take up too much room in the hold); when sold to the Regent of France, it fetched £125,000. Pitt had already invested in land, buying Boconnoc in Cornwall and Mawarden Court outside Salisbury; the interest of Mawarden, a modest enough house in itself, was that it controlled the defunct medieval borough of Old Sarum which retained the right to send two members to Parliament. 'Remember', Pitt once wrote from India, 'to buy no estate, but where there is a good house thrown into the bargain.' Soon he was improving his properties, with the same intemperate energy that drove other aspects of his affairs; he would die at Swallowfield Park in Berkshire, remodelled for him by John James.

Pitt thought his wife Jane was extravagant and reports of her behaviour at Bath caused a permanent rupture. The investment in Mawarden, however, paid off. Jane and Thomas's grandson William Pitt represented the non-existent residents of Old Sarum in Parliament, becoming prime minister.

The money taps of Empire had been turned on. They would water the architectural landscape of the mid- and late eighteenth century, bringing forth strange, sometimes wonderful blooms. Although the smell can wrinkle the nose, it gave country-house builders the heady sense that they were heirs to the imperial Rome that they were visiting on the Grand Tour.

⚘

The king was foreign and so were many of the leading figures in the arts. The German composer George Frideric Handel put on Italian operas, whose superstars were lanky Italian castrati: their sexual development arrested when they were choirboys, they sang in a high register but with the power of adult male lungs. Before William Hogarth, nearly all the most successful artists in Britain had been born overseas: as a decorative painter, Hogarth's father-in-law Sir James Thornhill, although employed at Chatsworth, was eclipsed in his art by foreigners such as Verrio and Louis Laguerre. Architecture was in British hands but the court style of Sir Christopher Wren was heavily influenced by France. Connoisseurs called for a new style to suit the new times – a new and British style (British, not just English, because, since the Act of Union of 1707, England and Scotland were now one). In 1712, the philosopher Lord Shaftesbury prophesied that peace would make 'united BRITAIN the principal Seat of Arts'. Over the next half-century, the goal of a national style in architecture would be pursued in a variety of ways and almost every development was justified by claims that it displayed national spirit. Two of the most prominent trends were first the so-called Palladian Revival, which quite literally became the house style of the British ruling class from the 1720s, and second (as we shall see in the next chapter) an antiquarianism that revelled in the remains of the past. They were accompanied by new ways of shaping gardens and landscape and experiencing nature which, if not nationalistic, were certainly home grown.

Andrea Palladio had been a sixteenth-century architect who worked in Venice and Vicenza. He studied the ruins of Antiquity and created a style based on proportion and Classical ornament; the effect was calm, spacious and cerebral. Although some of his villas were decorated with bravura frescoes, the architecture itself was reserved; this appealed to

English connoisseurs who, as Protestants, were suspicious of the emotionalism of the Baroque and its associations with the Church of Rome. The Grand Tour, an extended trip around European cities that completed a gentleman's education, was now easier to make since the wars had ended, and among rich young aristocrats a Continental journey became de rigueur. But physically visiting Palladio's buildings was not the only way to get acquainted with them, for in 1570 the architect published many of them, as well as plates of Roman buildings engraved from his own drawings, in a treatise called *I quattro libri dell'architettura* (The Four Books of Architecture). His principles were universal.

A movement named after a Venetian might not appear to be very national in origins but the Palladian Revival – a later term, although Pope uses the word 'Palladian' in his *Epistle to Lord Burlington* – was misnamed: it might just as well have been called an Inigo Jones Revival. Jones was not only British but had been closely associated with the Stuart court (a plus for those who wanted the Stuarts to return). As we have seen, Jones had himself studied Palladio. Palladio's compatriots, Serlio and Scamozzi, both of whom had published books, were also part of the mix. Added to which was the revival of the glories of Ancient Rome, a goal encouraged by the education of British gentlemen in the Classics. The leading men of the time saw themselves, in this age of military triumph and assertive patriotism, as the natural heirs to the Roman Empire. Were they not creating an Empire themselves?

Three things were needed to achieve the success of the new style. First, an English translation of *I quattro libri*. This was provided by the architect Giacomo Leoni in instalments between 1715 and 1720; Leoni had the advantage of himself being a Venetian. Secondly, the public had to be shown approved architectural examples that it could emulate. In the year that Leoni brought out the first volume of *The Architecture of A. Palladio, in Four Books*, the well-connected architect Colen Campbell published the first volume of *Vitruvius Britannicus*. Campbell, born in Nairnshire, was one of a galaxy of Scottish architects who would transform the country house during the eighteenth century, usually from offices in London, including James Gibbs, the Adam brothers, James Playfair and the bridge-builder, Robert Mylne.

Vitruvius Britannicus celebrated the greatest works of recent British architecture, many of which were country houses. The first volume was not unduly doctrinaire and the gentlemen and occasionally ladies who subscribed to it were of different political persuasions and not always friends. However, the second and third volumes promoted a more consistent architecture – plain walls, austere ornament and mathematical proportions were the note. The manner of the engravings, simplified to outlines, key details and plans, tended to make already severe buildings look even sparer. Thirdly, Palladianism needed a rich and sociable nobleman to promote it. One appeared in Richard Boyle, 3rd Earl of Burlington, self-proclaimed arbiter of taste.

Burlington's family had been Irish but his great-grandfather, the 1st Earl's marriage to the sole daughter of the 5th Earl of Cumberland brought them large estates in Yorkshire and the Lake Counties. On the death of the 2nd Earl, Burlington, aged nine, inherited three country houses and the London palace of Burlington House on Piccadilly. Architecture only came to him after a first love of music; he undertook a Grand Tour in 1714–15, from which he brought back some Italian musicians; on his return, aged barely twenty-one, he was made Lord Treasurer of Ireland and governor of County Cork. Some mystery surrounds the sudden passion that he developed for architecture and scholars now point to the role of other architecturally minded gentlemen (Sir Andrew Fountaine or the Earl of Pembroke) and Oxford dons. By 1719 he was sufficiently fired by his new enthusiasm to make a second Grand Tour to look at the works of Palladio (it has been claimed that the real purpose of this visit was to associate with the court in exile of the Old Pretender, James II's son, James Stuart, and that Burlington's subsequent buildings incorporate secret Jacobite symbols but this far-fetched theory has been exploded). In Rome, Burlington had already met the key, though mercurial, figure of William Kent. Kent was then a painter – not a very good one, but British and, more than that, like Burlington, a Yorkshireman. A gregarious, kaleidoscopic artist, who had the knack of being beloved by all, and an aloof aristocrat of fixed ideas and highbrow tastes: theirs may have been an attraction of opposites but the friendship lasted until Kent died in 1741. From the moment of his return to London, he lived in rooms at

Burlington House – with time out, presumably, to visit his long-standing mistress, the actress Elizabeth Buller, with whom he had two children. He was buried in Burlington's family vault at Chiswick.

While Burlington was on his first tour, his mother began to remodel Burlington House using the architect James Gibbs. Burlington sacked Gibbs and employed Campbell. Campbell had first trained as a lawyer and it showed; however, his pedantic nature came to suit Burlington, who, when his own ideas had developed, could mould him in his own image. In the end they parted company: Campbell had served his purpose for Burlington, who could stand on his own architectural feet.

For the country house, Palladianism *à la* Campbell would mean porticos, 'correct' ornament based on precedent, acres of bare external wall and a three-part composition which often entailed pavilions linked by quadrant wings (first used by William Winde on Buckingham House, the precursor of Buckingham Palace, then just outside London, in 1702–5). One pavilion usually contained the kitchen: this put it a long way from the dining room but reduced the risk of fire; the other pavilion might be the stables. Wanstead House in Essex, for the banker Robert Child, was a prime example; built in 1714–20 but so huge and glacial that it was demolished little more than a century later. Campbell would be dropped by Burlington in favour of Kent, who morphed from artist and *virtuoso* to architect and furniture designer with characteristic self-confidence and aplomb. However, it was probably Campbell who gave Burlington drawing lessons, enabling him to become, like the Earl of Pembroke, an architect in his own right. In 1717, Burlington designed a Bagnio, or bath house, in the grounds of Chiswick House, whose upper room he used as a study. Half a dozen years later, he began one of the most original and influential buildings ever constructed in Britain: his Villa at Chiswick (fig. 21).

The Chiswick Villa was a homage to Palladio's famous Villa Rotonda outside Vicenza, although with only one portico, on the entrance front, rather than four – there is less need for shade from the sun in Chiswick than on the Veneto. Originally, a large Jacobean house stood next to the Villa, fire-damaged but able to provide sleeping accommodation. So the Villa was purely for entertaining, architectural experiment and

FIG. 21 *Chiswick House, to the west of London, was designed by the gentleman architect Lord Burlington in 1723–9 as a homage to Andrea Palladio's Villa Rotonda in the Italian Veneto. Originally it was attached to a large Jacobean house and served as a showcase for Burlington's architectural ideas, in a severe style based on ideal proportions as seen in both Palladio and Inigo Jones.* © Historic England Archive

show. People could hardly help seeing it: it stood only a few feet from an important road into London on one side and is only a little more distant, on the other, from the Thames. Kent designed interiors; he provided the furniture, in the manner of the *saloni* of the Roman and Venetian aristocracy, lined with immense, gold-encrusted tables and chairs, supported on carved eagles, sea creatures and lions.

Chiswick possessed only a few score acres of land – a flea bite compared to the estates that Burlington owned in Yorkshire and Ireland. But that land could be gardened and Kent was on hand to produce a stream of enchanting sketches – a little dog pees on Lord Burlington's shoe, hares dance in the moonlight – in brown wash and rapid squiggles of line. Out went the straight sides of the canal. It was turned into an irregular lake, fed – for the short periods when the waterworks could produce enough flow – by a splashing cascade. Grass was brought up to the feet of the Villa, as though it were set in open countryside.

While in Rome, Il Signor or Kentino – as Kent was called – met not only Burlington but Thomas Coke, later created the 1st Earl of Leicester. Coke's parents had died when he was a child, leaving guardians to manage the estates he inherited; there was land in Suffolk, Buckinghamshire, Oxfordshire, Staffordshire, Dorset, Kent, Somerset and London as well as Norfolk. They did so conscientiously. There were no debts when Coke came of age and he was one of the richest commoners in the country. From an early age, he saw himself as a *virtuoso*. On his Grand Tour, begun at the age of fifteen, he bought sculpture, paintings, drawings, books and manuscripts. He also fell under Kent's spell. They were – despite the gulf in social position – soulmates. For all the splendour of his inheritance, Coke was a naturally boisterous man, irrepressibly witty and not at all inclined to stand on ceremony when dealing with people sharing his passion for the arts. He was irrepressible in other ways too. Despite the rosy condition of his estate when he came into it, he soon got into debt; trying to put himself right, he invested heavily in the South Sea Company and lost £35,000. Even so, he was determined to build a great country house. Architecture was his 'Amusement' (according to the architect Matthew Brettingham the Younger).

Several hands were involved in creating Holkham Hall, on the North Norfolk coast, and it is, as so often, difficult to disentangle the contributions each made (fig. 22). Essentially, Matthew Brettingham the Elder, a local man, was the executive architect. (Coke addressed letters to him as Honoured Sir, Great Sir, Most Illustrious Sir, or just Bret.) The designs came from Kent under Coke's close supervision – for the client was involved in every detail of the project. These appear then to have been vetted, since a letter of 1734 (to Brettingham) begins, 'It is wth. pleasure I can inform you our whole design is vastly approved of by Ld. Burlington, he says the insides plan is the best he ever saw.' The project began in 1734 but did not finish until 1765; by then Kent had been dead for twenty-four years and Coke himself for six.

The original intention was to face Holkham in Bath stone; this was abandoned in favour of the cheaper alternative of yellow brick, whose effect is austere. There is an awkwardness to the pavilions – each of them built like a villa, with pedimented centrepiece and wings – but the plan of which Burlington so much approved is heroic. The house is entered by

FIG. 22 *The Marble Hall at Holkham Hall, on the North Norfolk coast, evokes the splendour of Ancient Rome through an interpretation of the Egyptian Hall described by the first century B C military architect and engineer Vitruvius. William Kent designed it, with a ceiling derived from the ancient baths he had seen in Rome, adding drama by making the entrance at a level below that of the main floor, which is approached by steps. The material is not in fact marble but Staffordshire alabaster.* © Alamy

a great hall, but not of the medieval type – or of any type previously seen in Britain. It was surrounded by columns made of Staffordshire alabaster, a material similar to marble. The inspiration was less Palladio, whose villas were built of modest materials, than the vanished glory of Ancient Rome. In his treatise on architecture, the Roman architect Vitruvius had described an Egyptian Hall. Vitruvius's text is not illustrated, his description rudimentary and no Egyptian Hall has survived from the Ancient world. Here was an attempt to reconstruct one, though with added drama since, because Holkham has a basement floor, the hall is entered at a level lower than the colonnade, which soars above the visitor's head. A coffered ceiling recalls the Baths of Diocletian and Caracalla in Rome. Even today – and however often you see it – the effect is sensational.

This is an imperial space, immense and imposing, but also flamboyant and festive. The staircase leads up to the *piano nobile*, so called because it was the storey that contained the state rooms.

Georgian country houses were rich in collections that spoke of their owners' connoisseurship, wealth and self-image as inheritors of Rome's imperial tradition; the antique sculptures acquired by Leicester were displayed in a three-part Statue Gallery with niches around the walls specially designed for them to stand in. But it was Rome updated with what a foreign visitor, towards the end of the century, called 'every kind of comfort and convenience'. Holkham boasted an exceptional number of water closets and bathrooms (the bathroom in itself being a novel concept). The family wing contained three water closets. There were double-seaters elsewhere for upper servants. The bathroom in the family wing contained a 'mahogany bathing tub', presumably cold; a hot bath, and a 'biddeau'. Beneath the Marble Hall, in imitation of Roman precedent, Brettingham created a 'furnace . . . for the conveniency of warming it'.

The furnace reminds us of a drawback to marble as a material for Northern Europe. While its cooling properties were appropriate in Italy, they were hardly necessary in Britain. However, it appealed to men like Sir Robert Walpole whose imaginations were fired by Roman grandeur. At Houghton Hall in Norfolk, neighbours and political friends were overawed by the Marble Parlour, with its buffet made from marble of different colours. Marble was hard, cold, imposing, sumptuous and masculine. It was also extremely expensive and even the Onslows at Clandon could not afford it: the only area of real marble in their Marble Hall was the black-and-white floor, the rest being stucco worked by Italian craftsmen, whose exuberant human figures and swags spread from walls and fireplaces to the ceiling (hardly possible to decorate in heavy marble). Remembering the marble of Carrara, the Marble Hall was, except for the floor, entirely white. Owners who preferred more sumptuous effects could achieve them through the use of scagliola, a material developed in sixteenth-century Italy, using special plaster mixed with glue, marble dust and chips of marble which can then be polished. It convincingly imitates the richest of marbles, extravagantly veined and gorgeous in whatever colour was desired – green, purple or yellow.

FIG. 23 *The magnificence of Prime Minister Sir Robert Walpole's Houghton Hall in Norfolk must have overwhelmed his political guests and the local squires with whom he hunted. The masculine style of the dining room, known as the Marble Parlour, reflected its use by men, who would continue to drink after dinner when the ladies had withdrawn. Animals are seen being sacrificed to Diana, goddess of hunting, in the carved relief by Michael Rysbrack over the fireplace in the 1730s; the fireplace itself is decorated with a head of Bacchus, god of wine.* © Country Life Picture Library

At Houghton, the Marble Parlour was a dining room (fig. 23). Although dining rooms had existed since the mid seventeenth century, they came into their own during the Georgian period, when long, heavy dinners were a social ritual. While both sexes ate together, the ladies withdrew after dinner to leave the menfolk to their bottles. So until Robert Adam introduced a lighter, more delicate style, the decoration was male in character – one reason for choosing marble. Hard wall surfaces were often preferred to damask since they did not retain the smell of food. Immense wine coolers were commissioned for the essential accompaniment to the food. Direct access might be had to the cellar, while the sideboard that was splendidly heaped with silver contained a hidden supply of chamber-pots. Lord Blayney of Blayney Castle in Ireland would take 'all his merry men to a little adjoining room, which was called his own glory hole, and there we had such fun, such jolly stories, that it was difficult to leave our seats'.

In Scotland, Palladianism had a special significance as the Establishment style. Scotland had long been poor and seen as culturally remote; but in 1707 its debts had been settled as part of the deal that enabled union with England and members of the ruling elite wanted to shake off the past. The architect who embodied the new mood was William Adam: an energetic son of the minor gentry who was also a building contractor. A Scottish Burlington existed in Sir John Clerk of Penicuik, who admired Adam's 'enterprising temper'. Outside Edinburgh, Adam turned Hopetoun into a palace for his friend Charles Hope, 1st Earl of Hopetoun (fig. 24).

Lord Hopetoun came from a family of lawyers. He was only a baby when his father drowned in a shipwreck in 1682: the peerage was supposedly given in gratitude by the Duke of York, to whom Hope senior gave

FIG. 24 *Hopetoun House, outside Edinburgh and easily reached by Firth of Forth, began as a compact block by Sir William Bruce, 1699–1703, seen here in the foreground. This was commissioned by Lady Margaret Hope whose baby son had been created 1st Earl of Hopetoun after his father supposedly sacrificed his life to save the Duke of York in a shipwreck. From 1723, Lord Hopetoun employed William Adam to add quadrant wings and pavilions, embracing a forecourt.* © *Dylan Thomas*

up his seat in a rescue boat. Charles's mother Lady Margaret was determined to create a house worthy of her son's fortune and title, employing Sir William Bruce to build, as his last commission, 'a Portico, Hall and 4 very handsome Apartments'; over the hall was a 'noble Salon', as *Vitruvius Britannicus* describes. The plan of the main block was a Greek cross, with an octagonal staircase hall in the centre, externally marked by a tall cupola.

But parents do not always know what their children will like. This house, though rich in architecture, was compact. By the time the earl's fortune had been increased by a large payment from the secret service fund, in reward for his support of George I during the Jacobite Rebellion of 1715, he wanted to make a bigger statement. William Adam was commissioned to remodel the entrance front on an immense scale, adding, in approved Palladian style, quadrant wings which connect with pavilions, each seven bays across and surmounted by a domed turret. The wings open like the mandibles of a whale.

What a mighty effort it all was to build – too mighty for one lifetime, since the house was unfinished at the earl's death in 1742; he had not been able to walk up to his front door, since the grand perron or flight of steps was yet to be built. Work continued under Adam's sons, John, Robert and James Adam after his own death in 1748. The personable and socially ambitious Robert Adam would travel in Italy with the 2nd Earl's brother Charles. Working with his brothers, he would dominate country-house architecture throughout Britain in the 1760s and 1770s.

❧

We have seen Kent gardening at Chiswick. In the course of the eighteenth century, the landscape park would become a subject of intense interest, argument and expense to country-house owners. The aim was to create a seemingly natural effect, composed as though in a landscape painting. Kent is credited, by his friend the poet Alexander Pope, with having 'leaped the fence' and seen that 'all nature is a garden' – although the future George II's wife, Princess Caroline, had beaten him to it at Richmond Lodge, not far from Chiswick. The leap was made by means of a concealed ditch with a vertical wall on the side nearest the house and sometimes a fence at the bottom, known, from the exclamation of surprise people were supposed to have made on first seeing it, as a ha-ha. For the ha-ha was invisible except close to: looking out from the house, there appeared to be no division between the parkland beyond it and the grounds within. Sheep and cattle were kept at a respectful distance.

Kent's great set pieces were Stowe in Buckinghamshire and Rousham in Oxfordshire. Temples and statues were set amid the parkland to create an image of Arcadia – the land of idyllic Nature that, in Ancient mythology, had been home to the god Pan – such as had been created by the French painters of idealised Classical scenes, Nicolas Poussin and Claude Lorrain. Stowe, where Kent worked from the late 1730s, was more than an aesthetic experience: Viscount Cobham, bitter from the clash with the prime minister, Sir Robert Walpole, which ended his political career, used the estate to which he retired to vent his frustration through gardening. His landscape expressed his thoughts about politics, as well as other matters. Busts in the Temple of British Worthies – Cobham's heroes from King Alfred to Newton – look across the lake (envisaged as the river Styx) to the Temple of Ancient Virtue, containing statues of figures from the Ancient world. In an ironic gesture, the Temple of Modern Virtue was a fake ruin to evoke the fallen nature of the times, over which Walpole presided in the form of a headless torso. It was a garden of ideas.

Not all the ideas were seemly. Stowe also had a Garden of Love, whose temple was decorated with erotic ceiling paintings and Latin poetry: a space for assignations or male ribaldry. Propriety was restored in the Lady's Temple, allowed to Lady Cobham for the practice of domestic arts.

Holkham, Houghton, Hopetoun, Stowe – these Brobdingnagian piles were too grand to be imitated by ordinary mortals, but the Palladian formula could also be adapted to the needs of rich gentlemen rather than aristocrats. Typical of the good-sized but not palatial country houses of which so many were built after 1730 is Prior Park outside Bath (fig. 25).

Externally the house can easily be described. Set on a hill, whose slopes, as you walk down them, command a fine view of the city, it is a tripartite composition: in the centre of the façade is a great portico, with a blank pediment above it; plain wings of five bays each extend to either side. This is almost a quotation of the central part of Campbell's

FIG. 25 *This print shows Prior Park outside Bath, the home of Ralph Allen, designed by his friend John Wood the Elder in 1735–48. Alexander Pope advised on the gardens. Stone from Allen's quarry, used to build Bath, can be seen on the railed track, hidden from the windows of the house by a wall.* © *The Board of Trustees of the Science Museum*

Wanstead House, published (of course) in *Vitruvius Britannicus*. Curving galleries run off to distant pavilions. Internally Prior Park is a double pile, with two unusual features: a double-height chapel on the east side and, on the first floor, a long gallery from which to enjoy the view. For Prior Park was built for Ralph Allen, evidently pious, certainly good (according to Pope) and conscious of landscape.

Allen came from Cornwall. Humbly born, he made his first fortune from the postal service; in 1720, he obtained – at considerable expense – the right to farm the supply of post around Bath, which was being taken to and from London by improved post roads. (Farming of this kind was common practice; the 'farmer' bought a monopoly for a fixed price and kept any profit he could make over and above it.) Shrewdly, he then acquired the site of Prior Park from his brother-in-law. Not only did this provide a splendid place to build a mansion but the hill on which it stood, Combe Down, could be quarried. It provided much of the building stone for the spa town of Bath, then expanding to accommodate the visitors brought to it along the post roads which also carried Allen's mail. We have seen that Thomas Coke wanted to use Bath stone for Holkham. An eighteenth-century print of Prior Park shows stone being sent down the hill on a wooden railway track; this scene of industry is hidden from the windows of Allen's house by a wall – although there are still ladies admiring the sight, while a carriage passes by. Allen began to build Prior Park in 1734. For his architect, he called on his friend John Wood the Elder, with whom he had been developing Bath's streets and squares. But there were other influences at work, since Allen stayed with Lord Burlington at Chiswick (where he deplored the pagan nudity of the statues). At the bottom of the hill at Prior Park is a covered bridge derived from an unexecuted design by Palladio for the Rialto in Venice. The Burlington connection was made by Alexander Pope who often visited the Allens and no doubt encouraged the making of the park, with its walks weaving through woods, 'wilderness' area and wriggling 'Chinese' paths. He gave Mrs Allen the present of a grotto and the Allens' dog (another present) is buried in it.

Architecturally, landscape parks could be an area of experiment; a new style could be trialled in a folly without the expense of building a country house – and the possible consequences of living with a mistake. One of the last buildings commissioned for Stowe by Lord Cobham in 1741 was the triangular Temple of Liberty – or, as it was renamed, Temple to the Liberty of our Ancestors – built with an asymmetrical tower, battlemented pediment and other Gothic references by James Gibbs. Gibbs's interpretation of the Gothic style may seem fanciful to modern eyes but to Cobham's contemporaries the symbolism would have been clear. The meaning of Gothic had changed since the days when it had been favoured by Archbishop Laud. The Goths had been the Germanic tribe who sacked Rome in 410 AD; in imagination, they were associated with the supposedly democratic early inhabitants of Britain and, loosely, a medieval order in which the Magna Carta barons had put the king in his place. The Gothic Temple of Liberty therefore stood for government by constitution, as opposed to the tyranny of Rome – whether that took the form of Hanoverian high-handedness or, heaven forbid, the Roman Catholicism of the Jacobites. Cobham adorned it with statues of Saxon figures from whom he was supposedly descended.

We have seen that Gibbs, for whom the temple was but one incident in an exceptional career, worked briefly for Lord Burlington but was then cast into the outer darkness, unwarmed by the Palladian sun, where historians have been apt to leave him. He does not fit a narrative in which Burlingtonian values conquer all. But Burlington was not the only nobleman who formed an artistic circle and Gibbs, though dismissed from Burlington House, was welcomed by the Duke of Chandos and Edward Harley, 2nd Earl of Oxford. Scholars have begun to see Gibbs less as an odd man out and more as a central figure in an alternative interpretation of the early Georgian period, as other powerful patrons than Burlington, as well as connoisseurs and gentleman architects, emerge from the shadows. They have been overlooked because, ultimately, Palladianism swept the board.

Gibbs's career is exceptional because it began in the office of Carlo Fontana, Bernini's successor as architect to the Pope. Gibbs had gone to Rome from his native Scotland intending to become a Catholic priest; once there, he was so appalled by the rector of the Scots College that he changed his study to architecture. In 1708 he arrived in London, steeped – it has been assumed – in the spirit of the Roman Baroque style, all curves and theatre. It has only recently been appreciated that the Roman Baroque, as practised by Fontana, had become more restrained and aware of Classical precedent. Gibbs's time with Fontana made him one of very few British architects to have had the benefit of a formal architectural training. He was soon in demand for churches, university buildings and private houses; we have seen him helping to remodel Burlington House and adding domed caps to the corners of Houghton Hall. His greatest commission was Canons in Middlesex, for the Duke of Chandos (albeit, in the way of the time, he was not the only architect involved). This house was so stupendous that Chandos's spendthrift heir could not support it; it was demolished in 1747, a mere three years after the duke's death. To appreciate its splendour now you must visit the Church of St Lawrence at Little Stanmore, where the Chandos Mausoleum survives, or the chapel of Great Witley in Worcestershire, now the Church of Saint Michael and All Angels: such was the quality of Canons that its constituent parts were bought for reuse (Gibbs himself supervised the installation of the chapel fittings at Great Witley).

The demise of Canons wrote Chandos out of architectural history. However, the duke formed a miniature court of artists, musicians and *virtuosi* akin to Burlington's; Handel, who had previously been patronised by Burlington, composed anthems for the chapel. The finest materials and craftsmanship went into its construction. At Wimpole Hall, in Cambridgeshire, Gibbs worked for the 2nd Earl of Oxford, who assembled the Harleian collection of 7,000 manuscripts, 14,000 charters and 500 medieval rolls, now in the British Library. We have a description of some of the regulars at Wimpole travelling there from London from the painter James Thornhill; en route they drank Harley's 'healths over and over, as well in our civil as bacchanalian hours' and talked 'of building, pictures and may be towards the close of politics or religion'.

Ditchley House in Oxfordshire is one of the grandest and most intact of Gibbs's country houses. Built of a dusty yellow stone, it comprises quadrant wings, cupola-capped pavilions and the main house in the form of a deep H. The doorcase is of a form so much associated with this architect that it takes his name: a Gibbsian surround. The frame is embellished with blocks (so that it looks like a battlement on its side). Two feisty statues – there were originally to have been four – stand on the parapet that conceals the roof: Fame blowing a trumpet and Loyalty in Roman armour.

Gibbs presented himself as a man of taste, collecting works of art, assembling a library and publishing a pattern book that shows churches, public buildings, country houses, pavilions, church monuments and architectural details is an easy-to-assimilate form, with a number of plans: all designed by himself, it was the first publication of its kind. *A Book of Architecture Containing Designs of Buildings and Ornaments* had a wide influence, particularly in America where versions of St Martin-in-the-Fields are found up and down the East Coast. He also published the *Rules for Drawing the Several Parts of Architecture*, a guide that simplified the architectural orders for the benefit of craftsmen and amateurs.

The Book of Architecture, like other treatises of the time, reveals nothing about servants, since it focuses on the polite aspects of architecture: the design elements which would interest a lady or gentleman. And yet a country house could not have functioned without them; clearly it was accepted they would be there, crammed into whatever space was available, without many formally differentiated rooms. Often they slept where they could, on truckle beds that were put away during the day. Proper beds were scarce and the domestic historian Amanda Vickery has shown that a maid might share a bed with her mistress. This was a practical, not a sexual arrangement but created a bond of intimacy which, on the employer's part, turned to bitterness if the maid then ran away without warning, as servants often did. Privacy hardly existed for servants, and their employers found it almost as difficult to escape prying eyes. Reports of adultery trials reveal the cast of housemaids, laundry maids, porters and stewards, who had all made it their business to spy through keyholes, snoop around bedrooms and notice when a lady was or was not at home, and who visited. When Lord Abergavenny was informed of his wife's indiscretion by the steward, he did not spring the trap himself; instead it was left to the steward and two male servants to hide in a closet for three hours one morning until they could catch the pair in bed.

Gentlemen were often on close terms with their gamekeepers and grooms; but the male servants who had been universal in the Middle Ages were now expensive and many of their roles were now performed by young women. In some cases servants stayed with the same family for decades and were treated with affection and respect, as can be seen from the portraits that their employers commissioned at some expense. The most famous example is Erddig in North Wales, where a series, begun in the early eighteenth century and continued (in the form of photographs) until the twentieth, was accompanied by specially composed verses. The tradition seems to have begun with a portrait of a black coachboy who is mentioned in family records in the 1720s. A verse written by a later squire imagines the lad blowing his coach horn in praise of William Wilberforce, who campaigned for the abolition of slavery in the late eighteenth century and lived to see it enacted in 1807.

Sadly, we do not know the name of the boy or why he was at Erddig; its builder John Mellor was a London lawyer without known links to slavery. His presence, though, bears witness to an aspect of Britain's imperial success from which, for centuries, it averted its eyes. Slavery was not confined to the British Empire but existed throughout the world in the eighteenth century; we shall see that products of the economy of which it was part were to be found in every Georgian country house.

CHAPTER SIX

Mid-Georgian

Two ideas characterised the Georgian age: improvement and politeness. Improvement meant the application of science to agriculture and manufacturers, both of which became more efficient and profitable. The Agricultural Revolution, as it came to be known, had a particular relevance to the country house, since many gentlemen drew an income from the land; animals grew fatter, common land – on which peasants had previously grazed animals and kept beehives – was enclosed by private owners, and new landscapes were created. While the French, with whom Britain was constantly at war, were portrayed as effete, priest-ridden, badly fed and addicted to the character-sapping luxuries of the town, the English national figure was John Bull: an honest, plain-dealing but decidedly belligerent countryman (invented, as it happens, by a Scottish doctor and satirist). John Bull lived in plenty, dined off roast beef, rejoiced in hard riding across country and bone-breaking sports such as singlestick, took no nonsense from foreigners and if he thought at all, did so for himself. Politeness was an attempt to tame John Bull's more boorish tendencies. It provided a common standard of behaviour and language for the newly formed United Kingdom, with a dictionary (Dr Johnson's) to define the meaning of words and a common model of literary excellence, provided by the Latin authors of Augustan Rome.

A new word had come into the language (or an old one with a new meaning): taste. Taste was a gentlemanly attribute, it spoke of shared values and common assumptions. It was what every genteel householder aspired to display, during the new social ritual of visiting. For ladies in particular spent part of their day in paying social calls on friends and neighbours, leaving visiting cards on those who were out. This meant that the main rooms of the house could be inspected and judged at any moment. Home was not only the 'Theater' of its owner's 'Hospitality', as Sir Henry Wotton had described it in the seventeenth century, but a stage on which the rituals of social decorum were enacted, whenever an audience appeared. Grand country houses were also viewed by the increasing numbers of well-bred tourists, who could expect to be shown around by the housekeeper even if the family was not there. Eccentricity was deprecated, conformity to established norms esteemed.

The need to establish common values was reinforced by the second Jacobite Rebellion. In 1746, the tattered remnant of Bonnie Prince Charlie's army was crushed at the Battle of Culloden, but the attempt by the Young Pretender, grandson of James II, to supplant George II and put himself on the throne had gone better than anyone might have predicted: his force had reached Derby. While Bonnie Prince Charlie himself managed to escape, in characteristically romantic circumstances, the Highlands were brutally suppressed and their traditions outlawed. Highland lairds like the Dukes of Argyll who supported the Hanoverian regime were rewarded and a new image was fashioned for Scotland, which made Edinburgh, rebuilt on rational lines and full of rational people, the Athens of the North. Forced to look for livelihoods outside their native land, Scotsmen joined the army or went overseas. Britain's naval supremacy over France following its victory in the Seven Years War allowed the Empire to expand. The system by which captains were rewarded with prize money on the capture of enemy ships cultivated a fearsome spirit of aggression, and country houses were built on the proceeds. While George III tormented himself over the greatest disaster of his reign – 'America is lost!' he lamented in a private essay – the colony was less valuable to Britain than its possessions in the West Indies and India.

Coming to the throne in 1760, 'Farmer' George was unimaginative and, from 1789, intermittently mad, but he has been reassessed as a cultural figure. Not only did he amass a great library, assemble a sumptuous art collection, give his blessing to the infant Royal Academy of Arts and make a friend of the Dissenting potter Josiah Wedgwood (who, typically, gave him a device to measure the shrinkage of clay in a kiln). He was also a surprisingly skilled architectural draughtsman, having taken lessons from the architect Sir William Chambers three mornings a week as a young man. Unlike his eldest son, the future George IV, he did not build on a spectacular scale, but his reign saw an exceptional flourishing of the country house. Up-to-date architects borrowed features from the smart Neoclassicism of France, a style of severe geometry, Greek ornament and columns, just as French architects admired the English landscape park. Both countries were excited by the excavation of Pompeii and Herculaneum and other discoveries of Ancient monuments and sculpture being made in Italy and later Greece. Aesthetic subjects were a matter of consuming interest for the well-to-do and a subject of polite conversation.

In furniture, this was the Age of Mahogany. Until 1709, walnut had been the cabinetmaker's wood of choice but that year's harsh winter killed many trees. Fortunately the potential of mahogany was discovered just as the need for another wood appeared. Native to the islands of the Caribbean and Central America, mahogany trees grow to enormous size, spreading big leaves above the canopy of the rainforest. Their reddish-brown wood became the medium out of which Thomas Chippendale carved his ribbon backs, cabriole legs and claw feet for Dumfries House, Nostell Priory and numerous other country houses. Its rise was particularly associated with Robert Gillow, founder of a famous dynasty of cabinetmakers and upholsterers, who worked in Lancaster, a port on the river Lune. Not only did he import mahogany from Jamaica in logs, slabs or planks, used to fill up the holds of ships while more precious cargo was stored on top, but he sent back finished furniture that could be sold to sugar planters; he also invested in ships. The ships had once transported slaves and may still have done so; mahogany was one of the goods imported into Britain as part of the triangular trade.

Mahogany was an environmental disaster. Huge trees were felled until, by the mid-eighteenth century, there were none left in Jamaica and merchants turned to other forests around the Caribbean, which were similarly pillaged. It also entailed a human evil; the labour was provided by slaves. Indeed the word mahogany is thought to derive from a Nigerian word for King of Trees, used by slaves imported to the West Indies in the 1660s. All but the most old-fashioned country houses would have contained some piece of mahogany furniture by 1800, just as every country-house kitchen had its cone of sugar. Sugar was refined from sugar cane grown by slaves on plantations in the West Indies. Modern writers cannot turn their eyes from the distasteful economy of the Age of Taste: most Georgian country-house owners managed to ignore the human misery that was being suffered in distant countries – as successfully, it might be said, as Western consumers fail to remember the sweated conditions and oppressive regimes under which cheap garments and mobile devices can be produced today.

Contemporaries objected to plantation-owning families who bought country houses, because they could out-compete other landowners in ostentation. William Beckford senior, owner of twenty Jamaican estates, bought Fonthill in Wiltshire about 1744 and built a house there; it was of such pomp that the Wiltshire antiquarian Colt Hoare christened it Fonthill Splendens and the name stuck. But Beckford and his like were far from the only beneficiaries of slavery. Many country-house owners benefitted from investments in sugar plantations, ships that carried slaves or trading companies that provisioned the West Indies, or had younger sons fighting in the regiments and the Royal Navy that defended them. Its tentacles reached everywhere.

Legally the position of slavery in Britain was ambiguous: towards the end of the eighteenth century it was established that slaves could not be transported from Britain against their will but the trade around the Empire continued until 1807; previously it had been possible to buy slaves at Wapping and elsewhere. It is not known how many were sold or imported into Britain during the seventeenth and eighteenth centuries – perhaps a few thousand. Most of the black people working in Britain were men and some began as little children serving the great ladies of Charles II's court. They were as much a fashion item as the drinking chocolate that also came from the West Indies and were often given imposing Classical names like Socrates or Pompey. Occasionally gentlemen recognised the illegitimate children they had with slave women. The planter William Wells had a son with the slave he identifies in his will as 'my woman Juggy'; christened Nathaniel, he inherited Wells's fortune and bought Piercefield House in Monmouthshire. Riding to hounds beside such other Monmouthshire landowners as the Duke of Beaufort, he was at different times a justice of the peace, high sheriff, Deputy Lieutenant and an officer in the Yeoman Cavalry; his race and birth do not seem to have caused great comment. At Kenwood House in Hampstead, designed by Robert Adam, Lord and Lady Mansfield brought up Dido Elizabeth Belle on more or less equal terms with her second cousin Lady Elizabeth Murray; Dido was the illegitimate daughter of Mansfield's nephew Sir John Lindsay, a naval officer, by an enslaved woman in the West Indies. The equality of the girls was not complete: Lady Elizabeth married a gentleman and Dido a gentleman's steward. English society was so prejudiced against foreigners in general, along with Roman Catholics and the Scots and Irish, that black people appear not to have suffered worse discrimination than other groups. The great and humane man of letters Samuel Johnson employed a black servant, Francis Barber, and made him the principal beneficiary of his will.

The nabobs of the East India Company were as conspicuous as the sugar planters in Georgian Britain – if not more so, given the allusions that they made to the source of their wealth in architecture and decoration. While it is difficult to find a single work of architecture in Britain that evokes the West Indies (although occasional idealised references are made in decoration: a bust of an enslaved man figures in the Marble Hall at Clandon and the silversmith Paul de Lamerie decorated sugar boxes with scenes of cane fields), servants of the East India Company – successors to Thomas 'Diamond' Pitt – were less coy. Oakly Park was one of the many estates bought by the general and administrator, Robert Clive – 'Clive of India' – when he returned from the subcontinent 'all over estates and diamonds', as Horace Walpole put it. His greatest coup, while in India, had been to obtain from the Mughal emperor Shah Alam II the *Diwani* rights of tax collection, which even contemporaries regarded as extortion; Clive had the making of the grant recorded in a gigantic painting by Benjamin West – so big it could only be accommodated at first-floor level in the stair hall (remodelled by C.R. Cockerell in 1819–36). Clive's collection of Indian artefacts can now be seen at Powis Castle – golden hookahs inlaid with ebony, jewelled daggers, silken hangings, coats of elephant armour and enormous gems. 'Loot' is one of the many words that entered the English language from India, along with kedgeree, chutney and chintz.

Nabobs were the oligarchs of their day – depressingly richer than everyone else and, although Clive was the son of an impoverished gentry family, not all of them could claim even that. As the *Gentleman's Magazine* sarcastically put it in 1786,

> the East India Company providentially bring us home every year a sufficient number of a new sort of gentlemen, with new customs, manners, and *principles*, who fill the offices of the *old country gentlemen* . . . with so much better address.

The young men who sought a fortune in India did not always return rich: many did not return at all, having died from fever. And the number of nabobs was not as great as the fear of them suggested. But they were part of a larger phenomenon which affected the appearance not just of the country house but all affluent homes: what we would now call the globalisation of trade.

Indian goods, sometimes confused with Chinese, were not the only nabob taste. Chintz – a Hindi word for calico painted or printed with flowers: nothing to do with China – had been available since the seventeenth century. Gingham is another Indian word, although by the 1760s, ginghams were being manufactured in Manchester. Imported shawls, embroideries and ivory chess pieces fed an appetite for consumption that was served by an increasing number of London shops. Tea from China was served in Chinese porcelain cups – although English manufacturers were quick to spot the opportunity provided by the coming national beverage. Teapots took the form of elephants, oyster shells, houses, cabbages, pineapples; they were decorated with flowers, fossils, slogans ('No Stamp Act'), oriental patterns, portraits of Frederick the Great, transfer-printed with scenes of landscapes and lovers . . . The novelty of the product seemed to permit a degree of fantasy beyond that of other wares.

Born in Sweden, the architect Sir William Chambers (his title was Swedish although George III allowed it to be recognised in Britain) had visited Canton with the Swedish East India Company before studying architecture in France; his trip provided the material for *Designs of Chinese Buildings* in 1757. Just at this time the virtuoso woodcarver Luke Lightfoot began to decorate the niches, doorcases and chimneypieces at Claydon Hall in Buckinghamshire with a froth of swirling curves, Chinese fret and Chinamen drinking tea. Both Chambers's book and Lightfoot's carvings are an example of the Chinese taste, or *chinoiserie*, particularly associated with the Rococo: a style of sinuous, asymmetrical curves and counter-curves, involving decorative shells, tendrils and birds, which had originated in France. The Rococo never fully succeeded in jumping the English Channel, at a time of intense chauvinism, but it caught on with silversmiths, cabinetmakers and stuccadores, whose exuberant plasterwork was particularly popular in Ireland. Claydon is one of the few country houses where it forms a complete decorative scheme.

British industrialists fed the appetite for consumer products – many of which found their way into country houses – grew rich, and sometimes built their own country houses, generally close to their factories. These include Soho House (for the manufacturer of metal goods Matthew Boulton, near his prodigious Soho Works outside Birmingham), Etruria Hall (for the potter Josiah Wedgwood, near his Etruria Works in Staffordshire) and Willersley Castle (for the cotton spinner and inventor Sir Richard Arkwright, above his Cromford Mills in Derbyshire).

☙

Country-house owners displayed their knowledge, curiosity and world view through their parks. The interest that Kent, Pope, Burlington and

Princess Caroline took in gardening became a near-universal passion for country-house owners as the eighteenth century progressed. By 1826, the German fortune-hunting Prince von Pückler-Muskau could tell his (for tactical reasons, divorced) wife that it would take her 'at least four hundred and twenty years to see all the parks of England, of which there are undoubtedly at least a hundred thousand, for they swarm in every direction'. The Hon. Charles Hamilton spent so much on creating the garden of Painshill in Surrey that he was never able to build the country house with which he had hoped to complete his pocket estate on that important artery of communication, the Portsmouth Road.

The fourteenth child of the 6th Earl of Abercorn, Hamilton visited Italy twice, in 1727 and 1732, buying sculpture. A school friend had been the banker Henry Hoare, known as The Magnificent, who created the beautiful gardens at Stourhead from 1741, and like Hamilton, took inspiration from the landscape paintings of Claude, Gaspard Dughet and Salvator Rosa. But Hamilton lacked Hoare's means, and on his return from Italy, needed employment. He found it at the court of Frederick, Prince of Wales, who took a keen interest in landscape. This also brought him into contact with Lord Cobham, for whom William Kent had recently begun to design garden architecture at Stowe.

The land at Painshill – less than four hundred acres – was extremely unpromising. Contemporaries were appalled by the unproductive Surrey heaths amid which it was set and to Hamilton's visitors, one of his greatest achievements was to make what Horace Walpole described as 'a fine place out of a most accursed hill'. Weeds were ploughed up and burnt, sheep fed with turnips to provide manure. Hamilton's tree planting won praise from no less an authority than the Swedish botanist Carl Linnaeus who declared that 'a greater variety of the fir was to be found on this spot than in any other part of the world'. Another pioneering achievement was a vineyard, whose 'champagne' was an expensive novelty at a time when no other landowner attempted viticulture.

Experimental agriculture went hand in hand with the Picturesque. Arriving visitors were led to the edge of a vale and beheld a series of carefully curated views. Below them was a lake with a Chinese bridge, beyond a Turkish tent. They were standing in a Gothic temple (made of wood). It is like a garden of the Golden Age in which different styles can exist in harmony with each other, as though the lion were lying down with the lamb; albeit visitors may only have had a hazy idea of their origins – Indian, again, could be mistaken for Chinese. In the grotto, a gardener waited in the dank for visitors to approach, then switched on a pump to circulate dripping water – while the surface of a pool remained still, to produce reflections. (Grottoes were becoming a craze, often – as at Goodwood House in Sussex – decorated by ladies; the cost of the shells could be exorbitant.) At Painshill, plaster stalactites covered in wafers of shiny, sparkling quartz and other minerals descended from the roof of the grotto, amid which were amethyst and other crystals. Wonder at the natural world gave way to the introspection of a hermitage and the gloom of the Ruined Abbey (erected to hide a brickworks). The gaily decorated Turkish Tent evoked pleasure, while also recalling the Tent of Darius in which Alexander the Great gave freedom to the women and slaves of the defeated King Darius. Alexander's magnanimity was, perhaps, an implicit criticism of George II, still on the throne when the tent was erected in the 1750s; Prince Frederick had been banished from his court.

At some point, Hamilton must have consulted Robert Adam since designs by him (for ceilings and a pedestal) survive in the Soane Museum; but for the most part he was his own architect. That assiduous tourist and pontificator on the Picturesque, the Rev. William Gilpin, approved. 'This', he exclaimed of Painshill, 'is one of the most beautiful things of the kind that I have seen.'

Hamilton was a gentlemanly enthusiast; Lancelot 'Capability' Brown was a professional. Nobody did more towards the creation of those seemingly limitless numbers of landscape parks described by Pückler-Muskau than him. We know little of Brown the man, and he left scant documentation as to his ideas. But it must have taken someone of great determination, persuasive ability and tact to keep his powerful clients committed to his schemes, throughout the vicissitudes of political life and the nation's economic ups and downs.

Born in 1716, Brown was the leading exponent of a new idea in gardening. By dint of digging, moving earth, planting trees and sweeping away every vestige of the rigid Baroque garden, parklands beneath grey

English skies were made to resemble the Roman Campagna, as depicted by Claude Lorrain. Follies, of the kind seen at Painshill, played their part, but what Brown really liked was a combination of trees, hills, lakes and greensward; no flowers, no Turkish tents. His masterpiece is often regarded as the park at Blenheim, which is fitting: it was there that Vanbrugh improvised his theory of the Picturesque. By a stroke of irony, Woodstock Manor, which Vanbrugh had sought to restore, was torn down, its stones being used to build the Grand Bridge that Vanbrugh had designed – the avowed object of which was to lead to the manor house, which of course no longer existed. And so the road over the Grand Bridge went nowhere, while the bridge itself, spanning a puny and soon unfashionable canal, became the subject of ridicule. Remedy came in 1764 when the 4th Duke of Marlborough commissioned Brown to provide a suitably imposing sheet of water for the bridge to span. Brown would work at Blenheim for a decade.

Brown's career had been astounding. Having grown up in a Northumbrian village, he had begun his working life, aged sixteen, as a gardener at the house of the local squire. His break came two years after he journeyed south, when he was appointed as undergardener at Stowe, just at the time that it was being developed into Britain's first and greatest garden of allegory and ideas. By 1749, Brown, having imbibed Kent's ideas – and perhaps some of his self-confidence – could set up on his own. After a couple of years, he was continuously in demand. By the time of his death in 1783, he had 'improved' nearly one hundred and fifty estates, freeing country houses of the visual encumbrances that surrounded them (not only Baroque gardens but old villages and market towns) in order to develop their naturalistic 'capabilities' – hence his soubriquet of Capability Brown.

Under the hand of Brown and his contemporaries, the Baroque garden almost disappeared from the record; numerous villages which had previously lived beneath the wing of the local country house were destroyed, their inhabitants being rehoused – if they were lucky – in tidy model villages, such as Milton Abbas, with its street of thatched double cottages designed by Chambers. Milton Abbas replaced an ancient market town that had clustered around the skirts of Milton Abbey, rebuilt by Chambers in an unenthusiastically Gothic style with the ruin of the original abbey converted to a spectacular private chapel. We see Lord Milton himself in the chapel in a monument carved by Agostino Carlini, tenderly mourning the wife who predeceased him; he was inconsolable at her death and became a recluse. But he was also a difficult man, who fought a long battle with the population of the town he wanted to demolish, some of whom would not leave; he had the home of an obdurate solicitor flooded.

Milton's account at Hoare's Bank makes sorry reading. He was ruined by his building and landscape works; but Brown's Arcadias were not wholly impractical. They were adapted to the sheep and beef farming that was encouraged by agriculturalists like the 5th Duke of Bedford at Woburn Abbey and the 1st Earl of Leicester's great-nephew 'Coke of Norfolk' at Holkham Hall. The sport of fox hunting had begun in the mid-eighteenth century, using heavy horses that could get across boggy ground while supporting equally heavy riders. Well-drained parkland, however, could be galloped across, on Thoroughbred crosses. Clumps of trees sheltered foxes. Game birds could be walked up with a dog and shot at (not many, with the guns of the time, could have been hit). Timber had been in short supply since the seventeenth century. Growing it was both patriotic (it was needed for the navy) and profitable. There was method in what can at times seem landscape madness.

The monument at Milton Abbey, carved by Agostini, was designed by the most successful country-house architect of the 1760s and 1770s, Robert Adam, whom we have already met at Hopetoun and Painshill Park. Adam's career demonstrates the continuing supremacy of the Antique in architectural taste. Whereas architects and patrons of the previous generation had striven for a theoretical understanding of Ancient Rome, via Palladio and Vitruvius, any go-ahead young person now went directly to the ruins themselves. Archaeology became the inspiration of new styles.

The science of excavation was still primitive by modern standards and enterprising Italian charlatans faked or improved the statues for which gullible *milordi* were willing to pay high prices. But there was also genuine scholarship. In Rome, architectural students were now commonly to be seen on ladders measuring capitals and cornices to ensure that their dimensions were faithfully understood; and Adam's friend the great

Venetian engraver Giovanni Battista Piranesi was creating dramatic plates of both views and details, enriched by a farouche imagination which might exaggerate scale and richness (and made occasional mistakes). At home, Adam had been brought up in the circle of Sir John Clerk of Penicuik, an antiquarian who saw a continuum between the culture of the Roman Empire and the present day – anything that had occurred between those points being a barbaric aberration. Having helped his father William Adam on architectural and building projects, and met the clients who employed him, this ambitious young Scot was fully alive to the importance of a Grand Tour before he could launch himself on London as an architect.

Rome would play another role for Adam. Shrewdly, he saw the opportunity for a clever, knowledgeable young man to meet prospective clients in the less socially constrained conditions of Italy. By good fortune, he was able to make the journey with the Hon. Charles Hope, son of his father's client at Hopetoun. Unlike another hopeful Scot, Robert Mylne, who had walked to Rome, Adam rode in Hope's carriage and bought fine clothes along the way. Eager to be seen on equal terms with the aristocratic visitors, he shamelessly fibbed about his antecedents. He partied hard, but mostly he worked hard, studying the Baths of Diocletian and Caracalla and eventually producing a sumptuous volume on the *Ruins of the Palace of the Emperor Diocletian at Spalatro in Dalmatia.*

Adam returned from Italy in 1758. Not everyone responded favourably to his relentless 'self-puffing'; the king and queen preferred Chambers, who in time became Comptroller of the King's Works. Adam's one royal commission was for the firework display that celebrated the purchase of Buckingham Palace and he was never knighted. But the fashionable world went mad for him.

Today, the Georgian period can be disparaged as the age of brown furniture – all that mahogany – but Adam's style was anything but brown. His ceilings and furniture – he designed everything in an interior – coruscated with colour, shimmered with incident, glittered with gilding. They were the backdrop to entertainments crowded with people in equally glorious and strident colours: beautiful silks and, as was said of Lady Williams Wynn, wife of one of Adam's clients in the 1770s, 'quite dazzling' diamonds.

To the lighter style of decoration introduced by Kent in the 1740s, influenced by the Rococo, Adam added motifs such as ram's heads, garlands, festoons, husks and the wave pattern of the Vitruvian scroll seen on the sides of sarcophagi. Airy staircase balusters were created from swirls of wrought iron, ceilings were covered in a lace of low relief 'composition' pressed out of boxwood moulds (compo had the advantage of being cheaper than more boldly modelled plasterwork); the spindly lines of 'grotesques', derived from the recently excavated frescoes of Pompeii, brought wall surfaces to a state of nervy animation.

All this was new. As Adam put it with typical bravado in his *Works of Robert and James Adam*:

> The massive entablature, the ponderous compartment ceiling, the tabernacle frame, almost the only species of ornament formerly known, in this country, are now universally exploded, and in their place, we have adopted a beautiful variety of light mouldings, gracefully formed, delicately enriched and arranged with propriety and skill.

This amounted to 'a kind of revolution in the whole system of this useful and elegant art'. The idea that taste could be subject to revolutions was itself new.

One of the greatest of all Adam's many country houses is Syon House, to the west of London, commissioned by the 1st Duke of Northumberland (fig. 26). Beginning life as plain Hugh Smithson, the duke had become rich and ennobled through a series of inheritances and marriage, and was now a leading politician. Although Syon seems to modern eyes a large country house, to the duke and his architect it was simply a villa, only used for short periods and originally not hung with paintings. Adam's Grand Tour had been to good effect, as discussions may have started soon after his return; work began in 1762. Syon had once been a nunnery (its name derives from Mount Zion), built around a central square. Adam kept the gaunt exterior, giving it battlements and corner turrets, recalling the south front at Wilton. Inside, he quarried a series of spectacular interiors out of the crumbling Tudor pile. The cultivated duke 'expressed his desire that the whole might be executed

FIG. 26 *After Robert Adam – 'Bob the Roman' – returned from his Grand Tour of Italy and Dalmatia, he launched his prolific career with a series of spectacular commissions, one of the most inventive of which was Syon Park, to the west of London. Beyond the Ante Room, with gilded statues above scagliola (imitation marble) columns and trophies of arms and armour to either side of the doors, can be glimpsed copies of the* Dying Gaul *in the Capitoline Museum and the* Apollo Belvedere *in the Vatican.* © Country Life Picture Library

entirely in the antique style', according to Adam in the *Works*. That suited 'Bob the Roman', as he was sometimes known. In the plan, he put his study of the baths of Ancient Rome to good use, creating a sequence of rooms of contrasting shapes, with screens of columns and apses to give extra interest to the eye. Had he also looked at the plan of Holkham? Syon itself drove him to invention, since the existing house was irregular as well as dilapidated and Adam had to take account of oddly shaped spaces and changes of level. He succeeded, in his own words, in managing 'the inequality of levels . . . in such a manner as to increase the scenery and add to the movement, so that an apparent defect has been converted into a real beauty'. Revealing words. They show that Adam thought of architecture in terms of 'scenery', a term usually applied to the stage at that date; he liked to produce a series of effects. Similarly, 'movement' in the architecture kept the eye engaged, the visitor's interest sharpened; the stately interiors of the early years of the century had been static.

The first room that visitors encounter is an entrance hall thirty-four feet tall, with a coffered ceiling derived from Adam's study of the Roman baths. One end has an apse containing a marble copy of the *Apollo Belvedere* in the Vatican, the other a screen of columns with a bronze copy of the *Dying Gaul* in the Capitoline Museum. The screen ingeniously conceals a change in level, since to either side is a short flight of steps. Off the entrance hall is the Ante Room. It had not been possible to find sufficiently splendid marble for the columns in this room, so what appears to be *verde antico* is in fact scagliola – imitation marble. Scagliola was also used for the richly coloured floor (not a material friendly to modern high heels). Again, the columns are used to cunning effect: they divide off part of the rectangular room to make the surviving portion into a square. Gilded casts of Roman gods and goddesses stand on the entablature above the columns: contemporaries must have gaped at the sumptuous effect.

Whereas the ceiling of the entrance hall had been monumental, that of the drawing room is delicate, colourful and feminine. It looks like a mosaic of painted cameos, set within gilded octagonal frames – the effect is of endless repetition. Here as elsewhere, Adam drew on motifs from recent excavations in Italy: from Herculaneum come the figures on the many roundels on the ceiling of the Red Drawing Room which Chambers dismissively compared to 'skied dinner plates'. The old long gallery became a library, whose delicate filigree of ornament seems to ripple down the length of the room, like a theme and variations by Mozart. All was scenery, all was movement indeed.

The aristocrats who undertook the Grand Tour formed a club to celebrate their exposure to the Antique. The Society of Dilettanti had been founded in 1734 and made good the lack of an institution in Britain to rival the French and German Academies. They were not only interested in ruins and the purchase of old marbles: Italy was a playground to these rich young men, to whom nudity, sexual excess and bacchanalia were compelling aspects of the Ancient world. Like other groups of gilded youth, before and since, they thought they were above the narrow morality of the day. They might be depicted by painters like Pompeo Batoni surrounded by the culture they had come to admire, but not all of them were given to sightseeing and some spent their time in debauchery.

There was, though, a serious side to the Dilettanti. Many collected sculptures – or the surviving parts of sculptures, often improved, sometimes faked – that had recently been excavated. When they got home, they displayed these marbles in sculpture galleries which sometimes followed Holkham's in being formed of three interconnected rooms; Robert Adam built one of this type at Newby Hall in Yorkshire in the 1760s (fig. 27), Henry Holland another at Woburn Abbey in Bedfordshire in 1789–90. But the *beau idéal* of the sculpture gallery was designed by Henry Blundell of Ince Blundell to house the collection he formed, after the inspiration of his Lancashire neighbour Charles Townley, from the late 1770s. It dates from 1802–3 and takes the form of the Pantheon.

FIG. 27 *Travellers on the Grand Tour brought back Roman statues – often improved by having missing limbs, noses and heads carved to recreate an idea of the original – which could be displayed in sculpture galleries. At Newby Hall in Yorkshire, William Weddell began his gallery before he had acquired the famous collection of marbles that filled it. Robert Adam's plan may have been influenced by Holkham Hall although the top-lit central rotonda was probably inspired by ruins around Rome. © Country Life Picture Library*

Roman marbles are displayed in a setting expressly derived from the architecture of Ancient Rome.

The Dilettanti also promoted expeditions to record the architecture of the Ancient world. In 1750, Nicholas Revett, son of a Suffolk gentleman, and James Stuart, son of a poor Scottish sailor who was born in a seedy area of London, left Rome for Greece to collect material for what became *The Antiquities of Athens*; the cost of publication would be underwritten by the Dilettanti. Athens was the fountainhead of Classicism, from which flowed a purer stream than the overblown magnificence of imperial Rome. This view appalled the community of architects and dealers whom they left behind in Rome, who feared that a change of taste would eclipse their livelihoods. They need not have worried. Once Stuart had returned to England in 1754, gentlemen of taste eagerly subscribed to the book recording their work, only to find that the first volume took seven years to appear – and then it was confined to relatively minor monuments, such as the Choragic Monument of Lysicrates (in order that it could be measured, a local Athenian had obligingly pulled down a house) and the Tower of the Winds; such was the hunger for accurate representations of Greece that even these small works were widely copied. The three subsequent volumes only saw the light after Stuart's death in 1789. The fourth volume, containing the Parthenon, did not arrive until 1816.

Even so, the excitement generated by the first exposure to a new style of Classicism can be judged from Stuart's commissions. At Hagley, he built a Greek Doric temple in 1758–9 for the 1st Lord Lyttelton: Greek Doric is distinguished from Roman Doric in having flutes and no base. At Shugborough (fig. 28), for Thomas Anson, he erected copies of the Arch of Hadrian, the 'Lanthorn of Demosthenes' (as the Choragic Monument of Lysicrates was known) and the Tower of the Winds. New ideas were often first tried in landscape parks, whose follies were inspired by different periods of history and different cultures from around the world. In the end, Adam was let off the hook; Stuart did not start a full-blown Greek Revival. It was left to Charles Robert Cockerell, William Wilkins and Robert Smirke to inherit the Greek mantle during the Regency.

Adam parried the new interest in Greece by adopting the Etruscan

FIG. 28 *In 1762, James 'Athenian' Stuart and Nicholas Revett published the first volume of* The Antiquities of Athens, *showing accurate drawings of the monuments that they had measured in Greece. Stuart was commissioned to recreate three of them as follies in the landscape park at Shugborough Hall in Staffordshire – seen here is the Arch of Hadrian built in 131 AD by the Greece-loving Emperor Hadrian. They prefigured the Greek Revival that became popular during the Regency among architects who regarded the architecture of Ancient Greece as purer than that of the Roman Empire.* © National Trust

Style. This was misnamed, since the influences came from the painted interiors being revealed at Pompeii in the 1760s, and from Greek vases, of the kind collected by Sir William Hamilton and published in 1766–76. At the Earl Spencer's town palace overlooking Green Park, 'Athenian' Stuart, as he was known, created a Painted Room, with panels of grotesque decoration – arabesques derived from Raphael's murals in the Vatican *loggie* – interspersed with roundels and lunettes painted with motifs from Herculaneum, which were published from 1757. Adam rubbished it as 'pityfulissimo'; but was quick to copy the idea in the Etruscan Room at Osterley Park, west of London. He wrote to his brother James who was in Italy asking for 'any sketches of any painted ceilings at Herculaneum . . . I see that taste must come in.' Hence the Red Drawing Room at Syon.

Just as Classical architecture was becoming more archaeological, Gothic was becoming more antiquarian. Historians used to refer to the eighteenth-century Gothic Revival as Gothick (the usual spelling of Gothic in the Georgian period) with the patronising implication that it was un-serious: an example of the whimsy of the Rococo. Gothic, however, had deep roots. It had survived – or been revived – in odd pockets of the country, never having quite been snuffed out at the end of the Middle Ages. Before the Civil War, it was promoted by the High Church Anglican, Archbishop Laud: the religious community at Little Gidding in Huntingdonshire chose it for the façade of the church they built, which was visited by Charles I on three occasions. After the execution of Charles I, Lady Anne Clifford clung to the style in the churches and castles she restored or expanded in the north of England, as a symbol of undying royalism. Gothic was a style of somewhat unspecific antiquity: Lady Anne thought some of her castles were Roman and indeed some had been built on Roman sites. Following the Restoration, Bishop Cosin refitted Durham Cathedral in a Gothic style after the Scottish troops imprisoned there by Oliver Cromwell had burnt all the woodwork to keep warm; and no less a Classicist than Christopher Wren had a Gothic episode at Christ Church, Oxford, when he designed Tom Tower, wanting it to harmonise with the existing architecture of Cardinal Wolsey's college. Association also inspired Kent in 1733 to add a Gothic wing to the surviving gatehouse of Esher Place in Surrey, where Cardinal Wolsey had been kept under house arrest. 'Kent is Kentissime there!' exclaimed Horace Walpole.

Walpole seized the Gothic ball and ran with it at Strawberry Hill. His 'little Gothick castle' beside the Thames became the Gothic equivalent of Lord Burlington's Chiswick villa, a few miles further along the river. Effete and gossipy, Horace was a marked contrast to his father, the bullying prime minister Sir Robert Walpole, and Strawberry Hill (fig. 29), a cottage which evolved and grew from Walpole's purchase of it in 1747 until the 1790s, could hardly have been more different from Houghton. Neither Gothick nor Gothic is the right term to describe it; Walpole's taste was antiquarian. We know exactly what he thought because of his correspondence: vivacious, catty but immensely readable, and filling forty-three volumes in the definitive edition. He relished curiosities and fine workmanship; but what excited him above all were

FIG. 29 *The architecture of Horace Walpole's Tribune Room at Strawberry Hill, his villa at Twickenham, was derived from ecclesiastical sources such as St Alban's Abbey and York Minster. Originally called the Chapel, it was where he kept the greatest treasures of his collection, including miniatures and enamels. While his father Sir Robert Walpole was inspired by the splendours of Rome, Horace loved the romance of the Gothic past and stories from English history; this drawing was commissioned from the architect and antiquary John Carter in about 1789 to supplement the guidebook to Strawberry Hill which Walpole had printed on his own press. Courtesy of The Lewis Walpole Library, Yale University*

objects that enabled him to touch the past – a lock of Mary Tudor's hair, the Elizabethan magician Dr Dee's mirror, Cardinal Wolsey's red hat.

Walpole had inherited the lease of a London house, £5,000 in cash and the revenue of various sinecures which increased over the years: he was rich but not that rich. Fitfully, as money and inspiration allowed, Strawberry Hill became a showcase of Walpole's antiquarianism, a reaction against Italian grand masters and neo-Palladianism, rejoicing in the evocative oddities of the native English tradition. Rather than stun the senses with a blaze of opulence and order, Walpole wanted to intrigue the imagination with shadows, stained glass and the effects of age – just as John Soane would in the Regency. His was the first Georgian house to make a virtue of asymmetry, rather than Classical balance. 'The Grecian is only proper for magnificent and public buildings,' declared Walpole. '. . . I am almost as fond of the Sharawaggi, or Chinese want of symmetry, in buildings, as in grounds or gardens.'

What he hoped to achieve above anything was to give visitors the creeps, with a 'Gothic lanthorn with painted glass which casts a most venerable gloom on the stairs'. As the reference to Chinese asymmetry suggests, he was not remorselessly scholarly in his approach: medieval tombs, for example, were redesigned as chimneypieces. Yet there is no doubting Walpole's thoroughness. He was obsessively fascinated by the medieval past. In its present denuded state, the house gives no hint as to the richness and variety of Walpole's collections. Strawberry Hill was not the very earliest house to be built with pointed windows and battlements, but it quickly became the most famous. Walpole was an irresistibly likeable man and launched Gothic as a movement through his own personal charm. In scale and materials, his achievement was constrained by his means; William Beckford, the immensely rich builder of the *ne plus ultra* of Regency Gothic, Fonthill Abbey in Wiltshire, scorned Strawberry Hill as 'a miserable child's box – a species of gothic mousetrap'. But it had many imitators, such as the Earl of Charleville, who copied the fan vaulting for the gallery ceiling at Charleville Castle in County Offaly, Ireland, built in 1800–12.

Walpole, whom we know from his letter-writing so much better than his contemporaries, tends to obscure other Gothic initiatives in the mid-eighteenth century. These were various, if scattered. One of the greatest was Inveraray Castle in Argyll which Archibald, 3rd Duke of Argyll inherited from his brother, who was survived by four daughters but no son, in 1743. A bookish, untidy widower, he was already in his sixties and barely knew his Highland estates. He determined to make a visit, though he already knew from a survey that the ancient seat of the Campbells was falling down. When the duke succeeded in reaching Inveraray from Edinburgh in 1744, the London architect Roger Morris was in his retinue. The next year, at the outbreak of the 1745 Rebellion, the duke had to hurry back to London so fast that friction caused the axle of his coach to catch fire. But works had been set in train at Inveraray that would last for sixty years.

Built of the greenish local stone, Inveraray is a massive building, with towers at each corner and a central tower that rises above the battlements in the manner of Wollaton Hall in Nottinghamshire; the conical roofs on the corner towers are more Continental (or as we would say today, 'Disney') than British – but it is nevertheless undoubtedly a castle, regularised, in accordance with an aesthetic which could not escape the dictates of Classical symmetry. Not long before Duke Archibald and Morris had left London, Batty Langley, a failed architect who had turned to architectural publication, brought out the first edition of *Ancient Architecture Restored and Improved*, reissued in 1747 as *Gothic Architecture, Improved by Rules*. As the titles imply, this reconciled the (to the Georgian mind) chaos of medieval architecture with the expectations of a polite age. What Langley tried on paper Morris did in practice at Inveraray.

At just this time, Sanderson Miller, son of a wealthy merchant from Banbury, was building a thatched cottage at Edgehill. This was one of a number of works by Miller, around the estate that his father had bought there; his imagination was fired by the Battle of Edgehill which opened the Civil War. He gave his own house, Radway Grange, battlements and built an octagonal tower copied from Guy's Tower at Warwick Castle, rich in history, wreathed in legend and symbolic of England, in the county where Shakespeare was born. It was the first quotation from a medieval building. At Hagley, Miller built a ruined tower for Lord Lyttelton, remembered as amiable, absent-minded and benevolent, and for being briefly Lord Chancellor. Walpole thought it evoked 'the true rust of the Barons' Wars'. Lyttelton also built a Druid's Temple in the form of standing stones. With the crushing of the Jacobite Rebellion at Culloden in 1746, gentlemen could risk looking beneath the Celtic fringe and many were taken in by the poems supposedly written by the Highland bard Ossian, but actually composed by their 'translator' James Macpherson in the 1760s.

Chiswick, Strawberry Hill – they may seem to be the antithesis of each other but they had something in common. Both these influential showplaces were villas. That is to say, they were not really country houses at all, in the sense of headquarters of an agricultural estate. Neither had much land. They were near to London. In the case of Chiswick, Burlington did not even sleep there, but next door, in the Jacobean house. A generation before, it would have taken a determined traveller to see a remote country house, and during the Picturesque Movement they were placed at a further remove: the drive from Worcester Lodge to Badminton House is three miles long. Both Chiswick and Strawberry Hill, however, were highly visible. It was one reason for their influence on taste.

Villa was a foreign word, originally Latin but coming into use from the Italian (Jane Austen appears to have found it pretentious). Palladio was famous for the villas he designed outside Venice, and most villas designed in the first half of the eighteenth century were Classical. Most but not all: the villa invited stylistic experiment. As early as 1714 the Scottish travel writer John Macky described Twickenham as 'a Village remarkable for [its] abundance of Curious seats'. The numerous books by architects offering villa designs during the Regency offer a smorgasbord of possibilities: Tudor, Swiss, Indian, even Log Cabin.

Villas were often astylar: they had Classical proportions and pediments but the Order was implied, not visible. The master of the genre was Sir Robert Taylor, otherwise architect to the Bank of England and of the palatial Heveningham Hall in Suffolk. Convenient for London, his villas were often built by City men. They are of Palladian proportions. Taylor's Asgill House, in what is now a prominent position beside Twickenham Bridge (constructed in the twentieth century), has wings that appear to begin a pediment, in the centre of which is another pediment shape formed by the roof over the canted bay; this pediment-within-a-pediment motif was inspired by Palladio's church of Il Redentore in Venice (fig. 30). Nothing is wasted in the plan of this compact house, where an octagonal room in the centre of the garden front opens into the other main rooms, reducing the need for passages. The stairs, ingeniously fitted into a small oval space, lead up to an unexpectedly grand landing. Taylor achieves the Georgian ideal of elegance without ostentation.

♣

Conditions in Georgian Ireland were different from those on the British mainland. Still a colony, it was ruled by a Protestant Ascendancy which formed a small cadre in relation to the population as a whole. The estates

FIG. 30 *Sir Robert Taylor built Asgill House, near Richmond on the river Thames, for the self-made banker Sir Charles Asgill in the early 1760s. It is a villa, providing a compact house in the countryside near London, without a landed estate. This print of 1781 makes the surroundings look particularly idyllic.*

they occupied had, in many cases, once been owned by native lords, who had been dispossessed at some point, perhaps long ago, perhaps after 1688; the countryside was not as friendly to them as any English or many Scottish counties would have been, with their web of gentleman's residences, parsonages, villages, county towns and cathedral closes, full of people who might be visited or invited to the occasional ball. By contrast, what in Ireland was called the Big House was surrounded by people who spoke a different native tongue and were often regarded as untrustworthy, feckless and hostile. If the Anglo-Irish felt beleaguered, it was with reason. Those who lived permanently in Ireland might be deprived of the company of long-standing neighbours who had let their Irish properties and gone to live in England, where they still had connections and perhaps other houses. Isolation bred wild behaviour and more habitual drunkenness than the rest of the British Isles. For many, fox hunting was their reason for living.

When Ireland was incorporated into the newly formed United Kingdom of Great Britain in 1801, Dublin became the second city. It had already produced its own architects, notably the Sir Edward Lovett Pearce, an MP in the Irish House of Commons, whose father was a cousin of Vanbrugh. By the time of his death in 1733 while he was still only in his early thirties, he had become Ireland's leading Palladian, designing the brick villa of Bellamont Forest in County Cavan for his cousins, the Coote family, and Castletown House for William Conolly, the Speaker of the Irish House of Commons. Conolly had risen from obscure origins to make a fortune from buying or, as a lawyer, conveying Jacobite estates confiscated after 1688; at Castletown, a dozen miles from Dublin, he could entertain on the grandest scale to ensure his domination of politics as the chief 'undertaker' of British government business in the Irish parliament. Externally it was 'without orniments [*sic*] of any sort', according to Lady Anne Conolly, the English wife of the Speaker's nephew, though she thought it 'realy [*sic*] a charming [house] to live in'. The Speaker's wife, Katherine, liked gambling and among the rackety visitors was the actress Kitty Clive; she also liked Castletown, being proud of the fact that she almost never visited other people – she was so grand they came to her (this spared her the discomfort of travel, while saving her guests the cost of entertaining her).

The 1st Marquess of Abercorn had an English architect, John Soane, remodel Baronscourt in County Tyrone in 1791 to satisfy the instincts of a 'Magnifico'; but by birth, education and outlook Abercorn was English. The same might be said of the Ponsonby family at Bessborough, remodelled in an old-fashioned style in 1744, though by a native Irishman, the architect and painter Francis Bindon. Two years after it was finished in 1755, the 1st Earl of Bessborough died and his successors rarely visited. By contrast, the resident Dukes of Leinster were praised by an early nineteenth-century writer for their work at Carton, whose fine park was surrounded by 'comfortable slated farmhouses', well-drained land and 'a town laid out in the English style'. According to a later newspaper account, the 1st Duke wanted

> to have around him not an idle, sporting, presuming, carousing, set of squireens – but a comfortable, industrious, humble, but at the same time self-respecting yeomanry – a class of men so much wanting, and, alas, still so scarce in Ireland.

Irish country houses were famous for the exuberance of their plasterwork. Another obvious difference that would have struck English visitors as soon as the house came in view was the absence, quite often, of a portico (see fig. 31). In a land that was in other respects wedded to Palladianism, this omission could be explained by the weather. Invented beneath the baking suns of Greece, porticos were unsuited to a rainy climate, because the stones beneath them grew slippery with mould through lack of light. For ordinary purposes the family would not even use the front door, preferring a door convenient for the stables, where carriages might shelter from the wet. This was the equivalent of entering a modern house from the garage. Even beneath umbrellas – and a man carrying one was thought effeminate – it would have been a daunting task to climb a long flight of external steps in the rain, particularly for ladies in long dresses. John Nash's Killymoon Castle of 1801–3, which introduced the first porte cochère into Ireland, providing a covered space where carriages could stop next to the front door, was a revelation.

Understandably, damp and cold remained preoccupations inside Irish – as indeed other – country houses. As well as ordering soap and candles, the owner might have his room prepared for his arrival by ordering the housekeeper to sleep in it for the previous week. It was one way to air the bed. Inner warmth could be generated around the dining table, particularly by men who drank heavily after the ladies had left. Ladies such as Louisa Lennox, brought up at Goodwood and married at fifteen to Thomas Conolly, great-nephew of Speaker Conolly, got their own back by shopping (whether in person or by proxy, sending requests to family in England and France) and expensive interior decoration, creating a 'delightful pretty room . . . with blue paper and white knotted furniture in it', and another hung with white satin, in the attics of Castletown: 'in ye French taste', as Lady Shelburne noticed.

Previously country houses like Castletown had been the work of Irish architects but from the mid-eighteenth century, would-be builders looked to London. The process began at Marino House outside Dublin, where Sir William Chambers was employed to create a suave and delightful folly known as the Casino in 1758–76 – a project of nearly twenty years that had to compete for resources with the building of Charlemont's splendid

Dublin townhouse on Rutland Square and the nine years he spent living in London; it is a small but intense piece of geometry – very Neoclassical, very French – its volumes as tightly (if more interestingly) interlocked as a Rubik's Cube. After Chambers came Robert Adam and particularly James Wyatt – except that, apart from a single visit by Wyatt, they did not come: their many buildings were designed by correspondence. Drawings were sent that showed rooms in plan but with their walls folded flat, as though they were cardboard boxes: each wall was shown complete with its network of husks and garlands for local architects to follow. Plaster medallions could be bought ready-made. Ireland may not often have been graced by the presence of the architects who designed there, but its country houses joined the mainstream of British architecture.

FIG. 31 *Stair hall at Russborough House, County Wicklow, with stucco decoration by the Lanfrancini brothers, who were among the 'artificers from most parts of Europe . . . employed in this great work', recorded in 1746. The client, Lord Milltown, was the son of a brewer and property developer. Although sumptuous in joinery as well as plasterwork (note the inlaid stars of the landing), there are no human figures in the scheme for the walls, which is largely confined to flowers. This reflects contemporary taste in France.* © *Alamy*

CHAPTER SEVEN

Regency to William IV

G EORGE III and Queen Charlotte had fifteen children: a string of daughters and four wayward sons. Their way of life was financially prudent, domestic and not very different from any of their better-off subjects. George IV, who became the Prince Regent when his father went permanently mad in 1811, could not have been more different; self-indulgent and spendthrift, he had a catastrophic marriage but adored building, decoration and make-believe. Having commissioned works in the Neoclassical, Chinese and 'Hindoo' styles, he employed Jeffry Wyatt – whose sense of romance inspired a change of name to Wyatville – to reshape Windsor Castle, crenellating battlements, Gothicising windows and raising the Norman Round Tower by an extra thirty-five feet. Rarely has a monarch given such a strong if financially ruinous lead in matters of architectural taste. While the Regency itself only lasted from 1811 until George IV became king in 1820, in architecture the term is often taken to mean the period from 1790 until the death of George IV's brother, William IV, in 1837: appropriately enough, since during this time the Prince Regent was a leader of taste.

The era was dominated by the wars with France that followed the French Revolution of 1789. The Prince of Wales, as George IV then was, wept at the news of Trafalgar (he was easily moved to tears) and had the bullet that killed Nelson mounted in a silver locket. He exasperated the Duke of Wellington by pretending he had fought at the Battle of Waterloo in 1815 and even led a charge at Salamanca. Many sons of country houses went to fight in the wars and families at home were also affected. The price of wheat was kept high, causing hardship and discontent, particularly in industrial towns; this would break out in the demonstration, brutally suppressed by a regiment of drunken yeomanry (mounted militia), known as the Peterloo Massacre, which took place on St Peter's Fields, Manchester, in 1819. Unable to travel on the Continent, people who would otherwise have undertaken the Grand Tour began to discover the beauties of the Wye Valley and the Peak District, and to visit the country houses that they passed. The fall of the French aristocracy precipitated a golden age of collecting, as their houses were broken up. Cabinets by Boulle, made of ebony decorated with veneers of tortoiseshell and gilded or ormulu mounts, from the reign of Louis XIV, or up-to-date Neoclassical pieces, with their severe but elegant lines, were now eagerly acquired by those who could afford them, and some who could not.

The Regency country house was extravagant, glamorous, exotic and dramatic. It aimed to delight but also thrill. Architects discovered the ability to change mood through lighting. Light filtered into rooms through coloured glass or, in picture galleries, from overhead. A spirit of gigantism gripped the country house. At Knowsley Hall in Lancashire, the doors to the dining room were thirty feet high. A guest ironically asked Lady Derby if they were opened 'for every pat of butter that comes into the room?' She was delighted. Lively Lady Derby had been the talented actress Eliza Farren: no wonder her dining room was theatrical. Romanticism did not do things by halves. Dinner now took place in the evening. Robert Adam's light and delicate dining rooms were all very well when families ate their main meal in the mid-afternoon, while it was still light. The Regency needed richer decoration which would look well by candlelight and withstand the smoke from oil lamps.

When the 5th Duke of Rutland's heir, the Marquess of Granby, was christened in 1807, Belvoir Castle contained two hundred people and a fifty-gallon cistern of punch was kept brimming for four days. Over thirteen weeks in the early Victorian period 2,400 bottles of wine, 70 hogsheads of ale, 2,330 wax lights, 630 gallons of sperm oil and nearly 23,000 pounds of meat exclusive of game were consumed. This was hospitality on a scale that would have pleased James I.

But amid the excess we can also see the modern idea of the country house beginning to emerge. Continental visitors were surprised by the informality of Regency country houses, furnished with chairs and chaises longues on which it was no longer expected or even possible to sit up straight; some chairs could be mechanically adjusted for sprawling or reading. Prince von Pückler-Muskau observed that 'the practice of half lying instead of sitting; sometimes of lying at full length on the carpet at the feet of ladies' and other manners of lounging had become fashionable. Life at smart country houses was attended by the luxury expected in town.

Central heating makes an appearance. The Prince Regent himself led the charge from the Merlin chair in which he navigated the ground floor of the Royal Pavilion at Brighton when crippled by gout; underfloor heating provided the greenhouse temperatures he craved for his inflamed joints. Bathrooms and flushing lavatories became less exceptional. Gas lighting arrived as an alternative to oil, although to begin with, it seems, it was used outside the house to light up painted glass, for the enjoyment of those inside. This appealed to the Regency taste for coloured lights, mirrors and concealed lighting, seen to perfection in the work of Sir John Soane.

Greater attention was being paid to food, and there was a new way of serving it. Previously the fashion had been for *service à la française*, where a large number of dishes were placed on the table at once, in two courses, amid which might be a number of elaborately presented set pieces rising to a height of several feet to amaze the eye as well as the taste buds. This now gave way to *service à la russe*. With their fabled wealth, the Russian aristocracy could afford the large dinner services needed to offer each dish separately; this had the advantage that everyone had the chance to eat what they liked and sauces did not congeal.

Reached by long entrance drives, contrived to display the charms of the surrounding countryside and park, country houses formed more than ever their own world, out of the public eye. To some they offered a life of less artifice. You did not have to be a recluse like William Beckford to desire a degree of 'retirement'; it could simply mean living in the country and enjoying the pleasures of a garden. Retirement had been a theme for some time. For men it could be occasioned by loss of power (when they flounced off the public stage and created Horatian gardens as a critique of the new regime); women embraced it for religious reasons, because they had transgressed a moral code and needed a period of withdrawal as a prelude to rehabilitation, or because they genuinely preferred simplicity. 'What I wish is only to live one year in a less [grand] and more private way than we do now,' wrote Lady Holland to her sister in 1762, 'just as many people do of 2 or 3000 pounds a year.' Simplicity was only relative. The place of Lady Holland's retreat took the form of a mock castle on the Isle of Thanet called Kingsgate. With retirement went a desire for privacy. Corridors were added to Longleat in the 1820s.

Readers of the French philosopher Jean-Jacques Rousseau became more engaged with their progeny. Portraits began to show children looking lively and carefree. Even the rich and fashionable wanted to enjoy the intimacies of family life. Some society mothers made a point of breast-feeding their own babies. Formality gave way, sometimes, to looser and more friendly spaces. As the landscape gardener Humphry Repton put it:

> No more the Cedar Parlour's formal gloom
> With dullness chills, 'tis now the Living Room.

He illustrates these lines with a picture of a library in which a clergyman reads a book but others, including children, look at illustrated tomes, sketch, talk or walk through a broad doorway into an airy conservatory.

Not all Regency country houses were titanic in scale; many were comfortably sized and today seem easy to live in, with their elegant proportions and spare ornament. The main rooms have descended from the *piano nobile* to the ground floor. Tall windows with thin glazing bars go down to the ground, making it possible to walk straight out onto the terrace or lawn. We find houses that many people could imagine happily occupying in the twenty-first century.

Not so Fonthill Abbey. William Beckford abandoned Fonthill Splendens, built by his father, Alderman Beckford: materials from it were used to erect a new house. It was an extreme building. As (to quote Byron) 'England's wealthiest son', Beckford could give his imagination free rein. After a homosexual scandal at Powderham Castle in Devon, he had left England; on his return, he was shunned by society and lived as a recluse, building a twelve-foot fence around his estate to repel fox-hunting neighbours. And yet this man who distanced himself from the world and wanted to live as privately as possible built a house that flagrantly drew attention to itself. 'I am growing rich and mean to build towers,' he commented, after receiving exceptional profits from Jamaica. Fonthill Abbey would be built on a hill. James Wyatt, who began as Adam's imitator and rival in the 1770s but came to take his place as the busiest country-house architect in the 1780s and 1790s, designed it.

Nothing on the scale of the tower, which rose three hundred feet in the style of a cathedral spire, had been seen before in a country house. Beckford's front door alone was thirty-five feet high; to increase the drama, Beckford employed a dwarf to open it. As a connoisseur, he collected the weird, the exotic, the rich and the wonderful. Still-life paintings show Baroque pearls next to Chinese vases, lapis lazuli cups beside enamel reliquaries. A table from the Borghese Palace was veneered with opulent marbles and hardstones including jasper, onyx and lapis lazuli (it can be seen today at Charlecote Park). Twenty of his paintings are now in the National Gallery. Beckford's country house provided a case for it all. Since his beloved wife, Lady Margaret Gordon, had died in childbirth, he had the Abbey to himself. In 1825, the tower collapsed but by that time Beckford had moved on (he returned the purchase money to the buyer, a gunpowder contractor from Bengal). Poor management of Beckford's Jamaican estates caused his income to decline but, even so, he already had another tower on hand – the Lansdowne Tower outside Bath, which afforded him spectacular views. He wanted to enjoy his solitude in public.

Architecture resembled stage scenery even more than it had for Adam. Beckford actually employed David Garrick's set designer from the Drury Lane Theatre, Philip James de Loutherbourg, to make an Arabian fantasy inside Fonthill. A country house might now conjure up any style from history or around the world. Sezincote House in Gloucestershire was begun in about 1805 by the nabob Sir Charles Cockerell to the designs of his architect brother Samuel Pepys Cockerell. Sezincote combined the Indian motifs of onion domes, deep cornices, cusp-pointed windows and *chhatris* or little domed pavilions, originally to remember the dead – details cribbed from the volumes of *Oriental Scenery* published by Thomas and William Daniell from 1795. In Brighton, the Prince Regent's Pavilion acquired onion domes as well as minarets. A genuine Indian, Sake Deen Mahomed, was employed as the Prince's Shampooing Surgeon: shampoo being derived from a Hindi word for massage, which was in this case combined with a vapour bath.

Amid the welter of exotic or histrionic possibilities, the Greek style remained, in the word of the time, chaste. However, it did hybridise with the Picturesque, as could be seen, from 1804 onwards, at Grange Park, in Hampshire (fig. 32). This country house is both a building to look out of, over what are now golden fields of corn, and to look at, because with its great Greek Doric portico it is like a temple folly in a landscape park: a carefully placed incident in a Picturesque vision of Arcadia. It was built by a banker and a Cambridge mathematics don. The banker was Henry Drummond, a mercurial and many-talented man, who inherited the estate at the age of eighteen. The mathematics don-turned-architect was William Wilkins, a fellow of Caius College, who had also travelled in the Mediterranean and was a punctilious designer in the Greek style (although also, equally punctiliously, in Gothic).

Wilkins could sometimes be dry; at Grange Park he achieved poetry. He created a baseless Greek Doric portico which he attached to a short side of the building, where it makes little contribution to the plan but really does look like the front of a temple (although the columns are in fact not marble but brick covered in cement).

Drummond had got bored before the house was even finished; in 1817 he sold it to another banker, Alexander Baring, 1st Baron Ashburton,

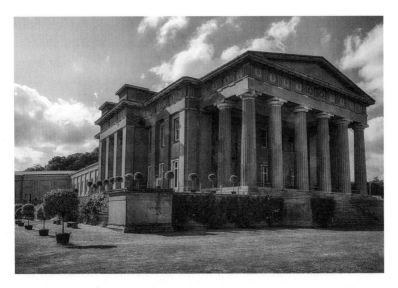

FIG. 32 *When bathed in a golden light and seen across the Hampshire countryside, William Wilkins's Grange Park is an image of Arcadia. The temple front of Greek Doric columns is precisely that: a front, with little practical value – but it does really look like an Ancient temple. Built in 1804, Grange Park was commissioned by the banker Henry Drummond, a mercurial man who sold it in 1817 to another banker Alexander Baring; the latter employed C.R. Cockerell to enlarge it. Courtesy of Lord Ashburton and The Grange, Hampshire*

who commissioned another Greek Revivalist, C.R. Cockerell (son of the architect of Sezincote), to add a wing. For the new dining room, Cockerell reproduced the Ionic order from the Temple of Apollo Epicurius at Bassae, which he had helped excavate.

To Sir John Soane, Wilkins's Greek fetishism led nowhere. Soane sought to penetrate to first principles and did not feel constrained by the need to follow precedent; instead he deconstructed the architectural language of the Ancient World and used the elements to make a new language of his own.

The son of a bricklayer, Soane was born in 1753; he married the niece of a wealthy man whose fortune meant that he could have abandoned his profession if he had chosen. But his was an obsessive nature, driven by a restless curiosity and intense spatial imagination. Before the French Revolution, all ambitious architects kept an eye on France. Soane, however, went further: he studied French architectural theory with its emphasis on the need to go back to the beginnings of architecture in order to understand what the motifs used in Classicism really mean. For they could be rationally explained, so the theorists maintained, as a means of codifying primitive methods of building. Architecture evolved, carrying with it this memory of the past. Architects who did not respect the underlying although hidden logic would look absurd. On the other hand, architects who understood the code could use it to invent new forms of architecture, which would stand in the same tradition as that begun in Ancient Greece. Soane's own country house, Pitzhanger Manor at Ealing, became a cabinet to display his ideas (fig. 33).

There was already a house at Pitzhanger when Soane bought the site in 1800. It had been designed by the architect under whom Soane had trained, George Dance. This gave it a special meaning to Soane, who used the architecture of his homes to represent his life and alter egos, forever

FIG. 33 *Joseph Gandy's watercolour of 1803 shows Sir John Soane's library and drawing room at his own country house, Pitzhanger Manor at Ealing, west of London. Influenced by architectural theory in France, Soane was a rationalist who sought to develop a Classical style from first principles. Mouldings are reduced to minimal lines, vaults and domes spring directly from the walls. On the table are Soane's plans for the Bank of England. © Sir John Soane's Museum, London*

gnawing his own entrails. The gateway to the mini-estate is in Soane's primitive style: a deliberately rustic version of a triumphal arch, made of red brick with pairs of unmoulded flint pilasters. On the way to the house, visitors passed fake ruins that Soane had supposedly excavated; he wrote a pseudo-antiquarian account of their discovery, speculating on what the temple they survived from might have looked like. Ruins preoccupied Soane's Romantic imagination and he employed the perspectivist Joseph Gandy to show how his own buildings would appear after the civilisation for which they were built had collapsed.

Pitzhanger's entrance front is modelled on the Arch of Constantine in Rome, an idea first used by Robert Adam on the garden front of Kedleston Hall in Derbyshire. At Pitzhanger, each of four free-standing Ionic columns supports a caryatid, or female figure standing in place of a column, copied from the temple on the Acropolis in Athens known as the Erechtheion. The Ionic order was thought of as female so the two elements – column and caryatid – are in dialogue. The caryatids were made from a kind of cast stone (actually ceramic) developed by Eleanor Coade about 1770 and may have been cast from an original brought back from Athens by Lord Elgin as part of the Elgin Marbles. Soane intended that Pitzhanger's entrance façade should be 'considered a picture, a sort of portrait' of himself, decorated with 'a number of detached pieces of ornament, such as eagles and wreaths, demiboys and foliage, columns and statues, pedestals and acroters, &c.' as memories of his time in Italy. The whole would 'give a faint idea of an Italian villa'.

Caryatids reappeared in the breakfast room, standing in recesses beneath a 'handkerchief' dome. Soane loved this form of dome, the curve sweeping up in a continuous line rather than being constructed from separate elements. It appealed to the radical in him, as a means of containing a circle (the dome) within a square (the space of the room). Alas, the dynasty for which Soane had built Pitzhanger was not to be: his children rebelled and the house was sold after ten years. Instead Soane worked and reworked his townhouse in Lincoln's Inn Fields, creating ever more complex and unexpected spatial effects and filling it with sculpture, paintings and the second-millennium BC sarcophagus of Pharaoh Seti I (he had to knock a hole in the wall to get it in).

Beckford was a collector, as were Soane and the 6th Duke of Devonshire at Chatsworth. The huge resources at the duke's disposal were matched by an obsession for decoration and the arrangement of houses. Known as the 'Bachelor Duke', he must have been the despair of aristocratic mothers with daughters to marry, since he was both inordinately rich and personally winning. He had an established mistress; it may have been that bad hearing dented his social confidence, although he was far from unconfident in other ways. When it came to the building and arrangement of his many houses, he showed panache.

What had been the gallery at Chatsworth – doubling as a ballroom – became the home to thirty thousand volumes, holding the four major libraries that he acquired. They include many rare books and opulent bindings, including from Lord Burlington's library, which the duke had inherited: Chatsworth still contains the largest collection of drawings by Inigo Jones. By the time of the duke's death in 1858, the house had become a carefully considered synthesis of Old Masters, Antique sculpture, minerals, gemstones, cameos, magnificent gardens, several glasshouses, the Emperor Fountain (the highest in the country) and decorative effects of untold and, to many people who had not been to the house, unimaginable splendour. Like the French food of the era, the result is delicious, spectacular and very rich.

The duke loved building and in Sir Jeffry Wyatville (knighted for his work at Windsor Castle) he had an architect whose company he enjoyed – a 'delightful man', as he wrote, 'good, simple like a child'. Wyatville had previously worked on Longleat House for the 2nd Marquess of Bath.

The duke's taste for highly coloured effects, involving rare and precious materials, was similar to Beckford's – although leavened with humour and Wyatville's good sense. A collection of Blue John, a purple and yellow mineral only found in Derbyshire, was set into a window:

> The stones were intended for a cabinet of minerals, and from their shape could only be arranged in a formal and not graceful pattern; and much did Sir Jeffry condemn the whole thing, which he pronounced to be the exact resemblance of his grandmother's counterpane.

The words are from the *Handbook* that the duke wrote to record his architectural and decorative interventions. It ranks high among the most charming productions of country-house literature.

The sense of medievalising romance that had caused Wyatville to lengthen his surname was fed by the novelist Sir Walter Scott, yet another collector. The son of an Edinburgh lawyer, Scott published his poem *The Lady of the Lake* in 1810; it sold twenty thousand copies. Two years later he installed his family in a farmhouse at Abbotsford on the river Tweed. With the phenomenal success of his novels, beginning with *Waverley* in 1814, the farmhouse would be transformed into a three-dimensional equivalent of the imaginative world of his fiction. Architecturally, the original building would disappear beneath the turrets and crow steps of a medieval mansion – one of the first examples of the Scots Baronial style that would sweep Scotland in the Victorian period. This provided the setting for a collection of objects that, like those of Horace Walpole at Strawberry Hill, told stories. Naturally the library of a writer contained books but Scott also used it to display such treasures as a lock of Bonnie Prince Charlie's hair, Robert Burns's tumbler (Scott met him once: the glass has verses scratched on it) and Rob Roy's purse. Elsewhere can be seen James VI's hunting bottle, Bonnie Dundee's pistol and a Celtic mask found in Galloway. Swords and breastplates spoke of the courage that brought men to battle long ago; stained glass enriched the mood of antiquity. These objects stirred Scott's imagination, which in turn inspired the Scottish country house to reinvent itself as a castle.

But Romanticism also pulled in the opposite direction from castles and Rob Roy, towards the simplicities of the natural and even primitive. Since the middle of the eighteenth century, Enlightenment philosophy had been trying to correct the social world by comparing it to the origins of mankind in Nature. This radical idea was turbocharged by the Romantic poets and provided an alternative self-image for the country house: not cloud-clapped towers or Classical porticos, but cottage simplicity. For the first time in the story of the country house, owners fell victim to inverted snobbery: it became fashionable for houses to ape the appearance of dwellings towards the bottom of the social scale, rather than at the top.

This can be seen at Endsleigh Cottage in Devon built for the 6th Duke of Bedford and his young wife, Georgiana, youngest daughter of the inveterately match-making Duchess of Gordon; the duke had not expected to inherit the estate but his brother, the 5th Duke – for whom Georgiana had been originally intended – died from a hernia while playing tennis. The 5th Duke had been an important figure in the drive to improve farming that is now called the Agricultural Revolution. By contrast, the 6th Duke was described by the diarist Charles Greville as 'a complete sensualist' who did not allow himself to be 'ruffled by the slightest self-denial'. Although large by ordinary standards, Endsleigh represented 'ultra-retirement': an escape from the grandeur and formality of Woburn Abbey with its platoon of liveried footmen. At Endsleigh, the Bedfords could live as a family (fig. 34).

Aged twenty-one, Georgiana was fifteen years younger than the duke, sexy and possessed of her mother's animal high spirits: house parties would echo with her romping games, during which candles and oranges might be thrown and exquisite furniture overturned. According to the duke, she liked

FIG. 34 *Endsleigh Cottage in Devon was built for the 6th Duke of Bedford and his young wife Georgiana. In reality, a substantial country house, its apparent bulk was reduced by the architect Sir Jeffry Wyatville, whose curving plan means that its full extent cannot usually be seen at a glance. This was a retreat from the formality of the duke's principal seat of Woburn Abbey.*

nothing better than to make others happy and comfortable. They loved each other and their children and wanted to live as a family. Georgiana was an advocate for breast-feeding. As they grew up, the duke wrote approvingly,

> The merry girls, and jumping, sporting boys,
> Make the old Abbey echo with their noise.

All that jumping and sporting – the nursery at Endsleigh was placed at some distance from the main house; nevertheless it gave onto a children's lawn which was overlooked by the duke and duchess's rooms. At the edge of the garden was a rill for sailing model boats. 'At this enchanting Retreat the most pleasing attention has been paid to the Comforts of Infancy and Youth,' wrote the landscape gardener Humphry Repton.

The Bedfords hit upon the site in 1809; it overlooked the steep sides of a picturesque but inaccessible valley which reminded the Scottish duchess of her own country. However grand they may have been in London, the Gordons threw off their formality in sporting lodges, ducal 'cottages' and turf-roofed shooting huts – and Georgiana never lost her taste for them. Once again, Wyatville was chosen as architect because of his work at Longleat, having built a small cottage orné there. Endsleigh was not small, but Wyatville broke the masses of the building so that it is only when you have walked some distance from the house, and are looking back at the whole, that you realise its size. The slinking plan makes the most of the views.

In 1813, the duke and duchess, with an entourage of nineteen and a cow to provide fresh milk for the children, left England for a two-year tour of the Continent, in the course of which they visited Napoleon, in exile on Elba, and bought Canova's statue *The Three Graces*, whose distilled Neoclassicism is about as far removed in taste as it is possible to imagine from Endsleigh. The house was ready for them when they returned.

⚜

A largely new type of room appeared in the conservatory. The word was first used by John Evelyn in the 1660s: a conservatory was where plants could be cared for, but not propagated. Tender orange trees were popular in the Baroque garden: grown in large pots, they would be placed symmetrically beside gravel walks during the summer and taken inside for the winter. Orangeries developed as rooms where they could be visited as well as stored. At the end of the eighteenth century, the conservatory became a room attached to the house itself. This was associated with the increasing popularity of growing flowers near the house and the development of the French window, giving direct access to the garden.

Various technical improvements paved the way. Panes of glass could be made in bigger sizes. Heating of different sorts had been developed, being usually provided by pipes. There were new plants coming into the country from foreign climes. They all spoke to the highly perfumed taste of the Regency for things rich and exotic. Mrs Philip Lybbe Powys, visiting a new house called The Temple in Berkshire in 1796, found it

> fitted up and furnish'd in so odd and superb a style, that one cannot help fancying oneself in one of those palaces mention'd in the Arabian Nights' Entertainment . . . at the farther end of a most magnificent greenhouse is an aviary full of all kinds of birds, flying loose in a large octagon of gilt wire, in which is a fountain in the centre, and in the evening 'tis illuminated by wax-lights, while the water falls down some rock-work in the form of a cascade.

As a place where couples could hide from public gaze behind burgeoning plants, they had a degree of intimacy which made them, according to novels, a popular place for proposals.

Before long, greenery had spilled out from the conservatory to appear in the form of large palms and ferns everywhere in the country house. With the introduction of plate glass, combined with commercial nurseries eager to grow the new plants being discovered on plant-hunting expeditions, the scene was set for the orchid craze that overtook some Victorian country-house owners, and the appearance of immense freestanding glasshouses, like that designed for the 6th Duke of Devonshire at Chatsworth by the great Sir Joseph Paxton, ducal gardener and architect of the Crystal Palace.

CHAPTER EIGHT

Early and High Victorian

THE year that Queen Victoria came to the throne, 1837, saw the opening of the first railway terminus in London, its presence marked by the splendid Euston Arch. Railways would transform the way Britain and the country house lived. Busy architects were perpetually on the move between clients, building sites and their London offices; a few Regency architects could travel far and wide by carriage but it was expensive, cumbersome and uncertain – Humphry Repton damaged his spine in a carriage accident and Wyatt died in one. Steam trains, and what became a comprehensive network of main lines and branch lines, enabled the Victorian professional classes to travel faster and more cheaply than their predecessors. It also became cheaper to use materials from distant places than local alternatives; mid-Victorian eyes accepted – perhaps relished – the brashness of industrially made brick. Country houses no longer seemed so distant from the capital. More families could decamp to Scotland for the start of the grouse-shooting season on the Glorious Twelfth of August. The people of Stamford, on the Great North Road, may have cheered when Lord Burghley's intervention meant that the railway went somewhere else, away from his park; but coaching was over, and with it the town's prosperity. Other country-house owners were more pragmatic; they arranged with the railway companies to have private halts, at which trains would stop as they needed them. By the end of the century, when some young gentlemen could no longer rely on inherited wealth and had to take jobs, the 'Saturday to Monday' became feasible. They could go down to the country for what would later be called weekends. It would not have been possible without the railways.

This was the age of steam and not just for trains. Britain had invented the steam engine and was the first to benefit. More cotton could be spun, more wool woven, more beer brewed, more heavy machinery manufactured and exported to the ready market that existed around the world. Coal powered all this industry. The grounds of Wentworth Woodhouse turned black from the coal dust from Lord Fitzwilliam's mines but its owner was made staggeringly rich. Coal powered the ships that took industrial products to the Empire. Previously Britain's most valuable overseas possession had been run on a freelance, ad hoc basis but the Indian Mutiny of 1857 – sparked when soldiers of the Bengal Native Infantry feared they had been issued with new cartridges wrapped in paper greased with cow and pig fat against their religious practices – badly rattled the British government. The East India Company was nationalised. In 1877, the prime minister, Benjamin Disraeli, declared the Queen Empress of India – a wildly popular move, which led to an Empire mania from the 1880s.

The bankers and financiers who oiled the wheels of commerce fared as well as bankers and financiers usually do in expansionist times; so did the railway promoters – and the suddenness and size of their fortunes made them the new nabobs. Tea, guano (dried bird droppings collected from islands off South America and used as fertiliser), biscuits, pianos, salt and ostrich feathers were other sources of the wealth behind the building of country houses.

None of them would have been possible without servants. In absolute numbers, they reached their peak in the Edwardian decade but as a proportion of the population, their zenith was the 1871 census, when 68,369 male servants and 1,207,378 female servants are recorded in employment. Labour in these years was cheap and a place in a country house, where as many as fifty indoor servants might be engaged, was better than working for a middle-class household, where a maid had more tasks to get through; since girls had few other employment opportunities, employers could take their pick. The number of men in service declined after 1851: footmen were always an extravagance, although exceptionally grand houses still had a liveried figure standing behind every chair at dinner until well into the twentieth century.

Mills and factories may have mechanised, but in the home innumerable things had to be done by hand and there was little motive to change while labour was cheap and plentiful. Hot water for baths had to be taken up from the basement to the bedroom floor, and for a large house party several dozen baths might have to be got ready in the hour before dinner – the same thing with the water for washing hands before and after meals. Grates had to be cleared; furniture, bibelots, picture frames, plant stands and all the other objects in an over-full drawing room had to be dusted. When the family rode, let alone hunted, the scrubbing of mud-spattered clothes was long, heavy work, especially when ladies' riding habits had to be cleaned; a young footman, serving in a house where the master hunted six days a week, later remembered that he would often not leave the brushing room until after midnight. The numerous outfits needed for a smart country-house party had to be packed in their swathes of tissue paper; and carrying the leather 'Saratoga' trunks, the dress baskets, the portmanteaux and the hat boxes was no mean task. Even a strapping lad of seventeen, six feet two inches tall, was advised to look for another place because it was felt he was too weak for the work.

When Queen Victoria ascended the throne, she was still a lively young woman – not the widow of Windsor dressed in black silk taffeta and mourning crape that she became after the death of the Prince Consort in 1861. Nevertheless, she led the nation in a change of mood, which is reflected in her country houses. She sold her luxury-loving uncle's Brighton Pavilion and built a different marine villa, ostensibly designed by the London developer and builder Thomas Cubitt but in reality master-minded by Prince Albert, on the Isle of Wight. The Royal Pavilion, on the edge of a seaside town, was too much on view. Osborne was also by the sea but private.

The queen's domestic requirements were not precisely those of her subjects; for example, she had her ladies-in-waiting and equerries to think about. But for the most part she wanted to live in the same way as the richer aristocrats and could afford to do so, being extremely rich in her own right. While she did not follow the Duchess of Bedford's example at Endsleigh and was a somewhat remote mother, Osborne was a family home, not a palace, and the provisions for the royal children were carefully considered. There was a light and airy nursery, lit by three windows on a curving bow (although little in the furniture or decoration related specifically to childhood, except for cane-sided cots and high chairs: whimsy of the type seen in the nursery wallpapers of Walter Crane and C.F.A. Voysey later in the century had yet to come in). Outside, improving play was the theme. As well as donkeys, miniature carriages and bathing in a specially constructed hull-less boat, to prevent the children from being washed out to sea, there was a garden with child-sized tools and wheelbarrows (so they could learn about agriculture), a Swiss Cottage (they cooked in the kitchen) and a museum (filled with natural history specimens collected from the beach as well as diplomatic gifts from abroad). The toy fort built for Prince Arthur, Duke of Connaught, helped shape the soldierly instincts of a future field marshal. Although a martinet and educationally hard taskmaster, Prince Albert was at his best with children. Visitors privileged to enter the royal nurseries could hardly believe the change that came over this stiff, aloof man when he played hide-and-seek. Queen Victoria never conquered her abhorrence of pregnancy and childbirth although she went through them nine times, and left the nursery regime to Lady Lyttelton, the Superintendent of the Royal Children (known to her charges as Laddle).

Neither Osborne nor the royal couple's other country house, Balmoral Castle, on the banks of the river Dee (fig. 35), is a great masterpiece (and Sandringham, rebuilt for the future Edward VII between 1870 and 1890, is even worse); but they are interesting in one respect: the difference in style.

FIG. 35 *On the banks of the Dee, Balmoral Castle was built for Queen Victoria and Prince Albert as an expression of their love for the Highlands. The architect William Smith of Aberdeen produced a rugged Scots Baronial country house – all towers, turrets, crowstepped gables and granite – which was thought to complement the landscape. Queen Victoria loved 'Scotch air, Scotch people, Scotch rivers, Scotch woods', and found deer stalking 'the most charming of amusements'. © Country Life Picture Library*

Osborne is Italianate, with walls rendered in stucco (plaster painted to look like stone) and two asymmetrically placed towers. Overlooking the sea, it evokes the Mediterranean; there is also quite a lot of Belgravia, which Cubitt had partly built, about it; as well as, from a bow window and awning, a dash of Hove. The best thing is the arrangement of the interior. The rooms are not particularly large but because the drawing room opens into the billiard room, which is at right angles but separated only by columns, it feels spacious. The arrangement is supposed to have allowed equerries and ladies-in-waiting to attend on the queen without crowding her, and once round the corner (being out of the royal presence) they could sit down.

Balmoral, designed by another underpowered architect, William Smith of Aberdeen, reflects the queen's love, as she once declared, of 'Scotch air, Scotch people, Scotch rivers, Scotch woods . . . deer stalking is the most charming of amusements.' There followed a cult of, and mania for, the Highlands. This owed much to Sir Walter Scott's novels and the celebrations that the novelist masterminded for George IV's visit to Edinburgh in 1822: the king squeezed into a kilt for the occasion and clan chiefs came in Highland regalia, newly designed on splendid and fanciful lines (the originals, banned after the Bonnie Prince Charlie's Jacobite Rebellion, had long since decayed). Tartan as we know it was born. In 1839, romantically minded aristocrats flocked to the Eglinton Tournament in Ayrshire, a re-enactment of a medieval pageant, blazing with heraldry, bright with armour, saturated with chivalry (alas, it rained). Sportsmen who had previously camped in little more than huts, tended by a farmer's wife, dreamt of castles, fully equipped, capable of entertaining large house parties and often purpose-built in the Scots Baronial style with towers, turrets and crowstepped gables, and grey with granite or harling. William Burn and David Bryce, at one point partners, made it their forte. Burn underwrote the publication of Robert Billings's *The Baronial and Ecclesiastical Antiquities of Scotland* to the tune of a thousand pounds, and quarried it for details.

To adapt P.G. Wodehouse, it is never difficult to distinguish between a Burn country house and a ray of sunshine; to modern eyes, Scots Baronial looks grim. We usually see it without the immaculately kept flower beds and plentiful servants in estate tweeds that would have brightened the scene. Picturesque theory dictated that castle-like architecture was appropriate to wild and rugged landscape settings, but the interior was less forbidding than the outside. Homely simplicity ruled. Despite the taste for old armour, furniture might be covered in sprigged chintz, there was a preference for comfortable upholstery over more formal settings, and tartan and stag's heads got everywhere. However elaborate the domestic arrangements needed to underpin such houses, the life in them was low-key.

For in Scotland, rambles around loch and burn, fishing, sailing, crawling through heather to shoot stags, and painting watercolours of the scenery filled the hours. It was where the Victorians could be themselves. Certainly this seems to have been one of the charms of Balmoral, not only for Queen Victoria but subsequent generations of the royal family.

Osborne, Balmoral: How does one explain that the same couple should build two such contrasting homes? Queen Victoria and Prince Albert were typical of their Picturesque sensibility. Style was not an absolute in itself but chosen to suit the location – something suggestive of sunny climes for the Isle of Wight, romantic castle architecture for Deeside. This was story-telling in stucco or stone, the home as domestic theatre. Other families may only have built one house but they could ask for whatever the wanted – usually, before 1870, within an Italianate or Gothic spectrum. Since the Regency, individual rooms within the same house had been decorated in different styles – Jacobean, Louis XV and South German Baroque in the case of Harlaxton Manor in Lincolnshire. The world was the rich man's oyster.

Planning was key to country houses that had to accommodate large numbers of guests and staff, as well as the owner and his family of many children and dependent relatives. This explains Burn's success: he pioneered a form of plan based on the convenience of the owner and his wife: from the moment they got up in the morning, they proceeded through a logical sequence of rooms, in the order they needed them. Their paths never crossed those accessing the State rooms in which guests were entertained, and their private quarters colonised more and more of the house, as well, perhaps, as part of the garden. There was often a door in the drawing room to reach them: only the family could go through it. Such understanding of their clients' needs gave Burn and Bryce the large practices that they enjoyed across Britain.

Victorian ideas of efficiency dictated that every function in the house should have its allotted space. The sort of servants' wing that had been exceptional during the Regency became standard for the Victorian country house. The comprehensive offices at Bearwood House in Berkshire are a case study of how one should be arranged, since the architect, Robert Kerr, wrote a treatise on *The Gentleman's House, or, How to Plan English Residences, from the Parsonage to the Palace*, in 1864. Professional men did not advertise but the book drew attention to Kerr's work: it was after seeing it that Bearwood's client, John Walter, owner of *The Times* newspaper, commissioned him. There is a butler's corridor, serving the dining room and billiard room; off it are the back stairs, which, as well as going up, lead down to the cellars. A lift was provided for luggage. The butler's own suite comprises a pantry and bedroom: he slept next to the plate safe. A men's corridor connects the cleaning room, brushing room, the footmen's room (small because nobody quite knew what footmen did), the gun room and the odd room, for the odd-job men. The kitchen, pantries, scullery and larder occupy one side of the kitchen, with the women's workroom, still room, storeroom and housekeeper's room on another. Off the housekeeper's corridor is the women's stair, since it was vital to separate the sexes; the men's stair is well away from it, off the cleaning room. Employers lived in horror of male and female servants meeting by chance or under any circumstance that was less than strictly controlled – and perhaps with some reason. When Lady Hervey-Bathurst enquired how a housemaid at Eastnor Castle in Herefordshire had been made pregnant at the servants' ball, the butler revealed that the deed had been done behind a curtain covering a bay window. (That, admittedly, was in the early twentieth century, although it is not known whether the couple had the benefit of the warm air rising through a brass grill in the floor from the new central heating system fitted in 1932.)

It was no less important to group the family's accommodation according to sexes who used it. Billiard rooms and libraries were generally regarded as male; drawing rooms, morning rooms, boudoirs and conservatories as female – although men were invited into the drawing room after dinner. Dining rooms were common ground, and Bearwood has, in addition, a large entrance hall (arranged like a medieval great hall) and a top-lit picture gallery. Unlike American houses, which ran on a feminine agenda, British houses revolved around the largely male pleasures of field sports. House parties would include a number of single men whose income was big enough to allow them to pursue a sociable life but not so big for them to marry anyone who was not an heiress. They might be accommodated in a bachelor wing from which a staircase might lead to the billiard room.

The billiard room reflected the specialisation affecting the whole house. Billiards was one of many aspects of the Victorian country house to have undergone a series of technical improvements by the mid-nineteenth century. Originally it had been an open-air game, played on grass, something like croquet: a memory of this survives in the green colour of the baize. It transferred to the table in the seventeenth century. In the eighteenth century, the blunt-ended stick (technically the billiard) was reversed and players used its tail or *queue* (hence 'cue') to strike the ball. During the Regency period, the rail around the table that stopped balls from running off was padded with leather; this would be replaced with rubber after the process of vulcanisation was discovered. Other improvements included the addition of a leather tip to the cue, the use of chalk to increase friction and the use of slate as the table surface.

This left Kerr with the question of where the table should be placed in a country house. One option was the hall: a large, otherwise empty space that, in the Victorian period, did not generally contain the footmen who would have waited there during the eighteenth century. Being always on the ground floor, it could take the weight of the table. But against these considerations was the problem of smoking. Victorian hostesses had a dread of smells emanating either from the kitchen (which was in consequence placed some way from the dining room with a long corridor with right-angled bends in between) or the cigar. Smoke in the hall would penetrate into every area of the house; besides the game would be interrupted by callers, forcing any men who were playing in shirtsleeves to climb back into their jackets. The noise of the balls was also disturbing. A better solution was to locate it next to the other male rooms in the house, such as the library, the study (if there was one) or the smoking room (which tended to replace the study during the Victorian period). These were served by a gentlemen's lavatory and might be connected with the bachelor bedrooms upstairs. This created an enclave for the men of the party. Ladies could enter: it was not unknown for them to play billiards. But the decoration – dark, leathern, solid – showed that it was not intended for the daintier sex. Kerr recommended fixed benches placed on a dais for better viewing of the game. For him, the great problem was how to give adequate light to the table: top lighting was preferred. There was an alternative position for the smoking room. To keep it absolutely at arm's length, it might be placed in a tower. The Oriental styles of decoration such as Arab, Moorish or Turkish evoked hubble-bubbles and other pleasures of the East.

A well-organised country house ran as though by magic. Servants did not obtrude. They might never be seen. Some owners were gripped by a morbid terror of encountering one of their own employees, who were instructed not to look family or guests in the eye. The 5th Duke of Portland, who inherited Welbeck Abbey in Nottinghamshire in 1854, built a network of tunnels, one of which is a mile and a half long, connected to an underground ballroom and chapel and with a railway to service the kitchen, apparently to avoid the horror of either seeing servants or being seen himself by anyone; the reason for this anxiety has never been satisfactorily explained. The tunnels were possible because of the new technology of gas lighting. Elaborate though they were, servants' wings ought not to draw attention to themselves, while the servants inside should not look onto the gardens. Designing a house so that all the many different people inside it could go about their lives without bumping into those they were meant not to meet, without being seen in the case of servants or being overlooked in the case of the family, involved considerable powers of three-dimensional geometry.

Sadly, at Bearwood the sophistication of the planning was not matched by the architecture, whose eclectic style – Tudorish, Jacobeanish – was of the sort that gives the Victorian country house a bad name. Glass could now be made in large sheets which Kerr uses without glazing bars, which compounds the harshness of the effect.

Charles Barry was a better architect: his Houses of Parliament are an image in stone of the British constitution and he fashioned a domestic identity for the richest echelon of the aristocracy by designing Trentham Hall in Staffordshire (fig. 36). His introduction to the 2nd Duke of Sutherland may have come through the duke's membership of the Travellers Club on Pall Mall, another of Barry's buildings. Trentham, which is in a similar but more sumptuous style, would set the standard for ducal country-house splendour for a generation.

The son of a stationer, Barry began his career with a firm of Lambeth surveyors. On coming of age, he made use of an inheritance to make a Grand Tour, leaving England in 1817. He got as far as Egypt and Syria, then came home via Rome and Florence, studying the architecture of the Renaissance palazzi. In 1830, he won the competition for the Travellers Club with a homage to Raphael's Palazzo Pandolfini in Florence.

FIG. 36 *In the welter of possibilities available to Victorian clients, the Italianate style seemed particularly suited to dukes. Trentham Hall in Staffordshire was reconstructed from an older house in 1834–40. Sir Charles Barry, architect of the Houses of Parliament, had studied the Renaissance palazzi of Florence and Rome. Pollution flowing along the river Trent eventually made it uninhabitable and it was demolished in 1907. Reproduced courtesy of Staffordshire Record Office*

The duke's grandfather and father had both married heiresses, one being the Countess of Sutherland, who inherited a million acres in Scotland. The 2nd Duke's choice of bride fell on Harriet Howard, daughter of the future Earl of Carlisle; he had met her as a girl at Castle Howard and they married as soon as she came out at the age of seventeen. This 'radiant' and 'inspiring' young girl threw herself into the whirl of social life in London. In the country she found 'one day is like another'; but she seems to have enjoyed building projects, decorating and entertaining, and her marriage provided all three – as well as eleven children. Though he was twenty years her senior, the age gap seems not to have mattered.

They chose Trentham in Staffordshire as their main country seat. There was already an eighteenth-century house on the site, designed by William Smith in 1707–10, which they decided to keep. This, however, was engulfed in a tide of new work that would cost, by 1841, the staggering sum of £123,000.

Italianate was not an entirely new style to England; John Nash had used it at Cronkhill in Shropshire in 1802. But Cronkhill, with its circular corner tower and arcaded loggia, recalled the farmhouses of the Campagna; it was built in Nash's favourite (and cheap) material of stucco with stone dressings. Trentham was a proper palace. Italian life is essentially urban and Barry took a form and vocabulary that he had observed in the cities of Rome and Florence, applying it to a country house, but grouping the parts according to Picturesque theory. A semi-circular corridor was attached to the entrance front, which led, rather strangely, to an entrance hall. The old house was given over to state rooms: an audience room-cum-library, the old library, saloon, drawing room, breakfast room and dining room, most of which form an enfilade along the south front; while Barry's principal addition is a family wing where the duke and duchess could retreat from the monster they had created.

What would otherwise have looked a loose assemblage of different structures was visually pulled together by a tall tower, containing a water tank. There was also a clock tower. The service rooms were underground; the footmen's bedrooms were in a separate building from those of the maids in the attics. A second campaign of work saw the addition of an orangery, a sculpture gallery, a bowling alley, swimming bath and 'ice wells' in a more rustic style that recalls Nash, although the materials are better. Unfortunately they are all that survive. Pollution washing down the Trent from Stoke-on-Trent made Trentham uninhabitable by later dukes and the greater part of it was demolished in 1907.

No record was made of the interiors, which were probably plainer than the exterior would suggest. While building Trentham, the duke and duchess were spending even more freely on the interiors of Stafford House (now Lancaster House), off the Mall, of which Queen Victoria, who was close to the duchess, said: 'I have come from my House to your Palace.' Behind the scenes, the difficulty of running such great houses with building work constantly in progress and a young duchess for whom domestic management was not a forte was considerable. On top of every-thing, the masons went on strike. It says much for the professional skills of Barry, the housekeeper Mrs Kirke and the steward Mr Webster that guests seem never to have noticed the chaos backstage.

The gardens at Trentham were even more influential than the house itself. The endlessly busy gardener and writer John Claudius Loudon was amazed by the transformation of a 'great dull flat place' into two terraces overlooking a lake. To construct the terraces Barry worked with William Andrews Nesfield, the king of the elaborate, bedded-out Victorian parterre who was employed at every great house in the kingdom during the middle years of the nineteenth century.

Before the second phase of Trentham had finished, the duke and duchess asked Barry to add a note of caprice to their Scottish seat, Dunrobin Castle in Sutherland. As Countess of Sutherland in her own right, the duke's mother had begun to improve her impoverished Highland estates in the first years of the century. The Highland Clearances have become so politicised that it is difficult to judge the countess objectively. It is at least possible she was motivated by the destitution of the Highlanders, who suffered frequently from famine, as well as a businesslike desire to put the estate on a firm financial footing; large families had been subsisting on land that could barely support them in a good year and caused them to starve in a bad one. Her solution was to move the population to specially constructed fishing villages on the coast. But the people would not move voluntarily, with gratitude: they had to be coerced, with the houses they had vacated being deliberately damaged to prevent them moving back in. Eventually many of the countess's clansmen solved her problem by emigrating to America. With these memories still raw, for the 2nd Duke to remodel the old castle as a place of romance, with the tall turrets of a miniature in the *Très Riches Heures du Duc de Berry*, was, to put it generously, brave. Unlike Balmoral, it does not try to look Scottish; Barry appears to have turned to the publications of the contemporary French champion of rational Gothic, Eugène Viollet-le-Duc for the details. Surrounded by terraces and parterres that step down to the waters of Dornoch Firth, it does succeed in looking glamorous. Whether it looks appropriate is open to debate.

Barry drew the plan and outline of the Houses of Parliament; it was Augustus Welby Northmore Pugin who designed the sculpture and crockets that encrust it and the furniture with which it is filled. Barry had little feeling for Gothic, but was pragmatic. Pugin, by contrast, was a believer, a polemicist and a zealot. He added fervour and moral seriousness to the Gothic style that had already appeared at Strawberry Hill and Fonthill Abbey. James Wyatt and his like were not merely wrong but wicked.

Shortly before his death aged forty in 1852, Pugin's doctor told him he had packed the work of a hundred years into his lifetime. He had designed scenery for London theatres. He had gone to sea and been ship-wrecked. He had bought and sold Gothic antiquities, brought home from the Continent in his lugger, the *Caroline*. He had written and published several books, championing Gothic as the only possible architecture for a Christian country. Standing at his drawing desk in his house The Grange at Ramsgate, without, for the most part, any assistant, he had produced the tsunami of decorative detail that washed bold Gothic pattern into every corner of the Houses of Parliament – statues, desks, ceiling bosses, lamps, wallpaper, thrones and inkwells. He had designed country houses for Catholic gentry and churches for Catholic worship. He had built his own church. All of which had been achieved against a background of money worries and personal tragedy, including the death of two wives and the mental deterioration that led him to die insane. Bullish, long-haired, apt to offend conventionally minded contemporaries by his rough clothes and eccentric absence of whiskers, Pugin was, by any standards, an extraordinary man.

Born in 1812, Pugin was the son of a French émigré, the draughtsman Auguste Pugin who passed on his skill with the pencil. From the age of fourteen, the younger Pugin was helping his father draw the architectural details. A generation whose historical sense had been awoken by the novels of Sir Walter Scott, with their photographically particular descriptions of places and things, was no longer satisfied by generalised Gothic refer-ences; it wanted detail. Pugin was soon given the job of designing Gothic furniture for Windsor Castle. It was a lot to expect of a fifteen-year-old; in Notre-Dame Cathedral in Paris he collapsed from overwork.

In his early twenties, Pugin converted to Roman Catholicism. This provided a direct link with what he regarded as the great Age of Faith which had preceded the Dissolution of the Monasteries, a time (as he saw it) when charity for the poor had gone hand in hand with sumptuous ritual and soaring architecture. This was practically an act of professional suicide, since it shut him off from church work for the Church of England. However, he built a number of country houses for rich Catholic gentlemen such as Charles Scarisbrick, who wanted a setting for his collection of Gothic carving.

A picture of Pugin's own house, The Grange, is given by his only pupil John Hardman Powell, nephew of the Birmingham metalworker John Hardman, who arrived in a desperate period after the death of Pugin's second wife in 1844. He found his greeting bluff but short. 'Compline at 8, supper at 9, bed at 10.' Religion permeated the house. It coexisted and intermingled with Pugin's other passions. 'In the Hall was a large figure of the Blessed Virgin niched in oak with folding doors,' he remembered, 'and a rack of favourite Telescopes, Sou'westers, and Tarpaulins.' The floor was laid with tessellated tiles, waterproof and resistant to hobnailed boots. Next door he erected, from his own money, St Augustine's Church, dedicated to St Augustine of Canterbury who had landed nearby in the sixth century. A house, a church – all that was needed to complete Pugin's vision of a revived Middle Ages was a monastery. He was unable to build it himself, but his son completed the project.

Pugin was an extremist but articulated an ideal that was widely shared. Religion, charity, architecture and life should be of a piece and medieval in inspiration; their architectural expression was a revival of the great hall – under whose rafters 'the Lords of the Manors used to assemble all their friends . . . while humbler guests partook their share of the bounty', as Pugin wrote. The vision of community spoke to an age fearful of the popular unrest threatened by Chartism and manifested in the Swing and Rebecca riots. It animated medievalising country houses like Bayons Manor in Lincolnshire, designed by the poet Tennyson's uncle Charles Tennyson d'Eyncourt for himself. One of the more sympathetic neighbours to Bayons – which had begun life as the modest Tealby Lodge – exclaimed, 'An old baronial hall; and the owner the second son of a Market Rasen attorney! It is too absurd.' To another visitor Tennyson d'Eyncourt's eldest son had whispered, 'it's all a romance.'

More than anything, the great hall symbolised family. Not only were Victorian families often large --the 1st Baron Tollemache of Peckforton Castle and Helmingham Hall had so many sons he could field his own cricket team – but they also had a growing consciousness of themselves as a unit, cemented by family prayers, services in the chapel and festivals such as Christmas, elevated to its present status as the great feast of the family during the Victorian period. Externally, Victorian country houses in the Gothic style can look forbidding; but in the privacy of the interior, the family could surround itself with ancestral portraits and other signs of antiquity, sometimes newly acquired, and enjoy a warm sense of its collective identity. This was based on a misreading of the medieval prototype, which shared the hospitality of the hall with all comers. The Victorians kept strangers at bay.

The greatest patron of the Gothic country house was the Marquess of Bute. His features stare out from the depths of a hood, belonging to robes of his own design for his position as Rector of St Andrews University; he looks monastic, even lugubrious. Letters show a rich vein of wit and he certainly enjoyed the effervescent company of his architect William Burges. But he was typical of many Victorian country-house owners, particularly those who built in the Gothic style, in being almost pathologically private. Whereas the Duke and Duchess of Sutherland loved the whirl of society and entertaining their friend Queen Victoria at Trentham, Bute hated meeting people he did not already know. He built for the sake of building and to the glory of God.

Bute's great-great-grandfather, the 3rd Earl of Bute, had been a prime minister under George III. Already rich, Bute's father, the 2nd Marquess, threw his energies and money into developing his Welsh estate, which included the site of Cardiff, where he undertook the heroic construction of Cardiff Docks. It nearly broke him but made his heir an extremely rich man. Unfortunately, the 2nd Marquess died suddenly, when Bute was less than six months old, leaving his personal affairs in disarray and his Scottish estate intestate. Bute's mother died when he was twelve and an unseemly struggle developed over the possession of this rich young adolescent; one claimant was his guardian, a general, whom he hated. He got his own back by converting to Roman Catholicism.

As soon as he had control of his own money, he started to rebuild Cardiff Castle (fig. 37), not as an archaeological exercise but a fantasy of medieval romance, from the brain of Burges, the 'soul-inspiring one', as he referred to him. Burges was not a religious man. Indeed, he was, in some ways, the antithesis of his patron, being gregarious, rumbustious, an opium user and a bohemian frequenter of low dives. But like Bute, he adored the architecture of an idealised Middle Ages as an escape from the ugliness of the soot-blackened nineteenth century. He loved churches for the theatre of their liturgy, the richness of their carving, the inventiveness of the metalwork, the colour of the stained glass – but not their teaching. While Burges had the highest respect for 'that wonderful man' Pugin, the world moved on. Pugin was a natural designer of two-dimensional ornament. Burges was a sensualist; his architecture was volumetric; he favoured the elegance of early French Gothic (partly, he said, because the Early English ornament beloved of Pugin was too quickly lost beneath the atmospheric grime of the Victorian city). Georgian architecture was 'damnable', but Gothic, in his hands, could be rich, colourful, enchanting, whimsical and fabulous.

Cardiff Castle was a Georgian building when Burges came to it. It had no fewer than six towers by the time he died in 1881. Inside one

FIG. 37 *Cardiff Castle in Wales is a dream of the Middle Ages created by the ebullient, myopic, opium-smoking William Burges. His love of colour, ornament and jokes dispelled the gloom that haunted some Gothic Revival country houses. His client was the enormously rich Catholic convert, the 3rd Marquess of Bute, whose father had built Cardiff Docks.* © Alamy

of them, the Clock Tower, he created a Winter Smoking Room entirely encrusted with decoration on the theme of time, with statues, murals and stained glass depicting the zodiac, the four seasons and the days of the week as represented in Norse mythology. Except for the playfulness, the completely imagined alternative world that it summons up recalls Wagner, who was writing the *Ring* Cycle while Cardiff Castle was building. And so it went on, with the Guest Tower, the Herbert Tower, the Beauchamp Tower, the Bute Tower, the Black Tower – Burges's imagination never flagged. The accommodation included a banqueting hall and a huge library, where monkeys can be seen disporting themselves around the Tree of Knowledge, one stealing an apple, while another pores dubiously over a book – a comment on Charles Darwin's *On the Origin of Species*. Bute died in 1900 on the Isle of Bute, his last years spent in 'slow meditative brooding', according to F.W.H. Myers, founder of the Society for Psychical Research, as he withdrew increasingly into the world of the fourteenth century to which he was temperamentally better suited than his own.

Architecturally, Bute had become an anachronism. Burges's younger contemporaries like William Eden Nesfield, son of the garden designer W.A. Nesfield, did not take their inspiration from churches (although they had one thing in common: both kept an office parrot). As young men, Nesfield and his informal partner Richard Norman Shaw both published books on French Gothic architecture but they rejected its influence in favour of the Home Counties. They spent their leisure hours on rambles through the English countryside, sketching cottages, farmhouses and pubs. Their observations of tile-hanging, leaded lights, half-hipped gables and timber-framing were synthesised to form the Old English style. Shaw's Grim's Dyke, in Harrow Weald, designed in 1870 for the librettist W.S. Gilbert, is a representative example: oversailed by tall, red-brick chimneys, it is a rhapsody of vernacular building materials, gables and jettied bays: nothing is centred, nothing regular. Old English was the forerunner of the Surrey style made popular by Lutyens in the 1890s. Inglenooks were de rigueur.

At the same time, Nesfield pioneered another style, which came to be known as Queen Anne Revival. This did not have a great deal to do with the architecture of Queen Anne's reign (fig. 38). Instead it was a

FIG. 38 *Around 1870 William Eden Nesfield reorganised Bodrhyddan Hall in North Wales, whose plan had become muddled over the years; it was a sign of a new approach towards old buildings that he tried to do so without dispelling the charm. The entrance front is new, in a manner inspired by the red brick architecture of the seventeenth century. Known as the Queen Anne Revival, this eclectic style could include influences from Japan. Like the hipped-roofed, slate-hung Old English Style, Queen Anne appealed to architects who did not want to derive their details solely from churches.* © *Bodrhyddan Hall*

nosegay plucked from several periods and places, principally the red-brick Classicism of the seventeenth century with fine leadwork. While the sash window had been anathema to Gothic Revivalists, the architects of the new style brought back both the sash and its glazing bars; the latter softened the effect of plate glass, which looked ugly when used as an adorned sheet.

Progressive architects were rediscovering the joy of craftsmanship as opposed to the harsh mechanical finishes produced by industrial techniques. At a time when British cities were being ringed by suburbs constructed from sharp factory-made brick from the Midlands, Nesfield and Shaw were careful to specify hand-made brick of old-fashioned proportions (long and thinner than the usual), in softer hues; this was skilfully modelled into panels showing coats of arms or vases of sunflowers. Indeed sunflowers, which would become the badge of Oscar Wilde and the Aesthetic Movement, crop up everywhere: on roof ridges, on the sides of dormers, beneath cornices. Another motif was provided by 'pies': circular discs, asymmetrically placed, derived from the Japanese art that Shaw and Nesfield had seen at the 1862 International Exhibition at South Kensington.

In 1868, Nesfield went to Hampton Court with the Hughes family of Kinmel in North Wales; Hugh Robert Hughes's fortune came from a copper mine. Hampton Court set the note for the rebuilding of Kinmel Hall, although there is more than a dash of French chateau in the steep pitch of the roofs. The quality of the detail is superb. The painter Simeon Solomon described Nesfield as 'one of our very best architects . . . a fat, jolly hearty fellow, genuinely good natured, very fond of smoking, and I deeply grieve to say of women'. He found the strain of practice too much for him, gave it up and died of cirrhosis of the liver in 1888.

Shaw, who had parted company from Nesfield in 1876, stayed the course and had become the doyen of the profession by the 1890s. Cragside in Northumberland is now owned by the National Trust. Built for the inventor and armaments manufacturer Lord Armstrong, it inspires images from folklore. Perched high above a ravine, it is a composition of dizzy towers and gables which give the impression of having been conjured by a magician's spell. The work grew as Armstrong's ideas changed from 1870 to 1883. What had been a plain mid-Victorian fishing lodge became ever more bristly, gnarled and fantastic. It was the first house in Britain lit by electric light. Many of the exceptional crop of good architects at the turn of the century had been assistants in Shaw's office.

Shaw and Nesfield were both born in the 1830s; so were William Morris and Philip Webb. Like Shaw and Nesfield, Morris and Webb began as Goths (they met in the office of George Edmund Street, a church architect who also designed the Law Courts) but moved on, spurred by their Ruskinian horror at the effects of industrialisation. Morris became the noisy engine house of the Arts and Crafts Movement, Webb the quieter superintendent who converted the superabundant energy and ideas into architecture.

Brawny, gregarious, red-haired, Morris threw himself at the task of improving his contemporaries' lives and taste. When he was not writing epic poetry, he was weaving textiles; when he was not weaving textiles, he was delivering lectures on his romantic brand of socialism; when he was not lecturing, he was writing utopian tracts, or founding the Society for the Protection of Ancient Buildings, or designing wallpaper (fig. 39). The nail which stabilised this fizzing Catherine wheel of energy was the home. Morris had a romantic concept of it, reinforced by his vision of the Middle Ages. Naturally his own homes were central to him.

The first was Red House at Bexleyheath, begun in 1859 by a twenty-five-year-old Morris, newly married to a beautiful young wife, Jane Burden. Designed by the austere and reticent Webb, the idiom was that of a Gothic Revival parsonage, combining red brick, pointed arches and sash windows. Artist friends who stayed with the Morrises were pressed

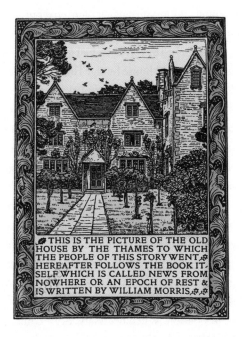

FIG. 39 *Kelmscott Manor, on the banks of the Thames in Gloucestershire, was William Morris's domestic ideal. In his utopian story,* News *from* Nowhere, *he wrote that it seemed to 'grow out of the soil' – a building that had no known architect but was instead the product of generations of anonymous craftsmen and the families who had lived in it for centuries. Fizzing with energy, Morris was the engine house of the Arts and Crafts Movement, to which both rural life and home-making were specially important.*

into service painting murals and decorating furniture on Arthurian themes. The painter Burne-Jones and his wife were meant to join them, building their own house to form an artistic community. It was not to be, but the need to furnish the Red House inspired Morris to found his own decorating firm called Morris, Marshall, Faulkner and Company in 1861, with offices in London. Morris's investments did badly; the firm in London took an increasing amount of his time. The heyday of Red House was over in less than six years. What fun it had been while it lasted.

In 1877 Morris and Webb founded the Society for the Protection of Ancient Buildings, principally as a bulwark against the over-restoration of churches by architects who 'scraped' the patina off the ancient stones. Medieval work was not only of architectural interest but made sacred by the hands of the craftsmen who had shaped it. The SPAB was important not just for the conservationist ideology it pioneered but as a meeting place for young architects and route of transmission for Morris's ideas; Webb gave practical guidance. In 1871, Morris had found a new domestic ideal in Kelmscott Manor, the old house by the Thames that seemed to 'grow out of the soil' as he described it in his utopian story *News from Nowhere*.

Unlike the ebullient and boisterous Morris, Webb was not a party animal and avoided the limelight. A socialist and an agnostic who followed Christian ethics, he trod an austere path, the character of which is reflected in his major surviving work, Standen in Sussex. His clients, James and Margaret Beale, were close to being his soulmates. Dissenters, the Beales were an old Birmingham dynasty of solicitors, working for the Midland Railway; James Beale came to London to handle the huge amount of legal work generated by the building of St Pancras station. By 1891, however, he was fifty, with thoughts that increasingly turned to golf, riding, croquet, fruit trees and what Kipling, another Sussex resident, called 'the wooded, dim / Blue goodness of the Weald', away from the smoke of London. When necessary, Beale could go up by train.

True to the SPAB creed, Webb respected the modest, tile-hung farmhouse that was already on site, repairing it and taking it as the theme from which the much larger Standen developed. Despite its size, the house is vernacular in spirit – the equivalent of a full-scale orchestral work created from a set of folk melodies. Stone quarried in the grounds, tawny Horsham bricks set off by reds, locally made tiles, weatherboarding: these are the ingredients of the composition, anchored by a square, plain water tower, clad in roughcast. There are leaded lights and sash windows, tall brick chimneystacks and lead flashing and pipes; but Webb strenuously avoids being picturesque. Each element is kept sternly separate from its neighbour in seemingly wilful awkwardness. The stone porch, which might so easily have been softened through moulding, remains big-boned and bare; the variety of crafts evident in the interior (some of them practised by the Beales in spare moments) do not compose into a harmonious whole. Standen did, however, achieve harmony of another kind. Family photographs show this to have been a happy home.

Home would be a watchword during the great flowering of domestic architecture in the years before and after 1900, in which the country house took centre stage.

CHAPTER NINE

Turn of the Century

T HE years 1890 to 1914 were a golden age of the country house. Not only was domestic architecture served by an exceptional richness of architectural talent but the rise of the professional classes, supplemented by wealth from industry and Empire, provided many opportunities to build. In the novels of Henry James, the country house evokes an ideal state of human existence which, after centuries of evolution, has reached a level as close to perfection as it is possible for mortals to achieve. George V did not have much of an eye for architecture but he and his generation had made life 'a masterpiece of well ordered, unostentatious elegant living', as his son the Duke of Windsor remembered a little sourly. The perfection of the British country house at the turn of the century was recognised by the Prussian government, which sent the architect and civil servant Hermann Muthesius to report on the advanced state of British domesticity: this he did, with Germanic thoroughness, in the three volumes of *Das Englische Haus*. Art architects such as Baillie Scott received commissions throughout Europe.

With hindsight, the Belle Epoque, as this era is called in France – the Gilded Age of the United States – seems a period of unruffled calm before the bursting of the storm clouds in 1914. This was not how it felt at the time. Although, from the 1880s, Britain went wild for Empire, the putting out of flags, the exhibitions, Jubilees and pageants, masked a time of industrial decline relative to her competitors. The cost of Empire became alarmingly apparent when the British army was humiliated by a force of rough-and-ready Boer farmers in South Africa; the jubilation throughout Britain that greeted the news that Mafeking had been relieved – 'to maffick' entered the language as a verb meaning to celebrate uproariously – could not calm consciences queasy at the barbarous methods by which the war had been pursued ('concentration camp' was coined to describe the place where women and children were herded as Boer farmsteads were destroyed). At home, labour relations deteriorated until hundreds of strikes were taking place each year in the Great Unrest of 1911–13. Landowners were targeted by Lloyd George's People's Budget of 1909 which sought to raise taxes to pay for old age pensions, measures that were bitterly opposed by the House of Lords; but the upper house was defeated and its powers reduced. To the Duke of Bedford, this was tantamount to socialism and in 1911 he announced that he would sell his estate in Devon, the first of what would be an avalanche of land sales after the First World War.

There were other changes. Electricity became the norm for new country houses, posing a dilemma for architects who had to find a means of treating the novel light source (bulbs were so weak that they were generally left unshaded – provoking displeasure from ladies who felt they had been mercilessly exposed to the glare of stage lighting). Vacuum cleaners, again powered from a central source with hoses plugged into outlets in the skirting board, began to make an appearance, apparently (according to advertisements) to the delight of footmen who no longer had to carry heavy rugs out to be beaten. The house telephone allowed orders to be given to distant servants without them having to hurry to the spot to hear what was needed. Laundries were equipped with washing machines, driven by belts and cranks connecting to a central engine as though in a factory; racks on wheels could be pulled in and out of heating chambers to dry clothes. In theory, all these novelties saved labour. This was becoming a consideration. Before the First World War the difficulty of finding and the cost of employing staff would present itself, to some minds, as a crisis. The peak, in terms of absolute numbers of servants, was reached in the 1901 census, when about 1.7 million women worked in domestic service; despite the growth of the middle classes, this figure declined to about 1.35 million in the course of the Edwardian decade. But even the 1901 figure is misleading: as a proportion of the growing population, it already showed a decline.

This caused not only a practical problem but an ethical reaction. As a character in Mrs Humphry Ward's *The Marriage of William Ashe* of 1905 put it, 'people are beginning to be ashamed of enormous houses and troops of servants'. The office wings that had made the Victorian country house so voluminous shrank. Even large houses were designed in quieter styles. Stridency, brashness, striving for effect – these were not qualities admired by the 'art architects' of the time, who preferred mellowness and soft tints. There were show-offs like the financier Whitaker Wright, who built a ballroom beneath the lake at Witley Court in Surrey, or Julius Drewe, who insisted that Lutyens build him a granite castle beside Dartmoor, but they did not end well; Wright committed suicide at the Royal Courts of Justice after being convicted for fraud, Castle Drogo was not finished until 1930, on a far smaller scale than planned, and soon leaked. The spirit of the turn-of-the-century country house was understatement.

The appearance of the safety bicycle in the 1880s began a revolution in transport and sheds were built to house bicycles at some country houses. It was a democratic development: people who could not have afforded a horse could bowl over the South Downs on a bicycle. By contrast, motor cars, becoming practical after 1900, were extremely expensive. Although speeds were slow and progress unreliable – burst tyres were inevitable – they caused alarm to old-school country-house families who predicted a fragmentation of rural society. Previously, country-house owners had been forced to rely on their neighbours for company: visiting was limited to a fixed radius by the distance the carriage horses could go and come back. Guests were expected to stay for a week. The motor car blew up the old rules. As that incorrigible motorist Mr Toad exclaimed, you could be 'Here today – in next week tomorrow!' According to *The Car Illustrated*, the Earl Fitzwilliam could hunt in Ireland, motor to Dublin, take the night boat to Manchester and then motor on to Wentworth Woodhouse, repeating the process in the opposite direction at the end of the day. Motoring was itself seen as a sport.

Early cars were expensive and required constant maintenance. So the motor house at Manderston House in Berwickshire, built in 1903, incorporated an engineer's shop in the basement, where a car could be virtually rebuilt if required. A lift bay in the floor would take the car down. In an age before roadside garages and spare parts, repairs had to be carried out by the chauffeur and replacement parts made either by him or the blacksmith. A canopy over the front provided shelter while polishing the bodywork; a drain in the floor disposed of spillages; and electric lighting to minimise the risk of fire. An inspection pit, an engineer's bench and a lathe were highly desirable. Heating was needed unless the cars were to be drained down on cold nights. The chauffeur, perhaps a repurposed coachman, often had a flat on the first floor. It was a sign of things to come that oil was financing country houses: Henri Deterding, the director general of Royal Dutch Petroleum, built Kelling Hall.

Motoring accidents were commonplace; horses bolted, cattle stampeded, dogs were run over. Motorists were thought to belong to that alien race: the plutocracy. For just as Georgian society had been rattled by the appearance of nabobs, so traditional country-house owners in the early twentieth century were alarmed by buccaneering millionaires from the gold and diamond mines of South Africa, the City, industry – even the high street, where the Home and Colonial Stores would build Castle Drogo and Lipton's tea funded challenges in the America's Cup yachting race. The world was going through a second phase of globalisation and fortunes were to be made.

Weetman Pearson, 1st Viscount Cowdray, transformed a family engineering firm into a colossus that bestrode the world, building docks and digging the Hudson River and the East River Tunnels in New York as well as the Gran Canal in Mexico City. From the last, Cowdray progressed to owning sixty per cent of the oil industry in Mexico, at the time the world's third biggest oil producer. The supporters that he chose for his coat of arms were a deep-sea diver and a Mexican peon. He bought or built several country houses, Paddockhurst and Cowdray Park in Sussex, Dunecht Castle and Castle Fraser in Aberdeenshire.

Sir Andrew Noble of Ardkinglas (fig. 40), on Loch Fyne, ran Lord Armstrong's armaments and engineering firm, inventing the Electro-Mechanical Chronoscope, which measured speeds inside a gun barrel. Frederick Merrilees of Goddards in Surrey owned a department store in St Petersburg, before marrying the heiress of the Union Castle Line. Walter Burns of North Mymms in Hertfordshire was the American financier J.P. Morgan's brother-in-law and ran his European operation. Robert Hudson, soap manufacturer, not only recast Medmenham Abbey on the Thames but built Danesfield House, on an astonishing scale, nearby; the architect of both was the publicity-shy W.H. Romaine-Walker who

FIG. 40 *Ardkinglas Castle, at the end of Loch Fynne, stands in a glorious situation, complemented by the choice of a greenish local stone flecked with gold. The cool, dark cream dressed stone around the doors and windows is from Dallatur. The architectural vocabulary of towers, turrets and crowstepped gables derives from the late sixteenth century, defensive in general appearance but not so castle-minded as not to have light-admitting windows. In this land of midges, the main rooms are on the first floor, where a loggia provides space to sit out. The ground floor was a male preserve of smoking room, billiards room, gun room and Sir Andrew's study. © Country Life Picture Library*

made a point of never speaking on the telephone and banning typewriters from the office. The steel magnate Lord Wimborne employed Lutyens to tinker endlessly and sometimes against his better judgement with the Manor House at Ashby St Ledgers, in Northamptonshire (Wimborne may have been the only private client who got the better of the ebullient and persuasive architect).

New money would have struggled to penetrate Queen Victoria's inner circle but the doors of the Marlborough House Set – the circle around the Prince and Princess of Wales – seemed always to be open to millionaires. When the Tsar of all the Russias visited Sandringham in the early 1890s, he was shocked to find that the future Edward VII kept company with financiers and Jews, who would not have been welcome at his own court. The exuberance of the new millionaires, who could afford every luxury, was painful to traditional estate owners, since the income from tenanted farms had been hit by an agricultural depression which began in the late 1870s and lasted until the Second World War, with only a short-lived interruption during the First.

In the middle years of the nineteenth century, it had been fashionable for improving landowners to invest in machinery. High Farming was the result. Operations were centralised in large, expensively built farmsteads, with steam-powered turnip cutters and threshing machines; pairs of traction engines were trundled out into the fields to pull ploughs across fields that were spread with imported guano. It is doubtful that these investments paid off but they appealed to the progressive mind. The depression was caused by the arrival of cheap imports by steamship (soon to be equipped with refrigeration) – grain from the expanding United States, beef from South America, sheep from the Antipodes. When it struck, landowners drew in their purse strings. There was little money in circulation, and poverty stalked the countryside. The Arts and Crafts Movement, which celebrated a rural, utopian vision, found the reality neglected and old-fashioned – which was just what they liked.

Young aristocrats whose inheritances were shrinking before their eyes found a new source of wealth appearing at exactly the right moment: American heiresses. When the thirty-one-year-old Sir Thomas George Fermor-Hesketh, 7th Baronet, steamed into San Francisco on his yacht at the end of a round-the-world tour with some friends in 1880, one of them described their time in port:

> Nothing could exceed the Kindness and Hospitality of everyone we met. Head gave us a dinner party – had some very pretty girls to meet us. We spent a most enjoyable evening, never left the house till 2.30. I met a Miss Crocker, a very nice girl with heaps of the needful. Francis got hooked on and has landed her I think. Hesketh has two on hand, both very nice . . . Can't make up his mind . . . I must say American girls are very pretty, dress well, have good feet, lots of fun & very sharp. Some have lots of money.

Sir Thomas married the richest one of the lot and remodelled Easton Neston in Northamptonshire. There followed a rush of transatlantic marriages, which, together with the input of men such as William Waldorf Astor who made Britain their home, transformed some country houses (Cliveden, Hever Castle, Blenheim, Floors Castle, Leeds Castle) and kept many others on their feet.

But not everyone could marry an American and some country-house owners were forced to sell land. And here again they might be lucky, if their holdings lay in a fashionable county or within easy reach of one of the big cities, because the decline of the traditional landed estate coincided with a new interest in the countryside from professional or self-made individuals who wanted to enjoy what it offered: gardening, a bit of fishing, sunsets and the newly popular game of golf. They did not want to tie up their money by buying more than a relatively small parcel of land – two or three farms, perhaps, to give a semblance of country life. In a series of five books before the First World War and a second series afterwards, the architectural editor of *Country Life* Lawrence Weaver celebrated the *Small Country Houses of Today*.

The small country house was progressive. While the Victorian country house had a different room for every purpose, the turn-of-the-century country house reverted to an older pattern; it was more economical, more friendly and suited the less rigid manners of the age for one space to fulfil several functions. This produced the living hall. It was somewhere to chat, to read newspapers, to tinkle the piano, to pass through – even for men to smoke in the presence of ladies. Gardens made of terraces and compartments that were rooms in themselves were considered part of the overall concept. Loggias were provided for the serving of meals; nights might be spent on an open-air sleeping balcony, now that fresh air was known to keep tuberculosis at bay.

Small country houses were a natural preserve for art architects like C.F.A. Voysey and M.H. Baillie Scott. They and Charles Rennie Mackintosh – whose only approach to a country house was The Hill House, a seaside villa for the publisher Walter Blackie – wanted to strip domestic interiors of their clutter; 'we cannot be too simple,' said Voysey. Published by *The Studio*, they were better known on the Continent than among major country-house clients at home.

Commissioned to design the furniture and decoration of rooms at the Grand Duke Ernst Ludwig of Hesse's Darmstadt palace in 1897, Baillie Scott went on to practise in Russia, Romania, Poland, Austria, Germany, France, Switzerland, Belgium, Italy, America, Canada, New Zealand and Peru. In Britain, one of his biggest projects was Blackwell, above Lake Windermere, a holiday home for the Manchester brewer Sir Edward Holt and his family. This was an ideal dwelling, whose carved beams, stencilled friezes, stained-glass windows, and even its wrought-iron light pendants take the beauties of Nature that surround the house and bring them, in elegantly stylised and harmonious form, inside.

Voysey, Baillie Scott and Mackintosh were avant-garde (see fig. 41). The majority of small country houses were designed by architects of a different stamp. They were loosely traditionalist, of a more or less Arts and Crafts hue, whose work, if not always exciting, is invariably well built out of materials that are pleasing to the eye. Lutyens, Sir Robert Lorimer and Detmar Blow; Ernest Newton, Guy Dawber and Arnold Mitchell; Walter Brierley, Weir Schultz and W. Curtis Green . . . not only are they remarkable architects but the appetite for this new type of country house, combined with the prosperity of the age, provided numerous commissions. The object was not to stand out but to blend in. Weaver described Alfred Powell's Long Copse – the most beautiful building in Surrey, according to the painter G.F. Watts – as not giving 'the feeling of having been devised. It seems rather to have happened.' He meant it as praise.

FIG. 41 *The turn of the twentieth century saw a great flourishing of country-house architecture in Britain. It was an era of sound building, when traditional styles were revered, crafts were revived and a particular thought was given to the 'small country house' built with only a few acres of land. One country house of this type was Perrycroft, on the edge of the Malvern Hills in Worcestershire, built by the radical C.F.A. Voysey for the Quaker MP J.W. Wilson, financial secretary to the Miners' Union. Completed in 1895, it is in a more picturesque idiom than Voysey would normally allow himself; he championed simplicity.* © *Country Life Picture Library*

Architects became so anxious not to appear brash that they increasingly kept whatever architecture was already on site or incorporated pre-used materials that bore the patina of age: silvery oak, weathered brick, ancient stone details. This was both romantic, in that it revelled in the softness of visual effect that suggests the passing of years; and rational, because the SPAB had strict views about the ethics of faking history. At Standen, Philip Webb had not wanted to make the pre-existing farmhouse appear an integral part of the country house he created. Not all owners or architects were so scrupulous. But as the twentieth century wore on, more and more owners would fall under the spell of old country houses, going out of their way to restore them when it might well have been cheaper and more practical to start again.

The architectural historian Timothy Brittain-Catlin has recently described this as the most striking development of the age. Many if not the majority of Edwardian country houses are makeovers of old buildings, whose fabric is not obliterated as it would have been in previous centuries, but lovingly restored, heightened and enlarged in the same style, out of aesthetic choice. This was a new way of seeing the country house and has never lost its appeal.

In 1884, the nineteen-year-old Ernest Gimson met William Morris, who had come to address the Leicester Secular Society in an event organised by Gimson's father. Morris's buoyancy was irresistible– talk flowed until 2 a.m. Before long, Gimson had become one of the standard-bearers of the Arts and Crafts Movement that Morris had founded. He rejected practice in London in an idealistic mission to reconnect with the pre-industrial traditions of the Cotswolds, then an agricultural backwater, hallowed by Morris's affection for Kelmscott. He and Sidney Barnsley moved to the hamlet of Pinbury, where they were joined by Sidney's brother Ernest and his family, to form the sort of artistic community of which Morris so much approved. Gimson revived the craft of Elizabethan plasterwork, pressed out of moulds, and would sometimes make furniture – although he had come to realise that his talents were better deployed as a designer, since professionally trained cabinetmakers had greater skill. Sidney Barnsley became a furniture maker. Ernest Barnsley continued as an architect, designing Rodmarton Manor a few miles away: everything was made by hand, in the old way, from materials found on the estate, and estate workers shared in the joy of creation by helping to craft furniture and textile hangings.

In 1898 Gimson designed Stoneywell Cottage, among the volcanic outcrops of Leicestershire's Charnwood Forest, as a holiday home for his brother and sister-in-law, Sydney and Jane Gimson. Morris's domestic ideal, Kelmscott Manor, the home of his later years, seemed to emanate organically from its site and Gimson was bent on creating a similar effect when he designed Stoneywell. It surges out of the living rock, parts of which burst into the interior in the form of steps. Stoneywell, like Rodmarton, was built as far as possible from materials found on site, including boulders of immense size – indeed it went further because the form of the building is dictated by the curving hump of rock beneath it, necessitating seven changes of internal level. As the name suggests, the ground is stony and there is a well, from which water was drawn: there would be no piped water until the Second World War. Originally, a thatched roof gave the appearance of a huge, sleeping animal, as it curled around the flattened S-shape of the plan. Incredibly for a middle-class turn-of-the-century house – and not very conveniently for any house – the only entrance is through the kitchen, by a heavily studded door recessed beneath a frowning brow of slate. Inside, the ground floor is an organism of three cells: pantry, kitchen and sitting room. All walls are white, all wood unpainted.

But the sum of an Arts and Crafts house is not only what it is made of, but how it is made. With Ernest based for at least some of the time in Gloucestershire, the all-important process of building the house was entrusted to the head mason, the young, ideologically impeccable Detmar Blow. Blow had drunk inspiration from the fountainhead – John Ruskin, whom he met while on a sketching trip in northern France. On learning that Blow wanted to become an architect, the white-bearded sage delivered his theory of the profession – which was that it should be avoided. Honest handwork was the thing. Physical labour not only dignified the individual who undertook it, but the involvement of men such as Blow would help to revive the old ways, followed in the medieval period and down to the eighteenth century, which gave the builder a creative role in his craft – a tradition snuffed out by the tyranny of architects' plans that had to be followed in every detail. Accordingly, on his return to England, Blow apprenticed himself to a builder in Newcastle-upon-Tyne. He would go on to build many country houses, particularly for the group of intellectual, free-living aristocrats called The Souls.

By far the most successful country-house architect of the 1890s and 1900s was Sir Edwin Lutyens. His houses – dozens of them – bear witness to the domestic ideal of those years, part dream and part technical and social innovation. The dream lay in the aesthetic loveliness of silvery oak and softly coloured, hand-made bricks and tiles, or locally quarried stone, set amid yew topiaries and billowing flower borders. Novelty came in the way of life, lit by electric light, convenient for the metropolis and served by that wonder of the times – the motor car. Even Mrs Gerald Streatfield of Fulbrook House, in the prime Lutyens county of Surrey, bought one: a 4½ h.p. Locomobile; her highest recorded speed, on a flat stretch of the Portsmouth Road, broke the national speed limit of 20 m.p.h.

It helped that Lutyens was, by temperament, a romantic himself: a man who moved in a self-created world of delight, entranced by geometry, wreathed in extravagant notions of chivalry, particularly towards women, whom he did not perhaps understand. He grew up in the Surrey Hills, the ninth son and tenth child of an Indian Army officer turned animal painter. Rheumatic illness prevented the young Lutyens from going to public school or playing ball games. Instead he roamed around the Surrey lanes and looked, storing what he saw in an exceptional visual memory which would provide the basis for his early style.

At the age of twenty, Ned – as Lutyens was known – went to a Surrey tea party and met Gertrude Jekyll. Miss Jekyll was by then forty-six: a daunting, myopic garden designer, shaped like a cottage loaf. Ned called her Aunt Bumps. From being an artist and expert craftswoman, Jekyll had only turned to gardening when failing eyesight made it impossible to continue embroidery. She knew William Morris and had strong ideas about architecture which, in due course, she instilled into her protégé, commissioning him to design a cottage for her, and then a house: the famous Munstead Wood, whose artistically composed borders, planted with broad masses of colour, were visited by every distinguished gardener and botanist of the age. Miss Jekyll introduced Ned to her friends, some of whom, like Princess Louise, a daughter of Queen Victoria who was married to the future Duke of Argyll, and Sir William Chance QC and his wife (they had first seen her perched on a ladder outside Munstead Wood, giving directions to workmen), needed country houses.

It was Jekyll who introduced Lutyens to the proprietor of a new magazine for which she was writing, *Country Life*. Edward Hudson and Ned hit it off. Huddy, as Ned would call him, was another shy man;

photographs show him looking like a lugubrious bloodhound. But he recognised Lutyens as a genius, and quickly commissioned him to build Deanery Garden, a magical house constructed of exquisitely laid, mulberry-coloured brick that hides behind an ancient wall in the Berkshire village of Sonning. An interior of handcrafted oak, still bearing the marks of the carpenter's adze, provided a poetic setting for his collection of old oak and walnut furniture. Then Huddy took the lease of a castle: Lindisfarne, on Holy Island off the coast of Northumberland. It was wildly impractical, particularly given that Huddy, the son of a London printer, was not a natural countryman. The effete Lytton Strachey got incipient claustrophobia there and hated the dawn fishing expeditions. But to Lutyens it was all thrilling. On a family holiday, Huddy had Lutyens's young daughters photographed in the style of Vermeer. A frequent guest was the hot-blooded Portuguese cellist Guilhermina Suggia with whom poor Huddy was infatuated. Lutyens designed the hall of his third country house, Plumpton Place, as a stage for her to perform.

Hudson 'boomed' Lutyens through *Country Life*: the magazine published almost every work Ned produced, and the publicity brought clients. One of them was Herbert Johnson, the stockbroker for whom Lutyens designed Marsh Court – an improbably white, fairy-like palace above the river Test in Hampshire, built (very impractically) of clunch, a kind of hardened chalk. Lutyens was never too busy to take on more work, and he could not afford to be. In 1897, he faced down his bride's less than enthusiastic mother to marry Lady Emily Lytton, whose father, the 1st Earl of Lytton, had been Viceroy of India. They could only marry after he had taken out an expensive insurance policy so that Lady Emily would be comfortably provided for if he died; it would be a struggle to meet the premiums on.

Around 1905, Lutyens plunged into Classicism. He called it 'a big game, a high game': ordinary people might find it 'dry bones but under the mind of Wren it glows and the stiff materials become as plastic clay'. Lutyens was excited by the geometry and rules, which meant 'hard thought all through'. Here was something more intellectually stimulating than the nostalgia of the Arts and Crafts Movement, whose origin lay in the Gothic Revival; not surprisingly, Arts and Crafts architects were appalled.

The country house which first revealed Lutyens's love of the 'high game' was Heathcote, built in what Lutyens himself called 'an ultra-suburban locality' outside Ilkley in Yorkshire (fig. 42). To achieve a greater grandeur in the façades than the height of the rooms would have permitted, Lutyens turned to the work of the sixteenth-century Venetian Mannerist architect Michele Sanmicheli whom he greatly admired. The cornice of the Doric order does not reflect the internal form of the building – a mismatch that a more academic Classicist would have regarded as poor form. Beneath the cornice is rustication, which merges with the Doric pilasters: a visual caprice which Lutyens often repeated in later buildings. The vigorous projections and recessions of the façade have the plasticity of sculpture. But a memory of the Arts and Crafts Movement

FIG. 42 *Heathcote was built by Edwin Lutyens, outside Ilkley in Yorkshire. Begun in 1906, it was one of his first out-and-out essays in the 'high game' of Classicism, inspired by the sixteenth-century Venetian mannerist architect Michele Sanmicheli. Despite the rustication, columns and other Classical feature, the planning of the house is unexpected: designed on a symmetrical axis, there is nevertheless no direct route from front door to the back of the house; to get to the garden, it is necessary to follow a circuitous route, which makes the house seem larger than it is and unfolds a succession of surprises. In the entrance vestibule, grand doors that one assumes give into equally grand rooms in fact lead to the pantry and service areas, which occupy space ingeniously stolen from the main part of the house. © Andrew W. Barnett – Source: The Lutyens Trust Photographic Archive*

survives in the choice of a coarse yellow local stone for the walls and the idiosyncrasy of the plan. The front door does not give into the centre of an entrance hall, as you would expect. Instead, the hall has been placed asymmetrically, with the front door at one end. Similarly, the drawing room in the centre of the garden front is only revealed after a circuitous route (or choice of routes), leading to pairs of doors that are again not axially placed but stand at either end. It is as though Lutyens wants to build the quirkiness of old country houses that have grown organically into one that is both new and Classical. An unblocked axis running straight through the house would have displayed everything to a first glance; the delayed reveal of a Lutyens plan heightens the suspense and makes a small house seem bigger.

Where Lutyens led, others followed. By the First World War, Classical architecture (of a more muted kind than at Heathcote) became a preferred style of the small country house: Georgian in inspiration, as befitted the reign of George V, crowned in 1911.

In 1912, Lutyens received the greatest of all country-house commissions when he was asked to build Viceroy's House in New Delhi. Here, for once in British domestic history, was a palace, built all of a piece, with a footprint that is bigger than Versailles. Professionally, spiritually and geographically, Viceroy's House stands at a great distance from the English lanes in which Lutyens had formed his first style.

Splendid as architecture, Viceroy's House had already been left behind by time when it was inaugurated in 1931: self-rule was happening, independence on its way and the huge building was cordially hated by the last viceroy and his wife, Lord and Lady Mountbatten. It had been conceived for a different era, a glimpse of which is provided by the photographers James Russell & Sons of Chichester. Every year they recorded the house parties for Goodwood Race Week at Goodwood House in West Sussex. Here was the smart set, in an Edwardian country house operating at full throttle. Correct dress was a preoccupation. In 1905, the king signalled a sartorial departure by wearing a homburg hat to the races, with a lounge suit (though not quite as we would understand the term, since it had a frock coat in place of a jacket). All the other guests staying with the 7th Duke of Richmond and Gordon that year wore the top hats and

FIG. 43 *King Edward VII and the Prince of Wales, future George V, leave Goodwood House, Sussex, for the racecourse in the first decade of the twentieth century. In this as other things they set the example for smart society, which operated to an elaborate ritual. So many changes of clothes were required for a week that some of the royal luggage was despatched in two special wagons, 'in size rather smaller than the ordinary pantechnicon', according to the king's chauffeur C. W. Stamper. The Trustees of the Goodwood Collection*

morning coats that had previously been de rigueur. The royal example was followed the next year, and by 1907, formality was thrown to the winds. Some of the younger set wore straw boaters, while the duke and others followed the royal lead by donning a homburg – although the king himself, perhaps mischievously, now sported a white bowler (fig. 43).

Race Week, which marked the end of the London Season, was an immovable fixture in Edward's diary and his host was usually the duke. They were the same age but not otherwise well suited. The duke had fought in the Boer War and remained, despite the art treasures and gilded decoration of Goodwood and Gordon Castle on the river Spey, 'a man of the simplest tastes'. The *Times* obituarist, writing in 1928, revealed that 'for many years past, he was accustomed to sleep on a small pallet-bed in a little narrow room overlooking the beautiful home park of the castle.' In Scotland he enjoyed stalking, walking up grouse and spending time in the Shankery, a room where fly books were sorted, reels oiled and hot scones made over a peat fire; a photograph shows him in three-piece suit and waders.

Edward VII probably preferred the livelier atmosphere that prevailed at another house faced in knapped flint: Goodwood's neighbour West Dean, where petite, myopic Mrs Willie James was the vivacious chatelaine. Some said that Evelyn James was the king's mistress although her son Edward James insisted that she was his daughter; Willie, her easy-going, half-American husband, is remembered for hunting big game in Africa with his more brilliant brother Frank, until the latter was killed by a wounded elephant. Whereas the duke was willing to invite the king's mistress Alice Keppel, married to an artillery officer, he drew the line at Lillie Langtry – an actress. She was, however, welcomed at West Dean, to which the Prince of Wales transferred his allegiance for the 1899 Race Week. The old 6th Duke was so mortified by this desertion that Edward, a fundamentally kind-hearted man, felt unable to repeat it.

The duke did what he could to cater to the king's tastes. A hint that the Temple of Neptune and Minerva obscured his guest's view of the orangery ensured its removal. Royal dislike of the Egyptian Dining Room caused it to be redecorated in *le goût Ritz*. Other rooms, in accordance with the aesthetic and social requirements of a great Edwardian country house, laced grandeur with intimacy. Furniture, often deep-sprung, was arranged in groups that promoted relaxed or intimate conversation among guests, shielded from the rest of the party by tall palms. The entrance hall, with its row of tall granite columns, served as a living hall, where family and guests could write letters, read the newspapers – left, with a cavalier disregard of their ink, on the silk arm of a sofa – and chat, before leaving for the races. The immense dining table, laid in the ballroom, groaned with heavy plate.

Food, prepared by a French chef called Rousseau, remembered as having a steel for sharpening knives hung at his side like a sword, was important. After 9 a.m. prayers came breakfast, offering grilled kidneys, fish, kedgeree or eggs, followed by devilled bones, chicken and goose, cold game pies, York ham, pickled fish and potted game, and any other spiced delicacy that Rousseau might concoct. By the 1890s, luncheon was accompanied by champagne. Afterwards, on other than race days, the ladies of the party wrapped themselves up in tweeds and furs to suffer the discomforts of exploration in a wagonette, to places of interest and country views. This stimulated an appetite for tea and flirtation, which continued until it was time to dress for dinner. After their Spartan baths, the ladies descended the staircase in a rustle of silk and brocade, their jewellery sparkling in the light from the big Palladian window and their alabaster complexions as pale as the antique marbles displayed beneath the pride of the picture collection. Dinner invariably consisted of two soups, chicken or duck 'with attendant etceteras to efface the absence of succulent putridity' (game, hung until high, was preferred in season), a roast joint with vegetables, sweets of a solid nature and a pungent savoury and dessert.

At the end of the evening, a tray would be sent to the queen's sitting room for her and her Lady of the Bedchamber, Charlotte Knollys, 'on which were crowded all sorts of delicious little things, and usually French plums of which she was fond'. The many changes of clothes meant a quantity of luggage that astonished the royal chauffeur C. W. Stamper.

It was soon over; the king and queen left, the party ended. The day after the last race, a private train drew into Chichester station: it took the duke and his family to Gordon Castle. Before long the Edwardian age itself had drawn to a close: the king died in 1911.

After the hot summer of 1914, the war that had been long expected broke out and those sons of country houses who were not already in the army rushed to enlist, in case they missed the glory. Most people thought that, like other wars, it would be over in a few months. After all, who wanted war? There was nothing much to fight about.

CHAPTER TEN

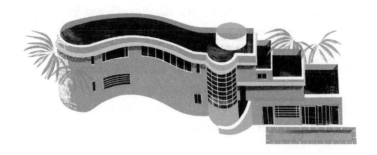

Between the Wars

OFFICERS suffered a disproportionately high number of deaths during the First World War. All those young subalterns leading their men from the front made a conspicuous target in their jodhpurs and top boots, with pistols rather than rifles in their hand; Eton's war memorial bears well over a thousand names. Among the fallen were many sons of country-house owners, such as Edward Horner, the last male member of his family: Lutyens designed the equestrian monument to him that stands in the church in Mells, in Somerset, as an image of Christian chivalry. At the back of the church, carved into the wall, is the Latin memorial to his brother-in-law Raymond Asquith, a Classicist and lawyer. Asquith was the son of the prime minister; his memorial evokes the other lodestone of public school education, Roman stoicism. 'All their young men are killed,' Lutyens wrote to his wife Lady Emily, on the day that he walked the village to choose a site for the war memorial.

The war had major consequences for the country house. Owners volunteered their property to become hospitals and convalescent homes, and purposeful chatelaines converted their luxurious motor cars into ambulances and set up field hospitals – which led to some extraordinary adventures for those who were overrun by the enemy. Building work was suspended for the duration (although not at Broome Park in Kent; the client was Lord Kitchener, Secretary of State for War). After the war, country-house architects could not restart their practices on the same lines. Some, like the Scottish architect John Kinross, the fastidious architect of Manderston House in Berwickshire, were glad of the commissions for war memorials for the children of their former clients, which helped to see them through. C.F.A. Voysey built no more houses after the First World War. Detmar Blow became a kind of factotum for the Duke of Westminster, helping administer the Grosvenor Estate in London until being ignominiously dismissed when the duke took a new wife – his third.

Before 1914, the only women to wear trousers were cyclists in bloomers. But attitudes on this and other matters had to change. 'Here is dawning a new era for womanhood and therefore the human race!' gasped one journalist, awed by the 'robust yet supple figures' and blooming cheeks of two hundred and fifty Land Girls marching through Dorchester. They had come to help on the farm, in a uniform of breeches and floppy hats.

People who feared a social revolution were right. One came after the war when women, who had proved that they could do the same jobs as men, eventually achieved equal voting rights. There was another taking place in the country house. War opened the eyes of servants to an alternative way of life. They could find employment in cities. Factory work, if monotonous, was cheerful. Girls could see whom they liked once they had clocked off. They did not want to go back to the country house, where the long hours, inflexible hierarchy and lack of privacy all grated. Pre-war anxiety escalated into a crisis for employers, struggling with post-war taxation. There was a rush to sell land and in 1921 the *Estates Gazette* announced that about a quarter of England and Wales had 'changed hands in four years': a transfer of ownership comparable to the Dissolution of the Monasteries. The landed interest was in retreat. In 1917 the Tory MP Arthur Lee gave Chequers in Buckinghamshire to the nation because it could no longer be expected that a prime minister would own his own country house.

With Britain blockaded, the government had wanted more food to be produced at home. After 1918, agriculture fell back into depression and the prestige of owning land hardly compensated for the responsibilities. By the time P.G. Wodehouse published *Thank You, Jeeves* in 1934, the plight of the 5th Baron Chuffnell of Chuffnell Regis – Bertie Wooster's friend Chuffy – was to be pitied. Like 'most fellows who own land', he was on his uppers and found Chuffnell Hall nothing but an encumbrance. Anyone willing to take it off his hands would have been rapturously embraced but who did want somewhere that big 'in these times'? The times were those of the Slump, as Britain called the Great Depression.

People who had fought or suffered during the war yearned for the Arcadia of a country house to heal mental wounds and reconnect with humane values: a private, self-created space. But what should this Arcadia be? There were wildly different approaches. Some people wanted to retreat to the cosiness of the Tudor past before aerial warfare and the artillery barrage. Some envied the technological sophistication of the United States and commissioned Hollywood-style bathrooms (Lutyens designed an onyx one for Lady Jersey, previously the American actress Virginia Cherrill, who had been briefly married to Cary Grant, for Middleton Park in Oxfordshire). Others welcomed a new, uncluttered form of architecture, open to the sun, redolent of a rational way of life, as appropriate to the better world they hoped to live in.

Few saw the solution as lying in the great country houses of the past. In some cases, the domestic machine rolled on under its own momentum, footmen, gold plate, shooting parties and all. But the engine of many was running down and a number went to the scrap heap. In 1921, Hamilton Palace in the Lowlands of Scotland – undermined by the Lanarkshire coalfields that were the source of the Duke of Hamilton's stupendous wealth – was pulled down. There would be hundreds more country-house demolitions to come over the next fifty years.

In Ireland, the struggle to secede from the United Kingdom, which the South achieved in 1919, was followed by civil war in 1922–3. During these years, more than 275 Irish country houses were burnt down or blown up, as revolutionaries gave vent to their hatred for the Big House, fuelled by memories of the Irish Potato Famine of 1845–9 and absentee landowners of all periods who evicted tenants or allowed them to be rack-rented by stewards.

It was a time of idealism and experiment, hedonism and disappointed hope. Above all it was a time of unease.

§

When the prime minister David Lloyd George wanted to discuss the Treaty of Versailles, which ended the First World War, with his French counterpart, Alexandre Millerand, the meetings took place at Port Lympne, Sir Philip Sassoon's country house on the Kent coast, within sight of France on a good day. It had been built in 1913–14 by Herbert Baker in what is called his Cape Dutch style (it is true that Baker had built literally hundreds of houses in South Africa but he came from Kent and knew that red brick and Flemish-looking curly gables was also indigenous to the county). The dining room had recently been decorated in a colourful Ballets Russes manner with murals by the Catalan artist José Maria Sert, with, as the former prime minister, H.H. Asquith put it, 'elephants in different attitudes'. Sassoon wrote with studied nonchalance, 'Personally, I think it monstrous.' But the position of the house delighted him. 'I am on the lip of the world,' he wrote to the novelist Mrs Henry Dudeney in 1918, '. . . How altruistic nature is. And this year the wild rampage of colour seems to be on tiptoe to soothe one's wretched heart.'

Describing the Franco-British conference, the future Fascist leader Oswald Mosley, then a Tory MP, depicted Lloyd George as living in the 'state of a Roman Emperor . . . regaled in the evening with the frankincense of admiring friends . . . [and] liberal applications of precious ointment from the voluptuous Orient.' The language reflects Mosley's anti-Semitism: the Sassoons were Sephardi Jews whose fortune had been made in Bombay. But his comment accurately evokes the world in which Sassoon moved, which was luxurious, arty and effete – all things that were red rags to most unreformed country-house owners, for whom interior decoration was not a manly activity. And yet in one respect the homosexual Sasoon's taste typified the age. It was mercurial. Exuberant and bursting with energy, Sassoon threw himself into new projects and could be a marvellous host; or he might be moody and rude. Signs of a manic depressive? To contemporaries the world itself was unsettled.

Sassoon projected his restlessness onto his house. The sides of a *trompe-l'oeil* tent painted by Rex Whistler lift to reveal a capriccio of favourite buildings. The homosexual painter Glyn Philpot supplied a Nubian frieze to replace the elephants. The architect Philip Tilden created a Moorish Courtyard and landscaped the gardens in an Imperial Roman manner, a bow to a Roman fort on the property. Meanwhile on the southern edge of Enfield Chase, outside London, Sassoon started another project, disinterring Trent Park from its unsympathetic Edwardian crust, to create an image of Georgian perfection. Anxiety at the destruction of Georgian London would lead to the foundation of the Georgian Group in 1937. Indeed, Trent Park was refaced with old bricks from the Duke of Devonshire's town palace, Devonshire House, which had been pulled down to make way for an office building. To Christopher Hussey, writing in 1931, Trent caught 'that indefinable and elusive quality, the spirit of a country house . . . an essence of cool, flowery, chintzy, elegant, unobtrusive rooms'.

Only a few country-house owners followed the creative lead Sassoon had given at Port Lympne but many came to share his taste for what is now called the long eighteenth century. Buscot Park, on the upper reaches of the river Thames, was re-Georgianised by the 2nd Lord Faringdon, who inherited in 1934. Faringdon had been one of the Bright Young Things. At a dinner to celebrate his impending wedding to Honor Philipps in 1927, friends poured sixteen gallons of petrol onto the river near Henley 'to set the Thames alight'. The marriage, however, only lasted four years. The Labour politician Hugh Dalton called him a 'pansy pacifist of whose private tendencies it might be slander to speak' – although he belonged to the same party. One of the murals on the outside of a new squash court-cum-theatre, painted by John Hastings, depicts daily life and the Progress of Socialism, Faringdon addressing an audience of rural folk from a farm cart, while behind him marches a procession that includes nurses and even a Sikh beneath the banner of the Faringdon Labour Party. The entrance hall at Buscot was decorated in the Regency Revival style and furnished with neo-Egyptian pieces by Thomas Hope.

An alternative historical reference was the age of Elizabeth. It spoke of Merrie England to men and women whose recent lives had lacked merriment; a time of national greatness, Shakespeare and pastoral imagery, far away from the angst brought on by the First World War. In his Mapp and Lucia novels, E.F. Benson pokes gentle fun at a community of genteel but generally impoverished people (sufficiently well off to employ a few servants, of course) who live the Tudor dream in conditions of self-conscious quaintness. The heroine Mrs Lucas – Lucia – has a garden containing only those plants mentioned in *The Winter's Tale*.

Timber-framed buildings, with their kit-like construction, could be dismantled, moved and re-erected with relative ease, provided care had been taken to number the beams. These and other architectural salvage could be incorporated into new ensembles. The taste for this had developed during the romantic Edwardian years but now reached the affluent middle classes. In 1929, the romantic Tudor look became the subject of P.A. Barron's *The House Desirable*, offering advice on how to persuade professional bricklayers, likely to take an awkward pride in the regularity of their work, to lay old bricks 'all wibbly wobbly', as a craftsman might have expressed it. He also suggests ways of winning round the district surveyor to the use of time-worn timbers and walls out of plumb. The master of the genre was Blunden Shadbolt.

In 1927, Lord Moyne (then Walter Guinness) began Bailiffscourt, on an estate of seven hundred and fifty acres on the Sussex coast. Moyne was a keen yachtsman and the seaside was good for the children. Lady Moyne appears to have led on aesthetic matters. Designs, architectural salvage and wormy furniture were supplied by the Oxford-educated antique dealer and author of *Old English Chintzes*, F.W. Phillips. The pseudo-medieval two-pronged forks and pewter plates were hammered out by the chauffeur in his spare time. Every guest room, noted the diarist and politician Chips Channon, 'is decorated to resemble the cell of a rather "pansy" monk'.

Old stones found in the walls of a demolished farmhouse that had stood on the site were carefully reassembled into their original doorcases and windows. Other features came from medieval structures brought from elsewhere. There was no conventional garden, only a meadow full of the wild flowers that Lady Moyne loved. Sir Philip Sassoon said that they were as expensive as orchids.

An exclusive club was formed by people who restored castles, often with American money. They included Lord Curzon, twice married to Americans, at Bodiam, and Olive, Lady Baillie, whose father had married a Whitney heiress, at Leeds Castle, in Kent. Work on Leeds Castle, using French decorators, continued into the 1960s with sublime disregard for the changing times.

The Prince of Wales, future Edward VIII, settled not on a castle but a mock fort in Windsor Great Park. Previously, for the summer of 1926, he had rented Small Downs House on the newly completed development of Sandwich Bay in Kent – near Royal St George's Golf Club – to be near his mistress Mrs Dudley Ward who took Fourth Green. It was what might be termed a Rhapsodic Tudor property, designed by Charles Biddulph-Pinchard, in which even the glass was old and 'slightly golden in tint', according to the *Architectural Review*. This was one of the ways that the prince – Betjeman's 'young man' arriving 'hatless from the air' – epitomised social change; and he would do so again when he created his own country house.

'What could you possibly want that queer old place for?' growled King George V when the Prince of Wales asked him for the eighteenth-century folly, Fort Belvedere in 1930 (fig. 44). 'Those damn week ends, I suppose.' He was right. Weekends, a shocking novelty to Victorian hostesses, became a social commonplace at the beginning of the twentieth century, when fewer men could afford to spend a week or more in the country at a time. While George V had been happy at 'dear old Sandringham, the place I love better than anywhere else in the world', his son wanted somewhere close to London, organised by his new mistress, the American Mrs Simpson, on American lines.

Edward loved the United States from the time that he was rapturously received there in 1919; he could escape the protocol that he found so irksome at home and the informality of American life was refreshing, after the fossilised rigidity of his father's court. His wardrobe – always important to him – soon contained sporting clothes in plangent checks, pullovers of vibrant hues, and soft collars; he affected an American accent, in preference to the previously fashionable faux cockney, and drank cocktails.

FIG. 44 *Fort Belvedere in Windsor Great Park, originally built in the 1820s, was converted by the future Edward VIII to a country house on modern lines after 1929. The Prince of Wales loved the Long Island homes of polo-playing friends that he had seen during his visits to the United States: they were luxurious, equipped with central heating and other conveniences, and built for fun, being unencumbered with the responsibilities and traditions of landownership. This photograph shows Edward's swimming pool, tennis court and polo stables.* © *Getty Images*

Fort Belvedere began as a triangular tower: one of the caprices of Virginia Water made for the Duke of Cumberland in the mid-eighteenth century. Wyatville transformed it into a toy fort in the 1820s. A projecting one-storey dining room would become the prince's drawing room. The house was so near London that the prince could make out the dome of St Paul's Cathedral through a telescope, but was nevertheless beyond the common gaze and the prying lenses of the press.

In 'fixing the place up', the prince followed his own ideas:

and, being mine, they were modern. Inside I introduced, to the extent that space and the old walls allowed, many of the creature conveniences that I had sampled and enjoyed in the New World – a bathroom to nearly every room, showers, a steam bath, built-in cupboards, central heating – the so-called modern comforts that were seldom found in profusion in British houses.

The prince had his domestic side. Since childhood, he had practised needlework. But the aspect of the Fort's revival which most appealed to him was the garden. Swathes of it had to be cleared. He learnt how to use a billhook and set about the laurels, taking out his frustration with the world as he slashed them down. It became a completely absorbing activity for a time, preferred to fox hunting and even golf. An outside swimming pool was constructed in 1931–2; a hard tennis court made alongside the battery. The Fort came to resemble the sports complexes with which rich men's country places in the United States were equipped.

Sometimes the prince played the bagpipes, sometimes the ukulele. He could smoke, relax and, if he wanted, throw gramophone records about the place, to see if they really lived up to their manufacturer's claim of being unbreakable. For someone who was otherwise almost always in the public eye, or under that of his family, it was a release. Here he could entertain whom he chose, how he chose.

After the prince became king, Fort Belvedere was further improved by the architect Giles Gilbert Scott. During the Abdication Crisis, Mrs Simpson moved in, leaving one night in December 1936 when, after a melancholy supper, she walked through the king's bedroom and out onto the lawn, without saying goodbye to any of the staff, but taking her jewellery. The abdication papers were signed by Edward VIII and his three brothers at Fort Belvedere a week later.

The Prince of Wales used Fort Belvedere as a villa and it is through villas that the story of the country house must be told in the inter-war period, since few people could afford – or wanted – places as big as Trent Park or Leeds Castle. This is particularly true of the flat-roofed, white-walled, generously windowed houses of the Modern Movement or International Style, which arrived from France and Germany at the end of the 1920s. Even large villas were few. In 1938, Evelyn Waugh deplored the 'villas like sewage farms, mansions like half-submerged Channel steamers . . . furnished with electric fires that blistered the ankles, windows that blinded the eyes', which had been erected in the course of the previous decade or so. He maintained that England's constitution was sufficiently strong to resist the microbial infection of Le Corbusier. There was something in what he said. An analysis of the thirty-three International Style houses (not all of them country houses) built in Britain before 1939 found that the clients were principally architects, artists, writers and scholars; a third were commissioned by businessmen or professional people. The old aristocracy was unrepresented; there was nobody of the wealth of Sir Philip Sassoon. Such buildings may have been Modern but had scarcely become a movement in Britain. Their white walls and flat roofs were better suited to the blue skies of the Mediterranean – and architectural photography – than British weather.

One of the largest of these villas is High and Over, at Amersham – chosen for its access to the Metropolitan Line – which became known locally as the 'aeroplane house'. Its client was the distinguished archaeologist Bernard Ashmole, descended from an uncle of the Elias Ashmole who founded the Ashmolean Museum in Oxford. He and his wife Dorothy had recently returned from Rome, where Ashmole had been director of the British School. There he had met Amyas Connell, a New Zealander who had trained at the Bartlett and was studying Michelangelo's buildings on the Campidoglio. 'His views on modern architecture were sensible,' Ashmole remembered in his *Autobiography*; 'he had studied the work of Le Corbusier and of modern German and Dutch architects, but dissented from the extreme view that a house was simply a machine for living in, unless beauty is considered part of living.' Dorothy bought twelve acres from the Shardeloes estate that was then being broken up. They found a spot above an old chalk pit: the form of the land suggested splayed wings (already tried in the butterfly plans of Edwardian architecture). The central hexagon provided a landing at the bottom and a nursery at the top. With main rooms opening with folding doors onto the hall, the whole ground floor except the kitchen could be made into one space, with vistas of more than sixty feet. Large windows to the south-east and south-west were arranged in continuous bands for the sake of the views and the sun.

There were difficulties from building with untried materials and a builder who was either incompetent or did not understand what was required of him; Ashmole blamed a mastoid abscess partly on the worry he suffered. But once finished, the 'airiness, lightness and spaciousness' and five-acre garden proved a hit with the family. He later came to regret that the house was too large for the conditions prevailing after the Second World War, 'but we had not the gift of prophecy'.

Gribloch in Stirlingshire is a rare example of a full-blown Modernist country house. Basil Spence built it for John Colville, whom he may have met through his work for the Empire Exhibition in Glasgow of 1938 (Colville was on the committee) although he had previously designed a Modern-meets-Scots Baronial country house called Quothquhan, in Lanarkshire, for a relative. In his early thirties and married to an American wife, Colville was the grandson of a steel magnate from Glasgow; he went to Spence after his previous country house burnt down. Gribloch looks south towards a glorious panorama of hills: two wings open to embrace a swimming pool. Inside, an oval staircase hall is lit by a mullioned window that takes up almost the whole façade. The service wing projects to the east, with the gun room off it; there is a game larder to one side and large spaces for both coal and heating fuel – this is Scotland after all.

The architect who epitomises the inter-war country house is Oliver Hill. At the age of eighteen, Hill hoped to become a pupil of his hero Lutyens. The latter advised him to work in a builder's yard; it would give him a knowledge of materials. The training grounded a young man whose upbringing had been somewhat rarefied: Whistler had decorated a room in the family's Bedfordshire country house with gold leaf glazed with grey-green. After eighteen months with a builder, Hill joined William Flockhart, a suave Scottish architect, who was capable of working in a variety of styles with equal assurance.

Hill's career had hardly got going before the First World War. In the decade afterwards, he showed himself adept at expressing the nostalgia and romanticism which seemed to provide a refuge for a shattered world. In Scotland, he built Cour House, a beetle-browed place of lowering walls which seemed to loom up like a cliff on the remote Kintyre peninsula. In the South of England, he beguiled clients with bucolic dreams, wavy weatherboarding and oak mullions snuggling down under a thatched roof. Dormer windows may peep out from a duvet of thatch and broad, stepped chimneys sail overhead, as though a declaration of domestic values. Unlike the zaniness of true Arts and Crafts houses, such as Stoneywell, it is too self-consciously picturesque to seem 'genuine'. These are villas, if not caprices. Hill's own home, Valewood Farm, in the Surrey Hills, was photographed with rows of outsized flagons on oak tables, a spinning wheel, a seventeenth-century brass chandelier and a warming pan hanging on a post. It was a stage set.

Hill shared this idyll with Christopher Hussey, architectural editor of *Country Life*, who introduced him to the Modernism that had begun to appear on the Continent. Hill, with his easy fluency, promptly went Modern – or perhaps it would be more accurate to say *moderne*: he absorbed French Art Deco along with Le Corbusier, the result being a stream of effortlessly suave London interiors and country houses that, like his Arts and Crafts work, do not ask to be taken too seriously. With its white walls, geometry and curves, Joldwynds in Surrey, which replaced a house by Philip Webb, is an ocean liner by a golf course. At Marylands, in Surrey, built after a trip to Spain, he created a hacienda on the North Downs, complete with green roof tiles imported, unexpectedly, from Sweden. It had been planned around an existing silver birch tree, and the octogenarian Gertrude Jekyll laid out the garden, the idea being, wrote Hill, 'to place the house in its lovely natural surroundings without any formal demarcation of house and garden beyond forecourt and steps'.

Hill was beguiling, not doctrinaire; he blamed the premature end to his career – he lived until 1968 – on Adolf Hitler.

CHAPTER ELEVEN

Post-War:
Recovery and Boom

IN the 1945 general election, Winston Churchill, the Conservatives' leader, was an imperialist who had been born at Blenheim Palace. The Labour leader Clement Attlee took a fatalistic view of the Raj; his birthplace had been Westcott, 18 Portinscale Road, in the London suburb of Putney. To Evelyn Waugh, standing in White's Club watching the results come in on the tickertape, the scale of Labour's epic victory was 'a prodigious surprise', which confirmed the gloom that he had expressed when writing *Brideshead Revisited* the year before. The country-house culture to which he had assimilated himself while at Oxford seemed at an end. The dome of Castle Howard, one of his inspirations, had been destroyed by a chimney fire in 1940 and would not be rebuilt until 1960–1. *Götterdämmerung* had come for the country house.

The extent of Labour's appeal should have been obvious. It offered welfare reform, the National Health, nationalisation and change to a country that was bombed out and bankrupt. Food would be rationed until 1954, clothing until 1949. The country house had been witheringly satirised by Noël Coward, whose song 'The Stately Homes of England' had first been heard as part of the musical *Operette* in 1938, sung by the significantly named Lords Elderley, Borrowmere, Sickert and Camp. The pre-war crisis was compounded by the war itself, when many were requisitioned. During the First World War, owners felt it their patriotic duty to turn a wing of the country house into a convalescent home: with the passing of the Emergency Powers (Defence) Act in 1939, they had no choice in the matter. Ralph Dutton, later Lord Sherborne, was given forty-eight hours to vacate Hinton Ampner in Hampshire, which he had just finished remodelling, to make way for a girls' school. It was 'a moment of intense bitterness'. In some country-house attics, stencilled names survive from the days of armed services' occupation.

Horror stories abound: grenades let off in the greenhouses; mahogany furniture smashed to make kindling; all the taps of Egginton Hall being left on when the troops left in 1945, causing a flood that brought down ceilings and forced the family to demolish the house and move into the stables. Broughton Castle in Oxfordshire had a comparatively lenient war: the Oak Room and great hall were piled from floor to ceiling with cases containing the insect collection from the Natural History Museum. However, even houses that were gently treated went unrepaired and some-times unmaintained; blocked gutters could cause dry rot, the strains of intensive occupation led to fires. Half of Melford Hall in Suffolk burnt after the Berkshire Regiment overloaded a fireplace in 1942; the west wing was so damaged by water that dry rot took hold. When owners returned after 1945, they found their homes in disarray or damaged, their parks dug up to grow food, their gardens overgrown. It took courage, willpower and faith in the future to unpack the furniture and move back in, particularly when building materials were still rationed. Building licences were not completely abolished until 1954.

It was a sign of the 'impending catastrophe' facing country houses that the Labour government appointed a committee to consider 'what general arrangements might be made by the Government for the preservation, maintenance and use of houses of outstanding historical or architectural interest'. Under the chairmanship of Sir Ernest Gowers, a newly retired civil servant, it reported in 1950 that taxation was the principal problem. The solution was to set up Historic Buildings Councils for England, Wales and Scotland with the power to make grants and loans. In return for the grant money, country-house owners would have to open their homes to the public for some days each year. An alternative for owners was the National Trust. Founded in 1895 to protect open spaces, it had responded to the looming debacle by establishing a country-house scheme in the late 1930s, enabling the Trust to accept the transfer of private property. Private owners were sometimes offered an exceptionally good deal: they could continue to live in their country houses, while upkeep was paid for by the Trust. Nevertheless, both grants and Trust accomplished what might now be seen a solution in keeping with the spirit of the times: nationalisation by another name.

Some class warriors in the Labour Party hated the country house for what it represented: the Minister of Fuel and Power, Manny Shinwell, vindictively insisted that an open-cast coal mine to be created in the park at Wentworth Woodhouse should run up to the doors of the house, making it uninhabitable by the 8th Earl Fitzwilliam and his family. But over the next half-century country-house owners often found that their woes were heard with a more sympathetic ear by Labour than the Conservatives. Labour were high tax but also high spend; they gave more generous grants. They recognised that country houses were a national responsibility; to the Tories, private property was primarily the responsibility of its owners.

New country houses told a story of retreat. Nearly all of those built in the four decades after the Second World War replaced previous ones, either because the latter had been burnt, or were too big, or had been damaged to the point that it did not seem worth repairing them. Owners withdrew into smaller spaces, suitable for an age of electric appliances and few staff. Dame Miriam Rothschild had the top floor of Ashton Wold in Northamptonshire removed, a lobotomy performed by the Hon. Claud Phillimore, an architect who specialised in shrinking large country houses or providing new dwellings on convenient if unexciting lines. Numerous owners of large country houses withdrew to the stables, which were converted to domestic use with lower ceilings. In Scotland, owners took the opportunity to liberate tower houses from the Scots

Baronial accretions which had overpowered the original architecture in the Victorian period. Wanting bricks for Sir Thomas Pilkington's new country house of Kings Walden Bury (fig. 45), Raymond Erith and his assistant Quinlan Terry went to a brickmaker in Sudbury, who used the same clay as that in Roman times. All but one of the kilns were full of pigs, which were more profitable. Terry was urged to keep a diary; they thought the job would be the last of its kind.

For one thing, some people hated the past. Although Britain had been on the winning side of the Second World War, it was now dismantling its Empire and trying to forge a new future; old styles, old buildings seemed an encumbrance. The Swinging Sixties had its fits of nostalgia (John Schlesinger's *Far From the Madding Crowd*, the maxi coat, *Sgt Pepper*) but the mood was not favourable to old, echoing, dry-rot infested mansions, without the conveniences of modern plumbing and kitchen gadgetry. In the early 1960s, the 5th Duke of Westminster demolished Alfred Waterhouse's vast main house at Eaton Hall in Cheshire, leaving the tower of the chapel to soar above a mass of devastation. He put in its place a white-walled Modernist building which, although large, looked too small for its setting; it was designed by his wife's brother-in-law John Dennys. It was remodelled in a French chateau style less than twenty years after it was finished.

Country houses had to become comfortable again if they were to survive as private homes. The person who made them so was the interior

FIG. 45 *In 1969 Sir Thomas Pilkington approached Raymond Erith to build a new country house at King's Walden Bury, in Hertfordshire. Erith took his inspiration from Palladio's villas on the Veneto, but was so convinced that no more country houses would be built on that scale that he suggested his assistant Quinlan Terry should keep a notebook to record the building. Terry commemorated the finished work in this linocut.* © *Quinlan Terry*

decorator Nancy Lancaster. Coming from Virginia, she had grown up among intrinsically elegant but down-at-heel Southern mansions, and so sympathised with the semi-derelict state of her clients' houses; as an American, she understood about bathrooms and central heating. Newly divorced from her second husband Ronnie Tree, in 1948 she bought Sybil Colefax's famous decorating firm, in which she was joined by the 'prince of decorators' John Fowler, an expert on the eighteenth century. Together they rekindled a sense of *savoir vivre* in the stately home.

Lancaster supposedly considered a hundred and fifty houses before buying her last home, Haseley Court in Oxfordshire, in 1954, still run down after use as a prisoner-of-war camp. There she copied the wallpaper for the Palladian Room from one at Drottningholm Palace in Sweden, after a sketch made for her by the King of Sweden. Looking out of his bedroom window in 1959, Cecil Beaton saw Nancy gardening and recorded his impression of the perfection she had achieved in his diary. It could be summed up as 'ENVY!!' In 1971, she moved out of the big house at Haseley, which had become too much even for such an avid lover of the domestic arts; her new residence – in harmony with the times – was the Coach House.

Lancaster had seen which way the wind would blow during the 1970s. Britain's economic and industrial difficulties made it the Sick Man of Europe. Taxation reached exorbitant heights – ninety-eight per cent when the surcharge on invested income was added to the top rate of income tax. The greyness of the decade can be seen in the smudgy black-and-white photographs in *Country Life*. The magazine's advertisement pages, celebrating the best that country property had to offer, show that the most aspirational dwelling was a convenient, newly built house, without much land, within an easy train ride to London and close to a golf course. Large country houses in remote counties were accompanied by the dread words 'suitable for institutional use'. Owners struggled with late-running trains, power cuts and postal strikes. The oil crisis of 1973, when the Arab oil-producing countries declared an oil embargo to punish states which had supported Israel during the Yom Kippur war, saw the price of petrol and heating fuel soar. This spelt disaster for country houses whose owners could not afford the oil to heat them. Cast-iron central radiators and pipes exploded when the water froze. The stock market, buoyant in the 1950s and 1960s, crashed. At West Green House in Hampshire, Alistair McAlpine, who later became Treasurer of the Tory Party, employed Quinlan Terry to build several follies, including an extravagantly purposeless column that bore a Latin inscription which translates as: 'This monument was built with a large sum of money, which would have otherwise fallen, sooner or later, into the hands of the tax-gatherers.' West Green was rented from the National Trust. Although a rich man from the family construction business, he was not tempted to sink money into buying a country house.

In 1974, the National Trust's expert on country houses, James Lees-Milne, was no more optimistic than Evelyn Waugh had been in 1945. 'The English country house is as archaic as the osprey,' which had become extinct in England in 1840.

> The few left fulfilling the purpose for which they were built are inex-orably doomed. The causes are only too well known: penal taxation and the dearth of domestic helpers. Furthermore the spirit of the age is against what is termed 'privilege'. God knows, the privilege of slaving in a palace without help and with responsibility for valuable contents is less than that of living carefree in a cosy cottage with every mod con.

Those words open the first essay in the catalogue accompanying an exhi-bition publicising the dire state to which the country house had fallen, held at the Victoria and Albert Museum. Called *The Destruction of the Country House*, it greeted visitors with the voice of architectural historian Sir John Summerson intoning a toll of the losses suffered in the century, since the onset of the Agricultural Depression of the 1870s. Exactly how many demolitions had taken place cannot be accurately computed, due to the difficulty of defining a country house, but a conservative estimate would be well over a thousand. 'Many was the time I stood in that exhi-bition watching the tears stream down the visitors' faces as they battled to come to terms with all that had gone,' wrote the museum's director Sir Roy Strong in his *Diaries*.

Both political parties recognised that there was a national interest in saving the country house, seen as a specially British achievement. It was also accepted that supporting the private owner – however distasteful to some politicians – was more cost-effective than ownership by the state. At Broughton Castle the 20th Baron Saye and Sele got a one hundred per cent grant from the Historic Buildings Council to replace the roof. When one of the officials who visited to inspect the house left his papers behind, they were found to say that the Twistleton-Wykeham-Fiennes family was 'notoriously impoverished'. The rate at which works of art were being sold to overseas museums and collectors caused consternation; the problem was not fully addressed until the advent of the National Lottery and the Heritage Lottery Fund, in 1994.

The revival of the country house began after the Conservative election victory in 1979. Although Mrs Thatcher was not herself enamoured of the old guard, indeed would have happily swept it away, the policies she introduced – wealth creation matched by lower taxes – made it possible for successful individuals to live in style. Income tax was cut to forty per cent. At the end of her decade in power, the property pages of *Country Life* were full of estates with sporting rights, beyond the Home Counties – and the more architecturally show-stopping the house was, the better. This was not only a reflection of the money available, although the Lawson Boom combined with the liberalisation of the City of London known as Big Bang meant that fortunes were being made on a new scale. Would-be owners regained their mojo. It was unlikely that property would be confiscated, or that assets, as well as income, would be taxed. They felt that they and their families would probably be able to afford to continue to live in the houses they restored or built for some time, perhaps generations. The way was shown by the Conservative cabinet minister Michael Heseltine who restored Thenford Hall in Northamptonshire, planted an arboretum and built a flamboyant Classical summer house. Some colleagues in the Tory Party sneered that the fellow had to buy his own furniture. But being an entrepreneur as well as a senior politician, he showed that, despite predictions, the spirit of the country house was not dead. It gave confidence to others.

In 1981, the *World of Interiors* magazine began publication, celebrating the distressed furniture and worn carpets of romantic country houses; stylists were suspected of scattering dust and fallen rose petals to complement the basket of freshly dug carrots that they placed in the kitchen. Country-house buyers looked for Sleeping Beauties, fragile and unmodernised, which they could kiss back into life in their own style, discreetly updating the services but cherishing irregularities and quirks. This baffled owners of an older generation, in whom hardship had bred an attitude of hard-nosed practicality. Even more extraordinary, in their eyes, was the move of old families to reoccupy country houses that had previously been let as institutions. Duncombe Park in Yorkshire, originally by Vanbrugh, was one example among many. After sixty years of use by a girls' school, it was remade into a family home for Lord and Lady Faversham.

The counterpart of the *Destruction of the Country House* exhibition which had characterised the 1970s was the *Treasure Houses of Britain*, a celebration of private country-house collections that opened in Washington in 1986. The catalogue evokes the wonder of the achievement, translated into the look of numerous Manhattan drawing rooms by fashionable decorators such as Mario Buatta. Ruched blinds could be seen hanging in the windows of terraced houses in Fulham and newly privatised council houses in the Midlands. As a cultural force, the country house was back on top.

To some, the 1980s were rather too much of a good thing for the country house. The rush of new money caused excesses. More pheasants were shot than anyone could eat. Expectations of comfort were not always to the benefit of old houses, many of which historically had been cold for much of the year and, by modern standards, unacceptably damp. Historically, nobody would have heated state rooms when not in use. But a younger generation of owners felt that a house was not fully habitable unless all of it could be used, simultaneously, throughout the year. Ancient walls dried out for the first time in their existence; panelling cracked as a result. Not all restorations were sensitive. Turning a major country house, which was probably listed, into a family home for the late twentieth century was, in any case, a costly and time-consuming undertaking. Old country houses were often too big for a single family to take on. A solution offered by the architect Kit Martin, pioneered at Gunton Hall in Norfolk in 1980 and subsequently applied to many other country houses, was to divide the existing buildings into as many as twenty dwellings, creating an instant community out of a forlorn and possibly abandoned wreck. In 1987, Roger Tempest took over the running of Broughton Hall in Yorkshire, which had been in his family since 1097 but was struggling to last out the twentieth century (his sister, Annie Tempest, reimagined it as Tottering Hall in her *Country Life* cartoon strip, 'Tottering-by-Gently'). Before long there were five hundred people working in the business park and this dynamic man had helped over three hundred traditional estates to see a bright future through his company, Rural Solutions.

An alternative to buying an old country house was building a new one. While this could be more expensive in the short term, the cost was at least predictable, unlike that of restoration, and the family got a home that was planned as they wanted, with all the modern gadgetry that they could wish, hidden (in the case of a Classical house) behind cornices and skirting boards. Only a few as yet preferred that option but their numbers would rise.

The architects who became synonymous with the country-house revival of the late-twentieth and twenty-first centuries were Raymond Erith and Quinlan Terry. Erith's practice had begun before the Second World War, when he designed two lodges in an austere Soanic style for Windsor Great Park; they were bombed a fortnight after completion, destroying what should have been a prime advertisement for the architect. The post-war years were lean and he considered giving up architecture altogether to become a farmer. Work picked up at the end of the 1950s when he was commissioned to reconstruct the most famous Georgian townhouses in Britain: 10, 11 and 12 Downing Street. But even after that plum job, his workload could be frustratingly mundane. He moved to Dedham in the beautiful country that Constable had painted on the Essex–Suffolk border: London with its tower blocks was not for him.

Terry had been a misfit at the Architectural Association, which like other architectural schools was dominated by Modernism. His outlook at that stage was influenced by the Arts and Crafts; conversion to Classicism came when he went to work with Erith in Dedham in the early 1960s. In 1973, Erith died and he took over the practice at a difficult time. But from 1978 he started to receive country-house commissions, starting with Newfield outside Ripon for the carpet manufacturer, Michael Abrahams. The design began with a building on the lines of Kings Walden Bury but in the course of it Mr Abrahams stayed at Twickenham and saw Marble Hill; this became the basis of the new house. Thinking carefully about the function of a country house at a time when few were being built, the client decided to forgo a big dining room; the entertainment that he gave, not least as Master of the West of Yore Hunt, would take place in the staircase hall. This would economise on space and cost. He was not the only owner – Sebastian de Ferranti, chairman of an electronics company, who built the rotunda of Henbury Hall in Cheshire, was another – to come to regret that he had not built bigger; his hesitancy, however, reflected the times.

The 1980s saw the emergence of a cadre of young architects, including John Simpson and Robert Adam, who championed a Classical Revival, their cause helped by the well-publicised interest of the Prince of Wales. This invited the opprobrium of the architectural establishment who could see nothing other than contemptible pastiche, but the royal backing gave confidence to clients. By the end of the century Terry had designed Ferne House in Wiltshire for Lord and Lady Rothermere, a Palladian mansion on a scale of which it would hardly have been possible to dream at any period since 1945. In 2006, wings were added, with the help of Terry's son Francis. In its parkland setting, this Palladian mansion, built of Portland stone, is a recreation of Arcadia in modern terms: a restatement of the enduring values of the country house. While the wings of Ferne were rising, work began on another exceptional house, Kilboy in County Tipperary for Tony Ryan of Ryanair.

The success of the Classical Revival was a disappointment for Modernists. They rarely had a chance to build full-blown country houses. A notable exception was built on the site of Wadhurst Park, home, at the end of the nineteenth century, to José Murrieta, one of three Spanish brothers who moved in the cosmopolitan orbit of the Prince of Wales (they lost their fortune when Argentina defaulted on bond payments). Around 1980, the Swedish chemist Dr Hans Rausing, one of the brothers behind Tetra Pak, commissioned a family home from John Outram, calling it simply The New House (fig. 46). The name was apt. Although the entrance court is broadly symmetrical, The New House looks nothing like a traditional country house. Single-storeyed, it has vaulted, green-coloured roofs; the walls are stripes of brown and white. At the corners are columns that are made from what the architect calls Blitzcrete – a kind of concrete containing crushed brick and other lumps of builders' rubble, which is then ground and polished; the effect is something like terrazzo. (When Outram asked the Cement and Concrete Association for information on concrete of this kind, he was sent a wartime pamphlet

FIG. 46 *The New House at Wadhurst, in Sussex, built by John Outram for the Swedish chemist and industrialist Dr Hans Rausing and his wife Märit in the mid-1980s, stands on the site of a previous country house that had been demolished, except for the shell of the conservatory, in 1952. Dr Rausing liked industrial processes, so Outram's previous experience designing factories and warehouses was oddly suitable. The finishes, however, are luxurious and include polychromatic concrete – nicknamed Blitzcrete by the architect since the information to make it came from a Second World War pamphlet for the construction of air-raid shelters. Courtesy of Wadhurst Park Estate*

on how to make air-raid shelters – hence the name.) Inside, quasi-industrial materials are used to similarly luxurious effect – polished stucco, burr elm veneer edged with aluminium. This is a Post-Modern house which stands in the Picturesque tradition, the site having been chosen for its views over a park which Dr Rausing managed for a deer herd. The roofless conservatory that is the one feature to survive from Wadhurst Park became an outdoor room – ivy growing up through boxes of lattice created green columns.

Encouragement was given to the building of outstanding new country houses, in whatever style, by the Secretary of State for the Environment, John Gummer, later Lord Deben. He inserted a clause into planning legislation to enable architecture of exceptional quality to gain permission where it would otherwise be denied, for example in the Green Belt. Several country houses have benefitted from this provision. After the triumph of Minimalism, promoted almost as the house style of New Labour following its election victory in 1997, a growing number of them have followed that or other Modern styles. In 2019, the RIBA West Midlands Award was given to the Ghost House by architects BPN, in the sunken garden of a demolished country house, meaning that most of the house is below ground level. It takes the form of a series of courtyards, using what the citation describes as a 'simple palette of materials' of concrete and black detailing that create 'dynamic and brutal spaces that challenge the very existence of a house'. Heavens.

CHAPTER TWELVE

Now

IN 2019, Firle Place in Sussex, fragile and beautiful, was cleared for the filming of *Emma*. Even the central heating radiators were dismantled, to be reinstated when Firle returned to its usual, dream-like, seemingly unaltered state. The riding house has been converted to semi-permanent kitchens for TV's *The Great Celebrity Bake-Off*. Country houses have, of necessity, become entrepreneurial, to meet the challenges and costs of the twenty-first century. Just as in 2001, ospreys returned to England, so owners who might have felt themselves to be an endangered species in the 1970s look to the future with optimism. A new generation is at the helm, often with young children. Taking on a country house is no longer regarded as totally odd.

Many country houses were demolished in the twentieth century and the members' organisation Historic Houses calculates that the backlog of repairs on those that survive is enormous. Most, though, are in better fettle than could have been predicted half a century ago and some, by historical standards, are miracles of comfort. New owners with high expectations of finish and technology spend heavily on restoration.

Build quality can be as high as anything done in the past. An American architect wept when he visited one of the several chapels built by Craig Hamilton in the grounds of a country house. He could not believe it was possible to achieve such perfection of materials and craftsmanship in the sublunary world. He found it akin to a spiritual experience – as he called it, 'transcendent'.

Such wonders cannot be achieved without large budgets and it was predicted that the financial winter of 2007–8 would blast the money tree. The gloom was unfounded. Spending continued, sometimes on a grand scale. The space needed by super-rich clients only increased. Home cinemas are the norm. Display space is needed for the collections of classic cars or contemporary art. Gyms and sauna suites can be extensive.

FIG. 47 *The Laskett, Herefordshire. Roy Strong and his wife Julia Trevelyan-Oman bought a three-acre field from a farmer and embarked on the creation of the largest formal garden in England to be made in the second half of the twentieth century. The inspiration was Hidcote Manor in the Cotswolds, the formal gardens of the Tudor and Stuart period and Renaissance Italy. Sir Roy remembers that 'for the first 15 years the only labour were two gardeners who came for one day once a fortnight': it was a difficult time for country-house owners. © Clive Nichols*

In the 1970s, Sir Roy Strong, then director of the Victoria and Albert Museum, and his wife, the theatre designer Julia Trevelyan-Oman, set out to create a garden in Herefordshire, reviving the formality of Baroque gardens: although packed with sculpture and follies, often with an auto-biographical content, it was not large – even today it is no more than four and a half acres (fig. 47). It could not be more because the Strongs had little help: early photographs show Sir Roy behind a Rotavator. Such homeliness belongs to a more frugal age, as does the garden's geometry. Inspired by estates such as Knepp Castle in Sussex and Alladale in Scotland, owners are increasingly beguiled by rewilding – an imprecise term which generally means allowing Nature to take care of itself within reason. They would rather look out onto a wild-flower meadow than a manicured lawn of no biodiversity interest. Indeed formality of all kinds is out of favour: as Martin Amis observes in his memoir *Experience*, 'it used to be cool to be posh' – a view incomprehensible to his children. In many country houses, baseball caps and contemporary art have taken the place of tweed suits and a mahogany dining table laden with silver.

Three houses sum up the state of play. The first is Ardfin on the Hebridean island of Jura, a spreading country house formed for a foreign client by Alireza Sagharchi of the architects Stanhope Gate. This is a remote location, but remoteness is not regarded as a disqualification so much as a charm, since it provides sixteen miles of shore, a view of Islay and privacy. What appears to be lawn is the first tee of an apparently natural links golf course, so discreetly designed that only the flags give the secret away. When the present owner acquired Ardfin in 2010, the lodge looked as bleak as only a neglected building in a distant Scottish location can do. It has now been more than trebled in size with new wings, seamlessly continuing the Scots Baronial idiom of the existing work, to become a comfortable and well-equipped country house with swimming pavilion, spa, shooting simulator, four-thousand-bottle wine cellar and cigar cave, garden structures and a small chapel in the grounds. Old steadings have been converted to provide a guest and entertainment complex, including a pro shop for golf. A courtyard has been glazed over, in case – perish the thought – it ever rains; giving off it are a ceilidh barn and a billiard room.

Inside the main house, Ardfin's decoration is everything you could wish of a Scottish sporting lodge. Dark-stained pine panelling, Victorian floor tiles, chintz coverings to soft furniture, floral wallpaper and mahogany chests of drawers – all combine, with the architecture, to create a sense of place, complementing the views of the coast that can be seen through every window. So here is a virtually new house that is sympathetic to the existing architecture; which has been provided with an income stream (since the steadings and golf course will be let out when the owner and family are not in residence); and whose relationship with the environment around it is paramount. These are all themes of the twenty-first-century country house.

My second example is Harewell Hall, which has been newly built (the last touches were added during the lockdown of 2020) by the architect John Simpson for himself and his family in Hampshire. This is on a different scale from the sporting estate of Ardfin, being essentially a villa in a village location, next to the church. While Simpson has already been mentioned as a leading Classical architect, this building is thatched. The centre is a double-height hall, with a roof made of green oak and a minstrels' gallery: the wood panelling provides an excellent acoustic for concerts. There is an imagined history to this house. Fictionally, the hall dates from the fifteenth century, when the village was owned by the nunnery of Wherwell Abbey; this building might have been used by visiting priests. Later the screens passage was rebuilt with columns; what is now the drawing room was added in the Georgian period. Beyond that is a swimming pool, in the form of a Baroque canal, with pergolas heaped with red and white roses to either side, laid out in false perspective. Like Ardfin, Harewell is sensitive to its setting; it is thatched because neighbours wanted the vernacular of the village to be continued. Rather than being dogmatic in style, the architect adapted to the conditions of the site – indeed, Simpson's genius here was to achieve planning permission for a substantial home on a site that, in other hands, might well not have got it. This illustrates a key feature of the twenty-first-century country house: its form is often determined by the need to get a scheme past the planning officers. Simpson argued that at one point in the distant past a building of some consequence had stood here, a fragment of which survived in the form of an old cottage. The narrative embedded in the architecture is also characteristic of today. We are seekers after identities and belonging. Houses are not only spaces but stories.

My third example is also from Hampshire. Little can Christopher Hussey have thought, when he published his classic *The Picturesque* in 1927, that it would bear such fruit as Downley House, a dramatically contemporary building. Hussey was inspired by his family's seat Scotney Castle and the view out to a ruin of the old castle, which was kept as feature when its successor was built. Downley House also began with a ruin, if not quite such a romantic one. The site originally belonged to the local big house, now a school, whose water supply came from a reservoir at the top of the hill, that was pumped from the well at Downley. The ruin was that of the engineer's house, reduced to little more than an ivy-covered wall. The architects Birds Portchmouth Russum kept this existing fragment and it became one of the generators of the design. Preserved, stripped of its ivy and planted with more beguiling climbing plants, it forms the protective wall of a courtyard garden.

The materials are Arts and Crafts, the relationship with the setting, in an Area of Outstanding Natural Beauty, necessarily sympathetic. Silvery oak and sandstone from Lambs Quarry, in Sussex, have been used to clad much of the exterior of the house, contrasting with passages of white render. Some of the roof is covered with a blanket of sedum that provides a habitat for both birds and insects. The garage and service rooms have been set into a shoulder of hillside, making them invisible beneath the turf. But the form has wow factor. In the centre is a reprise of the medieval great hall, double height and used for many different purposes, among which eating has pride of place.

Medieval great halls tended to be dark and confined. By contrast, the hall at Downley House runs from one side of the house to the other, each end being formed of a window wall. The glass of these windows can be made to vanish, opening the hall to the garden on summer days. This is the ultimate extension of the desire to live closer to landscape and Nature that began in the Regency and was continued in the Edwardian period, with its verandahs, dining loggias and sleeping balconies. The result might be compared to the cross passage of a tithe barn, where one set of towering double doors faces another. Yet the shape is quite different, having been suggested by the giant oak barrels known as *foudres* (the owners met while working in the wine business in New York). While the hall provides theatre, it also forms the central element of a tripartite plan: a shared common space that separates family rooms on the one side from guest rooms on the other. Privacy is maintained.

Here then is another house with an embodied story, a house close to Nature, a warm-hearted house that nevertheless provides the owners with space for themselves; a house that continues the Picturesque tradition that is so important to the British way of seeing. It is an Arcadia for the family who live there. Arcadia elsewhere may be on the retreat: this is, environmentally, a fallen world. But the Arcadia of the country house remains an ideal within the grasp of the human imagination. As the outer world becomes darker, demand for the beautiful and contemplative spaces, the garden settings, the *luxe, calme et volupté* that can be found – or created – within the moat or the park wall is set to remain high.

The most significant development of late-twentieth-century planning was the live-in kitchen. This reflects an age that did not routinely expect to employ cooks. Hardly any large country house could have operated without a cook before the 1970s. Unmodernised kitchens, designed for bevies of staff, were too inconvenient and gloomy for an owner's wife (it was likely to be the wife in that era) to use unaided. They might be some way from the dining room. But the 1980s saw the rise of specialist kitchen fitters, such as Smallbone, who made cabinets of a quality only seen in the drawing room, accompanied by a boom in upmarket food publishing, typified by the magazine *A La Carte*. Cooking might be complicated (no bish, bash, bosh as yet) but it could also be chic. In the 1990s, steel industrial-style cooking ranges became fashionable, giving the illusion that a home cook was equipped like a professional chef. To begin with, suppers served around a kitchen table were regarded as at best extremely informal, at worst inappropriate. These attitudes changed as people of all kinds spent more money on the design of their kitchens, making them more attractive to be in, as well as giving them more space. By the end of the century, kitchens with big tables for family meals were combined with a variable number of satellite rooms, for homework, television or other screen watching, and possibly games like snooker or table tennis. Builders of new country houses who entertain on a big scale might need a second kitchen for parties, at which the food will be prepared by caterers. For ordinary purposes, the live-in kitchen is the place to chillax.

With the rise of the kitchen went the death of the dining room. Most big country houses are still built with formal dining rooms; the number of people who will sit around the table at Christmas is one of the determinants of the size of the whole project. But dinner parties are not what they were. Who will polish the silver? With other forms of brown furniture, mahogany dining tables lost value in the salerooms: what was a status symbol to the yuppie generation of the 1980s is now a drug on the market. The rise of the live-in kitchen has been to the benefit of the new country house, compared to restorations, since it can be planned more conveniently, as integral to a project from the beginning. It can be difficult to accommodate such spaces in old and listed country houses, where state rooms may be too grand for kitchen use, as well as being difficult to open up. And so the family's most intensively used rooms in the house, focused on the kitchen, are likely be found in the old servants' wing. The priorities of yesteryear have been stood on their head.

Today, the space everybody needs is a home office. As ever, the style journalist Nicholas Coleridge, lately retired CEO of the publishing group Condé Nast but still chairman of the Victoria and Albert Museum among other things, is ahead of the game. In 2019 he fulfilled his ambition of building a folly at his home in Worcestershire. For architect he chose Quinlan Terry, who is not only the leading Classicist of his generation but has a special affinity with small, architecturally intense buildings. The inspiration in this case was the sixteenth-century summer house at Long Melford in Suffolk: a two-storey octagonal structure with corner buttresses. Brick was the obvious material to reflect Wolverton Hall (fig. 48). However, the folly is taller than the Long Melford building; the proportions have been improved and a viewing platform was provided at the top. There is an implied story to the folly. Although Wolverton was built in the eighteenth century, Mr Terry likes to imagine that historians

FIG. 48 *Folly built for Nicholas Coleridge at Wolverton House, Worcestershire, by Quinlan Terry. Terry, the leading Classicist of his generation, took inspiration from the Elizabethan summer house at Long Melford in Suffolk, which is similarly octagonal and built of brick. The room on the first floor contains Mr Coleridge's home office, which proved its worth during the Covid pandemic of 2020, the year of completion.* © Country Life Picture Library

of the future think that the folly belonged to a house that predated the present one.

But this is a folly with a purpose. While the ground floor serves as a dining room, the building's *raison d'être* is to be found on the first floor. Here is Mr Coleridge's study, with bookcases filled with the works of Coleridges past and present, above which are plaster heads from an art school which found that life drawing was redundant. The client could not have foreseen that he and his family would spend the spring of 2020 locked down at Wolverton and unable to leave it for seven weeks because of coronavirus – or that he himself would spend ten days in intensive care. But the folly provided the ideal setting for the Zoom calls by which business as well as social life was suddenly being transacted.

As yet, it is impossible to predict the impact of Covid-19 on the economy, or indeed the sense of confidence that is so important if clients are to commit to large building projects. Will they draw in their horns? If so, it could be that small, jewel-like pieces of architecture provide a more popular form of domestic self-expression than the ever-larger country houses we have seen in recent years.

And there is a wider significance. Not only is home-working bound to grow, it will be some time before we travel as much as we used to, as airlines struggle to recover their previous capacity. Life could become more local; there may well be a new focus on home. The city has been the loser from the pandemic, in that the buzz generated by people of all types and origins packed together (in the case of the London Tube) like sardines has gone – although – dare one believe? – the quieter pace, reduction in traffic and fall in pollution levels could make cities more attractive to be in. The countryside, by contrast, has gained. There it is easy to be socially distanced from other people, and gardens, during lockdown, were a great solace. Local networks are more resilient, because they have to be, and neighbours are more likely to know one another and help out.

The times are too uncertain to look very far into the future, but it is surely a safe bet, in these circumstances, that the country house will continue for many people to be an ideal. It has played many roles in the course of the story: medieval great hall, prodigy house, place of retirement, Baroque palace, Arcadian landscape, sublime fantasy, cottage orné, model of domesticity, Arts and Crafts utopia, inter-war pleasure dome, Neoclassical escape. What will its next avatar be? Covid stopped the world and caused a period of reflection, not least about the homes people were forced to spend so much more time in. They were already, perforce, thinking about the environment, because of climate change. As the world gets more crowded and Nature continues her retreat, luxury will be redefined. Silence will truly be golden. Seeing the diamond sparkle of stars against a black velvet sky will be precious to a generation whose night horizons usually have an orange sodium glow or halo of LED white. Hedgehogs, orchids, woods for the children to play in: these things will turn parents' minds towards country houses.

Country houses are one of a kind: perhaps that will attract a world on the hunt for 'authenticity'. More people will acquire craft skills as robots take other jobs. Their work will find its way into country houses although – a dilemma that William Morris would have recognised – it will have to compete in price with innovations such as laser cutting and 3-D printing. Those technologies will radically reduce the cost of making ornament. Goodbye to the Machine Aesthetic of Le Corbusier, predicated upon early-twentieth-century means of production which meant that factory-made goods of simple outline cost less than the froufrou of previous eras. Computers do not recognise economies of scale; anything is possible. On the other hand, it could be that owners want a closer bond with nature – spaces that merge with the outdoors, as we have seen at Downley House. The Edwardians liked to sleep in the open air, on balconies outside their bedrooms; that could come back.

Locked down in London, I followed social media posts from country houses where life seemed to have been relatively little affected by the restrictions that had turned the capital into a ghost town. Admittedly they had returned to a state of social relations more akin to the age of Jane Austen than the twenty-first century: family members had to rely on each other for company, since they were not allowed out. But this was not such a hardship as elsewhere, given the amount of space in the house, the grounds to walk in, the vegetables from the garden, the larders and freezers heaped with emergency supplies and perhaps a well-stocked cellar. From the number of new buyers entering the country property market, it seems that I was not alone in making this observation. The self-created utopia of the country house has acquired a new point. Who knows? Perhaps a refuge from a harsh outside world will be needed at other times as the twenty-first century wears on. The country house has often served that need before. Until then, let us celebrate its long continuity, admire the architecture and enjoy.

FURTHER READING

GENERAL

Bence-Jones, Mark, *Life in an Irish Country House*, 1996

Christie, Christopher, *The British Country House in the Eighteenth Century*, 2000

Cliffe, John Trevor, *The World of the Country House in Seventeenth-Century England*, 1999

Cooper, Nicholas, *The Opulent Eye: Late Victorian and Edwardian Taste in Interior Design*, 1976

Cooper, Nicholas, *Houses of the Gentry 1480–1680*, 1999

Cornforth, John, *The Quest for Comfort: English Interiors, 1790–1848*, 1978

Dixon Hunt, John and Peter Willis (eds), *The Genius of the Place: The English Landscape Garden 1620–1820*, 1988

Dresser, Madge and Andrew Hann (eds), *Slavery and the Country House*, 2013

Finn, Margot and Kate Smith (eds), *The East Inda Company at Home 1757–1857*, 2018

Fitzgerald, Desmond and James Peill, *The Irish Country House*, 2010

Fleming, Peter, *Family and Household in Medieval England*, 2001

Girouard, Mark, *Life in the English Country House*, 1978

Gomme, Andor and Alison Maguire, *Design and Plan in the Country House: From Castle Donjons to Palladian Boxes*, 2007

Gow, Ian, *Scottish Houses and Gardens*, 1997

Gow, Ian and Alistair Rowan (eds), *Scottish Country Houses, 1600–1994*, 1994

Jackson-Stops, Gervase, *The Treasure Houses of Britain*, 1985

Knox, James, *The Scottish Country House*, 2015

Macaulay, James, *The Classical Country House in Scotland, 1660–1800*, 1987

Mandler, Peter, *The Fall and Rise of the Stately Home*, 1997

McKean, Christopher, *The Scottish Chateau*, 2002

Musson, Jeremy, *The English Manor House*, 1999

Platt, Colin, *The Great Rebuildings of Tudor and Stuart England*, 1994

Purcell, Mark, *The Country House Library*, 2017

Somerville-Large, Peter, *The Irish Country House*, 1995

Stobart, Jon and Mark Rothery, *Consumption and the Country House*, 2016

Strong, Roy, *The Renaissance Garden in England*, 1979

Tinniswood, Adrian, *A Polite Tourist: A History of Country House Visiting*, 1998

Vickery, Amanda, *The Gentleman's Daughter: Women's Lives in Georgian England*, 1998

Vickery, Amanda, *Behind Closed Doors: At Home in Georgian England*, 2009

Wainwright, Clive, *The Romantic Interior: The British Collector at Home, 1750–1850*, 1989

Watkin, David, *The English Vision: Picturesque in Architecture, Landscape and Garden Design*, 1982

Wilson, Richard and Alan Mackley, *Creating Paradise: The Building of the English Country House, 1660–1880*, 2001

Wilton, Andrew and Ilaria Bignamini (eds), *Grand Tour: The Lure of Italy in the Eighteenth Century*, 1996

Worsley, Giles, *Classical Architecture in Britain: The Heroic Age*, 1995

MEDIEVAL

Emery, Anthony, *Dartington Hall*, 1970

Goodall, John, *The English Castle, 1066–1650*, 2011

Herlihy, David, *Medieval Households*, 1985

Mertes, Kate, *The English Noble Household 1250–1600*, 1988

Thompson, M.W., *The Medieval Hall: The Basis of Secular Domestic Life, 600–1600 AD*, 1995

For Margaret of Lincoln, see Louise J. Wilkinson, *Women in Thirteenth-century Lincolnshire*, 2007

For Bishop Grosseteste, see Philippa M. Hoskin, *Robert Grosseteste and the 13th-Century Diocese of Lincoln*, 2019

For Henry VIII's travelling chests, see Alden Gregory, 'The timber lodgings of King Henry VIII: Ephemeral architecture at war in the early sixteenth century', *Antiquaries Journal*, 6 May 2020, pp. 304–23

For Newton Castle, see Charles McKean, 'The Scottish Renaissance country seat in its setting', *Garden History*, vol. 31, no. 2 (Winter 2003), pp. 141–62

For Abbots Grange, see Alan Calder, 'From abbot to artist: The remarkable journey of Abbots Grange, Worcestershire', *Country Life*, 18 September 2019, pp. 68–72, 74

TUDOR AND ELIZABETHAN

Girouard, Mark, *Robert Smythson and the Elizabethan Country House*, 1983

Girouard, Mark, *Elizabethan Architecture: Its Rise and Fall, 1540–1640*, 2008

Henderson, Paula *The Tudor House and Garden*, 2005

Thurley, Simon, *The Royal Palaces of Tudor England: Architecture and Court Life, 1460–1547*, 1993

Thurley, Simon, *Hampton Court: A Social and Architectural History*, 2003

Wright, Jane A., *Brick Building in England from the Middle Ages to 1550*, 1972

For roofscapes, see Paula Henderson, 'Life at the top: 16th- and 17th-century roofscapes', *Country Life*, 3 January 1985, pp. 6–9

For long galleries, see Rosalys Coope, 'The "Long Gallery": Its origins, development, use and decoration', *Architectural History*, vol. 29 (1986), pp. 43–72, 74–84

EARLY STUART

Cooper, Nicholas, *The Jacobean Country House: From the Archives of Country Life*, 2006

Hart, Vaughan, *Inigo Jones: The Architect of Kings*, 2011

Worsley, Giles, *Inigo Jones and the European Classical Tradition*, 2007

For tower houses, see Rory Sherlock, 'The evolution of the Irish tower-house as a domestic space', *Proceedings of the Royal Irish Academy: Archaeology, Culture, History, Literature*, vol. 111C, Special Issue: *Domestic Life in Ireland* (2011), pp. 115–40

COMMONWEALTH TO QUEEN ANNE

Barber, Tabitha (ed.), *British Baroque: Power and Illusion*, 2020

Bold, John, *John Webb*, 1989

Downes, Kerry, *Sir John Vanbrugh: A Biography*, 1987

Fowler, Alastair (ed.), *The Country House Poem: Cabinet of Seventeenth Century Estate Poems and Related Items*, 1994

Hill, Oliver and John Cornforth, *English Country Houses: Caroline 1625–1685*, 1966

Mowl, Timothy and Brian Earnshaw, *Architecture Without Kings*, 1995

Rowell, Christopher, *Ham House: 400 Years of Collecting and Patronage*, 2013

For sash windows, see Hentie Louw and Robert Crayford, 'A constructional history of the sash-window *c.* 1670–*c.* 1725' (Part 1), *Architectural History*, vol. 41 (1998), pp. 82–130

For Roger Pratt, see Nigel Silcox-Crowe, 'Sir Roger Pratt 1620–1685', in Roderick Brown (ed.) *The Architectural Outsiders*, 1985

EARLY GEORGIAN

Barnard, Toby and Jane Clark, *Lord Burlington: Architecture, Art and Life*, 1994

Bending, Stephen, *Green Retreats: Gardens and Eighteenth-Century Culture*, 2013

Harris, John, *The Palladian Revival: Lord Burlington, his Villa and Garden at Chiswick*, 1995

Meir, Jennifer, *Sanderson Miller and his Landscapes*, 2006

Morel, Thierry and Andrew Moore, *Houghton Revisited: The Walpole Masterpieces from Catherine the Great's Hermitage*, 2013

Saumarez Smith, Charles, *The Building of Castle Howard*, 1990

Wilson, Michael I., *William Kent*, 2002

For Lord Burlington, see Alexander Echlin and William Kelley, 'A "Shaftesburian agenda"? Lord Burlington, Lord Shaftesbury and the intellectual origins of English Palladianism', *Architectural History*, vol. 59 (2016), pp. 221–52; Alexander Echlin, 'Was Lord Burlington a Jacobite?' *Burlington Magazine*, August 2019, pp. 626–37

For technology at Holkham, see Christine Hiskey, 'Palladian and practical: Country house technology at Holkham Hall', *Construction History*, vol. 22 (2007), pp. 3–25

For Holkham's authorship, see Frank Salmon, '"Our Great Master Kent" and the design of Holkham Hall: A reassessment', *Architectural History*, vol. 56 (2013), pp. 63–96

For James Gibbs, see William Aslet, 'A James Gibbs autobiography revisited: Rome and self-memorialisation in the Gibbs Manuscript in Sir John Soane's Museum', *Georgian Group Journal*, vol. 15 (2017), pp. 113–30;

William Aslet, 'On the threshold of the City: The Church of St Mary le Strand', *Country Life*, 7 November, 2018, pp. 56–61

MID-GEORGIAN

Arnold, Dana (ed.), *The Georgian Villa*, 1996

Binney, Marcus, *Sir Robert Taylor: From Rococo to Neoclassicism*, 1984

Brown, Jane, *The Omnipotent Magician: Lancelot 'Capability' Brown, 1716–1783*, 2011

Davoli, Silvia, *Lost Treasures of Strawberry Hill: Masterpieces from Horace Walpole's Collection*, 2018

Fleming, John, *Robert Adam and His Circle: In Edinburgh and Rome*, 1962

Harris, Eileen, *The Furniture of Robert Adam*, 1963

Harris, Eileen, *The Genius of Robert Adam: His Interiors,* 2001

Harris, John, *The Palladian Revival: Lord Burlington, his Villa and Garden at Chiswick*, 1995

Kelly, Jason, *The Society of Dilettanti: Archaeology and Identity in the British Enlightenment*, 2010

McCarthy, Patricia, *Life in the Country House in Georgian Ireland*, 2016

Mordaunt Crook, J., *The Greek Revival: Neoclassical Attitudes in British Architecture, 1760–1870*, new edition, 1995

Musson, Jeremy, *Robert Adam: Country House Design, Decoration, and the Art of Elegance*, 2017

Snodin, Michael, *Horace Walpole's Strawberry Hill*, 2009

Soros, Susan Weber (ed.), *James 'Athenian' Stuart: The Rediscovery of Antiquity*, 2006

Watkin, David, *The Architect King: George III and the Culture of the Enlightenment*, 2004

For mahogany, see Adam Bowett, 'The Jamaica trade: Gillow and the use of mahogany in the eighteenth century', *Regional Furniture*, vol. 12 (1998), pp. 14–57; Jennifer L. Anderson, *Mahogany*, 2012

REGENCY TO WILLIAM IV

Daniels, Stephen, *Humphry Repton: Landscape Gardening and the Geography of Georgian England*, 1999

Darley, Gillian, *John Soane: An Accidental Romantic*, 1999

Davidson, Keir, *Humphry Repton and the Russell Family*, 2018

Robinson, John Martin, *James Wyatt, 1746–1813: Architect to George III*, 2012

Robinson, John Martin, *The Regency Country House: From the Archives of Country Life*, 2009

Rutherford, Jessica, *A Prince's Passion: The Life of the Royal Pavilion*, 2003

Thompson, Melissa and Michael Borozdin-Bidnell, *Georgian and Regency Conservatories*, 2019

Watkin, David, *Thomas Hope and the Neo-Classical Idea, 1769–1831*, 1969

Watkin, David and Philip Hewat-Jaboor (eds), *Thomas Hope, Regency Designer*, 2008

For Prince von Pückler-Muskau, see Brennan, F. (trans.), *Pückler's Progress: The Adventures of Prince Pückler-Muskau in England, Wales and Ireland*, 1987

EARLY AND HIGH VICTORIAN

Crook, J. Mordaunt, *William Burges and the High Victorian Dream*, 1981

Franklin, Jill, *The Gentleman's Country House and its Plan, 1835–1914*, 1981

Girouard, Mark, *Sweetness and Light: The 'Queen Anne' Movement, 1860–1900*, 1977

Girouard, Mark, *The Victorian Country House*, 1979

Hannah, Rosemary, *The Grand Designer: The Third Marquess of Bute*, 2012

Hill, Rosemary, *God's Architect: Pugin and the Building of Romantic Britain*, 2008

Kirk, Sheila, *Philip Webb*, 2005

Miers, Mary, *Highland Retreats*, 2017

Saint, Andrew, *Richard Norman Shaw*, 1977

Weber, Susan, *E. W. Godwin: Aesthetic Movement Architect and Designer*, 1999

For Osborne and Balmoral, see Hermione Hobhouse, *Prince Albert: His Life and Work*, 1983; for the nurseries at Osborne, see Clive Aslet, 'Childhood at Osborne', *Country Life*, 1 December 1988, pp. 152–7

TURN OF THE CENTURY

Aslet, Clive, *The Last Country Houses*, 1982

Aslet, Clive *The Edwardian Country House*, 2012

Brittain-Catlin, Tim, *The Edwardians and their Houses*, 2020

Cornforth, John, *The Inspiration of the Past: Country House Taste in the Twentieth Century*, 1985

Cornforth, John, *Search for a Style: Country Life and Architecture, 1897–1935*, 1988

Drury, Michael, *Wandering Architects: In Pursuit of an Arts and Crafts Ideal*, 2016

Hussey, Christopher, *The Life of Sir Edwin Lutyens*, 1950

Stamp, Gavin, *Edwin Lutyens Country Houses: From the Archives of Country Life*, 2001

For Americans, see Clive Aslet, *An Exuberant Catalogue of Dreams: The Americans who Revived the Country House in Britain*, 2013

BETWEEN THE WARS

Powers, Alan, *Oliver Hill: Architect and Lover of Life, 1887–1968*, 1989

Stansky, Peter, *Sassoon: The Worlds of Philip and Sybil*, 2003

Stevenson, Jane, *Baroque Between the Wars: Alternative Style in the Arts, 1918–1939*, 2018

Tinniswood, Adrian, *The Long Weekend: Life in the English Country House, 1918–1939*, 2016

For Evelyn Waugh's views, see Evelyn Waugh, 'A call to the orders', *Country Life* supplement, 26 February 1938

For High and Over, see Bernard Ashmole, *An Autobiography*, 1994

For Gribloch, see Michael Hall, 'Gribloch, Stirlingshire', *Country Life*, 12 February 1998, pp. 54–9

POST-WAR: RECOVERY AND BOOM

Martin, John Robinson, *The Country House at War*, 1989

Musson, Jeremy, *Henbury: An Extraordinary House*, 2019

Powers, Alan, *The Twentieth Century House in Britain: From the Archives of Country Life*, 2004

Robinson, John Martin, *The Latest Country Houses, 1945–1983*, 1984

Seebohm, Caroline, *The Country House: A Wartime History, 1939–45*, 1989

Strong, Roy, Marcus Binney and John Harris, *The Destruction of the Country House*, 1974

Summers, Julie, *Our Uninvited Guests: The Secret Life of Britain's Country Houses 1939–45*, 2018

Wood, Martin, *Nancy Lancaster*, 2005

INDEX

Page numbers in *italic* refer to the illustrations